CULTURE AND ECONOMY

Culture and Economy

Contemporary perspectives

Edited by
ULLRICH KOCKEL
University of the West of England
Bristol

ASHGATE

Published by
Ashgate Publishing Limited
Gower House
Croft Road
Aldershot
Hampshire GU11 3HR
England

Ashgate Publishing Company
Suite 420
101 Cherry Street
Burlington, VT 05401-4405
USA

Ashgate website: http://www.ashgate.com

British Library Cataloguing in Publication Data
Culture and economy : contemporary perspectives
    1. Culture 2. Europe - Economic conditions - 1945- 3. Europe -
    Social life and customs - 1945-
    I. Kockel, Ullrich
    330.9 ' 4

Library of Congress Cataloging-in-Publication Data
Culture and economy : contemporary perspectives / edited by Ullrich Kockel.
        p. cm.
    Includes bibliographical references.
    ISBN 0-7546-1923-0 (alk. paper)
        1. Culture--Economic aspects. I. Kockel, Ullrich.

    HM621 .C8543 2002
    306.3--dc21

                                                                        2002026182

ISBN 0 7546 1923 0

Printed and bound in Great Britain by MPG Books Ltd, Bodmin, Cornwall

Contents

List of Figures and Tables

List of Contributors

Melissa L. Caldwell is Lecturer in Social Studies at Harvard University. She received a PhD in anthropology from Harvard in 2000, and is currently completing a book entitled *Not By Bread Alone: Social Security in the New Russia*. Her research interests include the anthropology of food, the politics of humanitarian aid, and church-state relations in post-socialist societies. She is co-editor, with James L. Watson, of the forthcoming book *Food: Producing and Consuming Cultures*.

Amy Goldenberg is a doctoral candidate in the Department of Folklore and Ethnomusicology at Indiana University. She has a Master's Degree in Slavic Literature and Linguistics from Ohio State University. Currently, she is engaged in research about Polish amber art.

Amy Hale is Visiting Assistant Professor in Humanities at the University of Central Florida. Her research interests include culture and economic regeneration and cultural tourism with a focus on contemporary Celtic identities in Cornwall. She is the co-editor of two books, *New Directions in Celtic Studies* (with Philip Payton) and *Inside Merlin's Cave* (with Tim Saunders and Alan M. Kent).

Kurt Hartwig is a doctoral candidate in Folklore at Indiana University, with minors in Slavic Languages and Literature and Performance Studies. He has received several grants, including a Fulbright-Hays Fellowship, under which he spent 2001 studying theatre in the Czech Republic. He works professionally in theatre and film production.

Angela Jancius is completing her doctoral dissertation with the Department of Anthropology at Michigan State University, where she is also teaching. She received a scholarship from the Alexander von Humboldt Foundation to support fieldwork in Leipzig. Her research interests include post-socialism, unemployment, the politics of labour, and welfare reform.

Reinhard Johler is Professor of Empirical Cultural Studies at the Ludwig-Uhland-Institut für Empirische Kulturwissenschaften, Eberhard-Karls-Universität Tübingen. His current research interests include migration, comparative European folk customs, and the process of Europeanisation. A regular contributor to journals of European ethnology, his books include *Die Formierung eines Brauches. Der Funken- und Holepfannsonntag. Studien aus Vorarlberg, Liechtenstein, Tirol, Südtirol und dem Trentino* (2000).

Ann Kennard is Principal Lecturer in German and European Studies in the School of European Studies, University of the West of England, Bristol. Her early research included Polish foreign trade, and relations between the *Comecon* and the EC. For some years now she has published on cross-border co-operation between Poland and Germany, and more recently has broadened out to include the wider central and east European context in anticipation of EU enlargement.

Ullrich Kockel is Professor of European Studies and Director of the Centre for European Studies, University of the West of England, Bristol. In 2001-03, he is convenor of the ESRC Research Seminar in European Ethnology. His books include *Regional Culture and Economic Development: Explorations in European Ethnology* (2002), and *Borderline Cases: The Ethnic Frontiers of European Integration* (1999).

Mónica Lindh de Montoya is a researcher at the Department of Social Anthropology, Stockholm University, where she received her PhD. She has carried out research on rural development and is the author of *Progress, Hunger and Envy: Commercial Agriculture, Marketing and Social Transformation in the Venezuelan Andes* (1996). Her research interests centre on the field of economic anthropology, and she is currently researching small investors in the Stockholm stock market.

Johannes Moser is Head of Department for Folk Life Studies (Volkskunde) at the Institut für Sächsische Geschichte und Volkskunde in Dresden. His main research interests include economic anthropology, especially work and unemployment; youth culture, and urban community studies. He is the editor of *Jugendkulturen. Recherchen in Frankfurt am Main und London* (2000).

Antonio Miguel Nogués is Chair of Anthropological Studies and Professor of the Anthropology of Leisure and Tourism, and Political Anthropology at Miguel Hernández University, Spain. He was an associated researcher at the Amsterdamse School voor Sociaal Wetenschappelijk Onderzoek (1995), and a Visiting Professor at Escola Superior de Gestão, Hotelaria e Turismo of the Universidade do Algarve (1997).

Máiréad Nic Craith holds the Chair of Irish Culture and Language at the newly established Academy for Irish Cultural Heritages in the University of Ulster. Her research interests include culture and identity politics, European influences on Irish culture, and regional diversity in the context of EU integration. Her many books include *Plural Identities, Singular Narratives: The Case of Northern Ireland* (2002).

Jane Saville is a Senior Lecturer in English and European Studies at the University of the West of England, Bristol. A professional EFL (English as a Foreign Language) teacher, and co-editor, with G. M. Blue and J. Milton, of *Assessing English for Academic Purposes* (2000), she also has an MSc in Development Studies. Her research interests include political and socio-economic aspects of language teaching and policy.

Vida Savoniakaitė is Senior Researcher in the Department of Ethnology at the Lithuanian Institute of History. Her research interests include ethnic identity of traditional society and migrants communities, local culture, and anthropological perspectives on the multi-medial present. She is the author of *Textiles in Rural Culture* (1998), and, more recently, *Creative Work and Traditions* (2002).

1 Culture and Economy: A Brief Introduction

Ullrich Kockel

Since the mid-1980s – the period leading up to the Maastricht Treaty and the re-invention of the 'European Economic Community' (EEC) as 'European Union' (EU) – 'culture' has become something of a buzzword in European integration and regional planning, and at the same time a kind of battle cry for regions and groups seeking a greater measure of self-determination. For many of the so-called 'peripheral' regions, 'culture' is considered the only viable resource they have for economic development. Yet the actual concept of 'culture', as used in this context, has remained rather oblique. At the same time, neo-liberal economics has become the dominant paradigm across a wide range of cultural contexts, while the cultural contingency of that paradigm itself is being obscured.

Having come to European ethnology from a background in economics, I find this trend particularly fascinating. In much of twentieth century discourse, 'culture' and 'economy' have been represented in juxtaposition, if not indeed as an outright contradiction of terms. The spectrum of debate ranges from the formalist-substantivist dispute in economic anthropology to the Frankfurt School's critique of the 'cultural industry', to the *fin de siècle* 'cultural turn' in practically every humanities and social sciences discipline. Towards the end of the century this debate became increasingly esoteric, as the fashionable constructionist approach to just about everything encouraged the hegemony of literary criticism as the chief epistemology of these disciplines, requiring the textualisation of the practices and phenomena of everyday life for analytical purposes. From the perspective of European ethnology, Orvar Löfgren (2001) and others have criticised this ontologisation of 'text' to the neglect of 'lived experience', which they regard as the proper ontological foundation for cultural inquiry. At the same time, 'culture' at precisely the level of lived experience became more and more instrumentalised and commodified.

The area where these processes attracted most attention initially was probably tourism, as many regions located some distance away from the sun-and-sand mainstays of mass tourism saw the promotion of 'heritage' or 'cultural' tourism as a viable alternative, to make up for a shortfall in industrial development (cf. Kockel 1994). With this type of tourism – together with the increasing affordability of far-flung exotic destinations – reducing the income of traditional sun-and-sand resorts, these have also begun to discover their culture and heritage as a resource for development (see Nogués in this volume).

As research on culture and economy accelerated, it soon became clear that, on the one hand, the instrumentalisation and commodification of 'culture' is by no means restricted to tourism while, on the other hand, there are other, equally if not more complex issues concerning the relationship between culture and economy that needed to be examined, and from different disciplinary perspectives paying greater attention to people's lived experience than to any trendy analytic text (cf. Kockel 2002). The 1990s saw the growth of practical concerns with regard to this problematic, as they found expression, for example, in the conferences organised under the EU's PACTE programme (Kilday 1998). By the end of the decade, research in this field had reached a stage where it seemed necessary to try and survey work in progress with a view to identifying key strands of a research programme. This is mainly being done through workshops and conferences, and first outputs from these are beginning to appear in print (e.g., du Gay and Pryke 2002). The present volume brings together contributions from two such meetings, as well as a number of invited essays.

Culture and Economy in Contemporary Europe

At the 2000 conference of the European Association of Social Anthropologists (EASA) in Kraków, a panel surveyed theories and practices that shape cultural and economic relationships in Europe at the threshold of the twenty-first century. The contributors investigated the culture/economy nexus within a specifically European context primarily from three angles. Case studies of territorially and non-territorially based groups shed light on the everyday practices associated with the envaluation of culture in the context and for the purposes of economic development. These were complemented by case studies of organisations and institutions involved in the design and implementation of economic strategies and policies at various levels, scrutinising the concepts of 'culture' and 'economy' employed at the level of policy decision making.

A third perspective was offered by theoretical contributions examining aspects of economy, such as the market, or *homo oeconomicus*, as cultural constructs in their historical context, considering 'mainstream' economics as well as 'folk' models of the economy. Critics of neo-liberal economics have often pointed out that it seems to have assumed the role of a secular religion, and this critique of the cultural function of economics led to the theme for a second meeting.

Economics as Folklore

Anthropologists and economic historians working with an ethnological perspective have long argued that the economy is culturally contingent. Taking this argument one step further, a panel at the 2001 conference of the International Society for Ethnology and Folklore (SIEF) in Budapest examined the premise that economics as we commonly know it – that is, the dominant neo-liberal paradigm that pervades policy making and lays claim to being a universal explanatory framework for all spheres of life – can itself be analysed in much the same way as other oral or literary traditions of everyday life, that is, as folklore. Economics abounds with superstitions and moral imperatives in disguise, affirming the societal code of values and conduct we are supposed to live by. Thus it serves as a quasi-religious belief system in our secularised world. The legitimacy of such systems is maintained either by their congruence with experienced, everyday actuality, or by powerful interests.

Contributions to this session concentrated on two aspects. Case studies of aspects of everyday life investigated how people try to make sense of economic 'imperatives' in their lived experience. How effectively is the code of values and conduct transmitted in everyday practice? How is it adapted and changed in economic interaction? How far, and in what forms, does it penetrate into various non-economic spheres of life? To what extent is the economic belief system congruent with the experienced, everyday actuality at the local level? What contribution does it make to the construction of localities, local identities, or power structures, and to their interaction across local and wider contexts? What are the power structures that maintain or modify the hegemonic view at this level, how do they work, and what determines their success or failure?

Some contributions looked at economic discourse itself in its academic, media and public policy form, analysing a range of economic texts with the tools of folklore study. The purpose of this was to establish whether and to what extent treating economics as folklore can shed light on some of the pressing socio-economic problems of contemporary life. Intended as a critique of ideology, the discussion aimed to highlight the contribution European ethnology might be able to make to a better understanding of issues and processes that will shape our everyday lives in the new century. The session also raised questions regarding the production of ethnological knowledge, and the consequent (potential) role of the ethnologist in the shaping of political processes. This, together with questions raised by contributions on the stock market (de Montoya and Hartwig in this volume), and on heritage-related policy (Hale, Johler, Nic Craith and Nogués in this volume), has led to the theme for a further workshop, on 'Heritage Futures', at the 2002 EASA conference in Copenhagen.

Outline of the Book

The present volume brings together, revised and thematically arranged, contributions to the first two workshops. Several interesting papers could not be included, for various reasons. A number of additional essays were invited, to cover specific aspects of the overall theme. The volume presents different disciplinary perspectives, with most contributors coming from social/cultural anthropology, European ethnology, folklore, or a combination of these. Other disciplines include economics, geography, history and linguistics.

Social Economy in Transition

The first three essays examine instances of the transition between different economic circumstances. Caldwell's study of food poverty in Russia puts the impact of the celebrated 'end of history' under the ethnographic microscope, looking at a society where the certainty of work with its however limited prospects of life-chances has radically disappeared. Foreign aid policies are shown as being informed by circumstances and models of the economy that are quite removed from the everyday lived experience of local people in Moscow. Thus the food aid issue 'represents a larger debate over the relation between economy and society'.

While the poverty witnessed in Moscow does not (yet) have its parallels in the Austrian town of Eisenerz, Moser's study of a declining Alpine mining community highlights underlying processes of change that are not entirely dissimilar. In both cases, global market forces are seen as having destroyed the certainties that came with an established mode of production and exchange. In the Austrian case, these certainties had a basis in the reliance on a single industrial sector rather than, overtly at least, a particular political system. For people who are struggling to survive economically, the distinction may be purely academic, the point being that, in both cases, they have lost what they regarded as the bedrock of their social economy.

The changing meaning of work as a result of much wider economic transformation is a theme continued by Jancius, who looks at work creation schemes in the context of post-Communism. Her case study of Leipzig shows a society where the unification of political territories into a new German state has not only replaced the political system of the eastern part with that of the western one, but swept away many, if perhaps not all of the remnants of the social market economy that once made West Germany a *Wirtschaftswunderland*. At the same time, we see individuals and organisations trying to balance a vaguely remembered social ethic that underpinned that economy with the 'rags to riches' folk tales of neo-liberalism, to create an interpretive framework that might help them cope with their changed circumstances.

Images of the Market

The next three chapters draw our attention from the changing fortunes of individuals in a transitory social economy more to the market itself. Elevated to the status of a divine principle by economic ideologues who persistently misread the moral philosophy of Adam Smith as gospel, the market is presented both in textbooks and in political broadcasts as the panacea for all (or most) that is considered wrong in modern society. Good examples of how markets are supposed to function are found in regular marketing events, such as trade fairs, and in more regular activities, such as the daily trading at the stock exchange.

Montoya discusses how culture affects perceptions of financial markets among shareholders in Sweden, and how this influences shareholders' actions within these markets. Visions of a 'society of shareholders' clash with other ideals of society, including those of the contemporary radical critics of global capitalism, but also the concept, strongly developed in Sweden, of a socially responsible economy. In her conclusion, the author refers to the same ideological balancing act earlier contributors identify, between communal and individual goals of economic activity.

Hartwig's ethnography of shareholders in one particular US stock market company reveals some of the superstitions with which people approach trading in this particular market. Given that the stock market has considerably more bearing on people's life-chances than the average spring bazaar at a community centre (which otherwise may also serve as a good example of how markets may function), this chapter serves as a salutary reminder that there is more than one kind of rationality, and that *homo oeconomicus* does not become 'irrational' economic man (or woman) just because he or she relies on a bit of magic to deliver the goods.

After the lofty heights of financial markets, Goldenberg's essay takes us back to the former Eastern Bloc, and to trade in material objects, in this case art and craft products using precious stone. Her study of a trade fair casts light on how the Polish amber industry tries to continue its craft tradition in a globalising economy, while illustrating the construction of place with reference to a particular combination of culture and economy, a theme that is picked up again in the next group of essays.

Constructing Places and Spaces by Culture Contact

Keeping the focus on craft traditions in a globalising economy – in this case textile production – and remaining in the former Eastern Bloc, Savoniakaitė takes the case of emigrants to examine how, in situations of culture contact conditioned by economic change, the interplay of economy and culture can erode and, at the same time, protect cultural traditions by creating in-between spaces where, in this instance, emigrants produce 'heritage' goods to meet a demand in their homeland. While this helps to preserve certain traditional styles, it lets migrants engage creatively with the host society. Textile styles and patterns become signs of belonging elsewhere in space and time, but, if one follows the author's argument, this rooted-ness is looking forward at least as much as backward. Migrants can thus live quasi with one foot in each of two cultural worlds. In the first decade after the end of the Soviet Union, this diversity may have been especially appreciated. Whether the utopian vision of a postmodern identikit as a solution to problems of assimilation and acculturation will survive the resurgence of xenophobia across Europe remains to be seen.

Fear of the Other, as xenophobia may be translated, has characterised intercultural relations in many borders regions for a long time, and the Polish borders are no exception here. Kennard examines the Euroregions that have been created along these borders in preparation for Poland's accession to the EU to assess how co-operation across a state border, inspired if not exactly forced by economic benefits expected from EU membership, is used to support cultural interchange in areas marked by a long and violent history of ethnic and political conflict. It is worth considering, in this context, the similarities and differences between those regions straddling the border with Germany, and those that connect with other Slavonic countries.

Culture contact of a different kind is the subject of Nogués' discussion of tourism-related policies in Andalusia. Once one of the sun-spots of international tourism, the region has been trying in recent years to re-invent itself as a cultural tourism product. The study explores how the Andalusian territory is being converted into spaces and places where the tourist and the local negotiate new Andalusias, which are a commodified version of the region, but at the same time have the potential for being more than that. To utilise this potential creatively is, Nogués suggests, one of the key challenges for policy makers.

'Branding' Culture

As culture is being turned into a commodity for consumption, regions trying to capitalise on their culture and heritage are concerned with developing their specific brand for marketing their product globally. Hale considers the case of Cornwall, a region on the 'Celtic Fringe' of northwest Europe. Tradition in Cornwall means the Celtic past, but also includes an image of the region as a cradle of the industrial revolution. In popular perception, the two images are not easily reconciled. To some extent, this has to do with a different kind of 'branding' – the stigmatising of the Celtic regions and their traditional culture as 'backward', and associated with poverty.

Nic Craith demonstrates this type of branding with specific reference to another Celtic region, Ireland. Her essay shows how stigmatisation of the language in particular went hand in hand with the depopulation of the island through famine and emigration. Whereas 'Irish culture' as a brand has been doing very well in the global market place for some time, this does not extend to 'Irish' as a language. Given the global success of 'Irish' as a brand, the author makes a case for including the language more proactively. Her conclusion highlights what is perhaps the greatest impediment to such a strategy – the everyday use of English, with its connotations of modernity and prosperity, in preference to Irish, associated with poverty and backwardness. Disregard for its linguistic heritage makes

Ireland, in the author's view, merely an island off the shore of its cultural 'mainland', that is, Great Britain.

From a development studies perspective, Saville examines the global association of indigenous languages with poverty in contrast to the perceived link between English and prosperity. She reviews the situation in a number of developing countries with regard to language policies and elite attitudes, and looks in detail at the representation of English as a source of social and economic advancement. The language issue, both in the Irish/European and in the Third World context, emphasises a point already indicated by other essays – that the utilisation of any aspect of culture as a resource for development is decisively shaped by prevailing power relationships. This in itself is nothing new, and various campaigns for indigenous languages have used a vocabulary of 'empowerment' for a long time. What is new, however, is that 'culture' has become an economic commodity of considerable earning power, as well as a key political issue.

Recognition of linguistic rights may help to promote social and economic equity, as Saville argues. Moreover, language holds the key to culture. In this sense, the more proactive use of lesser-used languages like Irish may indeed unearth a treasure. In economist-speak, treasure hunts are described as 'futures markets', and there may well be such 'futures markets' for culture and heritage in which people invest heavily despite considerable risk because the prospect of a major pay-off makes it all seem worthwhile.

Heritage Futures

In recent years, the EU has been one of the main investors in such 'futures', largely in pursuit of a European identity rooted in a common cultural heritage. Taking the EXPO in Hanover as his starting point, Johler questions contemporary identity politics and the role of the EU in the production of cultural heritage and traditions, which he describes as 'scarce goods in the field of global economy'. This leads him to postulate 'a more dynamic concept of cultural heritage', and call for 'new thoughts and ideas from us European ethnologists'. In many ways, the signposts for the way ahead point back towards the disciplinary history of European ethnology and its as good as forgotten connection with political economy and governance (Kockel 2002). In the final chapter, Nic Craith and Kockel outline an agenda for interdisciplinary research in the field of culture and economy, drawing from the discussion in this volume and other work. A key item on this agenda is the detailed examination of 'heritage futures', which provides the theme for a panel at the 2002 EASA conference. The panel is addressing questions such as whether and how culture may be utilised as a resource for the twenty-first century; whether this necessarily means commodification; who will win in the gamble, who will lose, and what implications all that may have for economy, society and – not least of all – culture itself.

References

du Gay, P. and Pryke, M. (eds) (2002), *Cultural Economy: Cultural Analysis and Commercial Life*, Sage.

Kilday, A. (ed.) (1998), *Culture and Economic Development in the Regions of Europe*, Ectarc.

Kiss, R. and Paládi-Kovács, A. (eds) (2001), *Times – Places – Passages: Ethnological Approaches in the New Millennium*, Institute of Ethnology, Hungarian Academy of Sciences.

Kockel, U. (ed.) (1994), *Culture, Tourism and Development: The Case of Ireland*, Liverpool.

Kockel, U. (2002), *Regional Culture and Economic Development: Explorations in European Ethnology*, Ashgate.

Löfgren, O. (2001), 'European Ethnology in the Jungles of "The New Economy"', in Kiss and Paládi-Kovács, 11-23.

2 The Social Economy of Food Poverty in Russia

Melissa L. Caldwell

In spring 1998, an elderly man hobbled along a sidewalk in downtown Moscow, not far from Red Square and the Kremlin. Dressed in a dark, well-worn overcoat and black fedora, the man slowly picked his way along the uneven pavement in front of brightly lit cafés and elite fashion boutiques. As pedestrians rushed past, he turned his stooped body to face them, extending his trembling hand beseechingly for spare coins. A piece of cardboard hung at the end of a string looped around his neck; the hand-lettered sign read simply, *Golodnyi*, or 'hungry' (also, 'the hungry one'). On the other side of the street stood McDonald's, an American pizza restaurant, and sleek buildings housing the main offices for a number of large international corporations. In their shadows several children slept at the feet of a woman who held up a small sign on which she had written a short blessing for those who might donate a few rubles to help feed her children.

During the transition from state socialism to market capitalism that has marked the last ten years since the dissolution of the Soviet Union in 1991, one of the most fundamental changes affecting daily life has been the way in which economic practices have been transformed from a system marked by shortages to one with supermarkets and automated banking machines on every corner. At the same time, economic-based disparities have increased, and juxtapositions of poverty and commercial wealth – such as those mentioned above – have become even more visible. Such contrasts were only heightened in the months following Russia's financial crisis in August 1998, when federal authorities devalued the rouble, a move that sparked plunging exchange rates (the rouble to US$ exchange rate plummeted. from approximately 6:1 to 15:1 within hours; by June 2000, the value was 25:1), bankruptcies, inflation, and the continued withholding of salaries and pensions by the federal bank.

In this chapter I explore the ways in which food poverty in Russia today has been theorised, both by foreign observers, policy makers, aid workers, and scholars, as well as by Russians themselves. This inquiry gets at the heart of larger questions concerning the intersections of society and economy in post-socialist Russia. Specifically, what distinguishes social and economic practices from each other? How do they in turn inform and constitute each other? And to what extent are such fundamental economic activities as procuring food intrinsically dependent on community articulation and legitimation? By comparing the experiences and narratives of Muscovite food aid participants with the observations of foreign media and policy analysts, I describe how the 'economy of discourses' (Foucault 1990: 11) and 'economy of practices' (Bourdieu 1990: 122) produced by these perspectives reflect competing models about the nature of food poverty in Russia today. At the same time that outsiders more generally associate poverty and food aid with economic conditions, Russian recipients and domestic aid workers approach them as social markers. The dialectic that emerges from these rhetorical conflicts frames a larger debate over the relationship between the economic and the social.

I begin with a discussion of the ways in which food poverty, among other forms of material hardship, has been theorised in the social science literature. From this I delve into the specific issue of how food poverty is variously represented and contested by Russians and non-Russians. First, I outline how outside analysts have detailed the correlation between food aid and economic conditions in Russia. This is followed by a description of Muscovites' interpretations of their involvement with food aid programs. Drawing from these competing discourses, I illustrate the intersections of the social and the economic. The data on which this inquiry is based derive from fourteen months of ethnographic fieldwork conducted in Moscow between fall 1997 and summer 1999.

Supplemental materials are drawn from newspaper and journal articles, as well as public debates administered on 'Johnson's Russia List', a list-serve and Internet discussion group for Russian studies.

My primary field site was a soup kitchen program administered by the Christian Church of Moscow (CCM), an international Protestant congregation in Moscow. I have given pseudonyms to the Christian Church of Moscow and to members of this community in an effort to protect their privacy. It is important to note that CCM staff maintain that their intent is to provide food, not religious instruction, to recipients.

The congregation's 300 members include North American and European diplomats, corporate executives, and their families; African diplomats, students, and refugees; and a small group of Russian participants. Church members run four daily soup kitchens that provide hot meals to 1,500 Muscovites. CCM staff have contracted with private cafeterias to provide the necessary space, cooks, dishes, and other facilities. Meals generally consist of a bowl of soup, meat, potatoes, bread, and tea. On special holidays and over long breaks when the cafeterias are closed (e.g., New Year), CCM soup kitchen clients receive supplemental packages of cereal grains, sugar, flour, oil, and other staples. CCM volunteers serve meals, clear tables, and solicit outside donations for the program. Although several volunteers are Muscovites who are also program recipients, most are foreigners who live in Moscow. Approximately one-half of the volunteers are North American and western European expatriates and their families; the rest are students and refugees from sub-Saharan Africa. Members of the CCM congregation estimate that there are approximately 3,000 Africans currently living in Moscow. Owing to recent racial tensions against people with dark skin (including people from the Caucasus, Central Asia, Africa, and East Asia), the position of these students and refugees in Russian society is precarious.

The daily routines, administrative procedures, and community profile of the CCM program closely resemble those at other food programs I have visited in Moscow, including soup kitchens organised by local church groups, a Red Cross after-school soup kitchen for children, a regional senior citizen centre, and a soup kitchen for the homeless.

Like their counterparts in other food aid programs, CCM staff collaborate with social workers from regional welfare agencies and veterans' councils to identify individuals with the most constrained economic resources – generally people receiving government stipends. In Russia's current subsidy system, which has been continued from the Soviet period, people are assigned status within a graduated hierarchy based on social experience: for instance, retiree (pensioner), veteran of labour or war, survivor of the blockade of Leningrad during World War II, invalid with a certain class of disability, and so on. Varying pension amounts are then assigned to these categories. CCM clients are representative of aid recipients throughout Moscow as most have status as pensioners, invalids, or veterans, and receive the smallest monthly pension amounts, typically sums of 500-600 rubles (approximately US$83-100 in June 1998, US$25-30 in June 1999, US$18-21 in June 2000).

Imagining Food Poverty

For the most part, the social sciences literature on food poverty (including scarcity, hunger, malnutrition, starvation, and famine) has provided external analyses of either materialist causes (Drèze and Sen 1989; Kates 1995) or the biomedical effects on the victims (Scheper-Hughes cites a specific example of this in 1992: 548 n.8). Most case studies are drawn from Third World nations, although the contributors to *First World Hunger* (Riches 1997) have explored the relationships between the politics of welfare reform and hunger in First World nations. As an important corrective to theories such as these, anthropologist Johan Pottier (1999: 10) has argued for the necessity of including the perspectives of those directly involved in and affected by food shortages: 'How does expert opinion compare with the perceptions and strategies of vulnerable groups and individuals?' Ethnographic attention to local social actors thus has not only provided a bottom-up approach, but has also complicated our understandings of food poverty by combining material concerns with experiential, symbolic, and practice-oriented approaches (see, for example, Aretxaga 1997; Brownell 1995; Glasser 1988; Prindle 1979; Scheper-Hughes 1992; Yan 1996).

Nevertheless, despite the plethora of research on aspects of food poverty throughout the world (for extensive overviews of this literature, see Dirks 1980; Pottier 1999; Scheper-Hughes 1992), the specific intersections of economic capital and social relations remain understudied. Most work addressing these issues focuses on their causal relationships: social relations alternately compensate for a lack of economic capital or redistribute what little capital exists in a community (Prindle 1979; Yan 1996); or a lack of economic capital disrupts social relations (Hastrup 1993). What has been omitted is the following question: to what extent are economic capital and social relations convergent? In the rest of this article I explore this question by comparing the competing narratives about food poverty that have emerged in Russia during the last several years.

The Politics of Scarcity in Russia

In both popular and academic discourses, much of Russian and Soviet social history during the twentieth century has been closely linked with themes of shortage. Several scholars explicitly situated the events of the revolutionary periods of the early 1900s with shortages of bread, among other foodstuffs. Representative book titles include: *The Fight for Bread* (*Bor'ba za khleb*) (Davydov 1971); *War, Bread, and Revolution* (*Voina, Khleb i Revoliutsiia*) (Kitanina 1985); *Bread and Authority, 1914-1921* (Lih 1990); and *Bread and Justice: State and Society in Petrograd, 1917-1922* (McAuley 1991). The 1920s and early 1930s were characterised by severe agricultural losses, widespread famine, and social aid programs. Although natural environmental conditions certainly factored into these problems, Robert Conquest (1986) has argued that the poor harvests were caused by Communist Party policies on collectivisation. Meanwhile, Kingsbury and Fairchild (1935) suggested that shortages of consumer goods resulted from shortcomings in production systems.

This period was followed by severe deprivations during and after World War II. Later, in the 1960s, although food and other consumer goods were more readily available, Khrushchev reflected (1964) that the market remained unable to provide customers with the goods they wanted. During the Brezhnev period of the 1970s and 1980s, grain losses and low economic growth also contributed to periodic shortages (see Kroncher 1979; Pipes 1984; Ries 1997). Finally, both the restructuring of perestroika during the late 1980s and the transition to market capitalism in the 1990s have also been associated with a decline in the national economy and shortages of both consumer goods and money (Burawoy, Krotov, Lytkina 2000; Ericson 1995).

Scarcity provides an important frame of reference for understanding and analysing the events of everyday life in Russia. Yet as these examples demonstrate, there is not a single, unifying narrative about scarcity and the way it has been experienced by Russians. At times scarcity has been theorised as a political condition, at others as an economic one. Thus, close examination of the various ways in which scarcity continues to be theorised in the 1990s provides a valuable lens for investigating how both outsiders and insiders understand everyday life in Russia.

The Outsiders' Perspective: Material Scarcity

In the 1990s outside observers who comment on food poverty in Russia have generally sought to identify underlying causes. In most cases these factors are political and economic problems that have emerged with Russia's transition to democracy and market capitalism. In the early 1990s, a reporter for *Business Week* predicted that a widespread industrial depression and massive unemployment in Russia would lead to hunger and riots and perhaps even to another coup (Brady 1992). Five years later, an American newspaper article reported: 'With their wages months overdue, millions of Russians [were] learning new survival skills ... giving blood for money and making pancakes out of potato peelings' (*The*

Chattanooga Times 1997: A2). A Moscow-based journalist reported in *The Independent* that, even before August 1998,

> ... miners, doctors and other workers have been surviving for months without any wages at all, ... people regularly faint from hunger in trolley buses, [and] neighbours are reduced to stealing cabbages from each other's gardens to feed their children (Womack 1998).

Other accounts note the situations of elderly Russians who allegedly cannot afford to buy food. A previous minister with the CCM congregation wrote in a fundraising brochure that was distributed to churches throughout North America that elderly soup kitchen recipients were in danger of starving because of the government's precarious financial situation. The minister described the relationship between one recipient and the government in this way: 'She is hopeless, the government is broke, and the days of Communism don't look so bad through the hunger pangs of memory' (Ammons n.d.). Meanwhile, several foreign volunteers in the CCM soup kitchens argued that food poverty had resulted directly from atheistic communism.

Following the August 1998 financial crisis rumours circulated throughout Moscow and the international media about the impending withdrawal of foreign companies from the Russian market, as well as delays in payment of wages and pensions. The effects of these moves would include a decrease in available foodstuffs and other consumer goods and an increase in the possibility of widespread hunger. In the midst of this financial 'crisis' (*krizis*) (as this period came to be known in popular discourse), North American scholars convened an Internet forum on 'Johnson's Russia List' to discuss the likelihood that bad harvests would further contribute to hunger conditions.

Rumours circulating in the English-language community reported that elderly people had begun eating their pets and that villagers in the provinces outside Moscow were organising vigilante groups to seek out and punish suspected food thieves. Meanwhile, friends and colleagues back in the United States related the dire images of food lines and empty store shelves that were depicted on American television and in American newspapers. A journalist writing for *USA Today*

cited an International Youth Foundation bulletin that claimed
that the rouble crash in August 1998 strained family budgets
to the extent that '14 million of Russia's 38 million children
[were] literally starving' (Babakian 1999).

Although the 'crisis' was primarily an official banking
matter, foreign media quickly focused on its significance as
evidence for a more fundamental calamity in Russia. An
article in the *Chicago Tribune* reported that the appearance of
soup lines in December 1998 was 'a stark reminder of how far
and how hard this former superpower's economy [had] fallen'
(McGuire 1998: 1). In an announcement that the U.S.
government would send food aid to Russia, American
President Bill Clinton commented that 'this program will help
sustain Russians through a serious food shortage ... as well
as their country's continuing economic distress' (Clinton
1998). A well-known American professor of Russian history
even suggested that Russia might demodernise (Cohen 1998).

Themes of blame and responsibility also characterise the
narratives of foreign observers. In many cases, these
perspectives retain the emphasis on material factors by
alluding to Russians' supposedly reckless – and even immoral
– economic practices. One analyst in the *Journal of Commerce*
suggested that Russia would never successfully reform itself
owing to the 'abnormality' of the local economy, particularly
the pervasive practice of barter to distribute domestic goods
(Steele 1998). A contributor to *The Economist* speculated that
post-crisis hunger was 'less because of shortages of food or
fuel than because of bad government.' The writer further
predicted that foreign interventionist food aid would hurt
Russia by 'encouraging corruption' (November 14, 1998).
Lawrence Summers, US Secretary of the Treasury, argued
that potential food shortages and civil unrest could result
from Russia's political woes and vowed that American aid
would be contingent upon Russian officials' acknowledgment
of local problems and their guarantees to conform to US
examples (cited in Coleman 1998). Finally, American policy
makers delayed promised food aid to Russia because of
disagreements with Russian officials over the proper ways to
distribute the aid to needy people (Slavin 1998).

This theme of a moral economy appeared strikingly in American scholar Jerry Hough's August 1998 comments to *The Los Angeles Times*:

> We [i.e., the United States of America; MC] need a major humanitarian program – not a loan, but a gift – of food and medicine to get the Russians through the winter. It is not only in our vital interest, but a moral duty given our role in imposing our brand of economic reform since 1991 (reprinted in Johnson's Russia List #2316).

Hough's comments sparked a sharp response from Leonid Bershidsky, editor of *Kapital Weekly*:

> Thanks, but no thanks. Humanitarian aid from the West came to Russia in 1991 and 1992; not only was it not appreciated by most people (who threw away the powdered milk and wondered at the biscuits in [German; MC] army survival kits that got sent here), but it helped create an image of the West as a place that pretends kindness by dumping stuff in Russia that is not needed by donors. There is plenty of food and medicine to 'last Russians through the winter' (printed in Johnson's Russia List #2316).

In response to concerns about widespread food poverty in Russia, foreign charities have sponsored and implemented a variety of aid programs ranging from soup kitchens and food packages to homeless shelters, domestic abuse hotlines, and children's centres. Common to these programs is a specific, generalised image of Russia's poor. Foreign aid workers appeal to potential donors abroad with detailed descriptions and illustrations of wizened, toothless, rag-wearing Russian pensioners, or of malnourished, listless orphans. A videotape that the CCM uses for fundraising purposes contains scenes of a poorly dressed, elderly woman begging on the sidewalk. In October 1998, International and Russian Red Cross workers promoted their winter appeal efforts in Russia with an informational letter that argued 'the financial crisis sweeping Russia and her neighbours has left millions of people struggling to survive in deteriorating economic and social circumstances' (Russian Red Cross Society 1998: 1). At the press conference to introduce the appeal, representatives drew visitors' attention to the image on the project's official poster: an elderly woman, bundled in thin coat and scarf, her swollen legs and feet in slippers, standing in front of a rundown building with unruly weeds growing on the front stoop. The caption read (author's translation): 'Living is difficult …. In the winter it will be even more difficult.'

Thus, in the discourses of outsiders, food poverty is conceptualised as belonging to a specific set of political and economic conditions: severe material constraints and an inefficient, even backward, state bureaucracy. At the same time, these foreign observers also associate food poverty with a well-defined social group whose members possess specific physical characteristics. This generalised image of tangible, material circumstances then becomes both a model of and a model for representing the Russian experience.

The Insiders' Perspective: Social Scarcity

Although conceptions of food poverty provide important referents to Russian current events, perspectives that privilege this aspect overlook the complexities and inconsistencies that comprise the everyday lives of Russians. At the very least, these narratives ignore the perspectives of Muscovites themselves. An intriguing counterpoint to the speculations of outsiders' about the impact of the 1998 crisis emerged from the reactions of Muscovites who both criticised the pessimism of non-Russian observers and denied the likelihood of either food scarcities or widespread hunger.

Muscovites articulated a number of reasons to support their optimism. Several respondents mentioned the continued presence of inexpensive food products in the markets, while others remarked on the widespread availability of summer gardens as means by which people could feed themselves. One member of the CCM congregation reported that his in-laws had not received their salaries for at least a year but were not hungry because they knew how to farm their gardens. World War II veterans who attended CCM soup kitchens listed edible food products, such as mushrooms, berries, and herbs, which could be gathered from the forest during lean times. Others described the strategies they had employed at various times during the Soviet period when a centralised system of production and distribution had frequently created shortage conditions. To procure needed goods and services, consumers created elaborate social practices such as communal shopping efforts; black market speculation; bribery; and informal exchange networks of relatives, neighbours, friends, and friends of friends. Verdery (1996) offers a detailed discussion of socialist economies of shortage, while Nancy Ries (1997: 36) has described for the perestroika period Muscovite's narratives about shortages and their strategies for dealing with them (see also Ledeneva's 1998 analysis of Russian exchange practices). The possibility that Muscovites were somewhat reluctant or embarrassed to discuss their present material circumstances was not supported by the willingness and great detail with which people articulated their financial and material resources. Numerous conversations and interviews quickly progressed to comparisons of prices, wages, and pensions.

Nevertheless, despite the openness with which Muscovites discussed scarcities and economic hardships, especially when talking about the past, respondents hesitated to confirm the current existence of hunger in Russia. During one of my visits to a CCM soup kitchen, I met a middle-aged man who was not a participant in the program but rather a paying customer in the café at the other end of the room. The man approached me and asked me what had brought me to the cafeteria. In response to my explanation that I was researching the soup kitchen program, the man became irate and told me that I was mistaken. There was no hunger in that place, he argued. When I pointed out the soup kitchen activities that were taking place around him (at that moment two different soup kitchens were operating within the cafeteria, one for CCM recipients and one for Red Cross recipients), the man maintained that neither the programs, nor the need for them existed in Moscow. When I refused to leave (I had been granted permission by CCM staff), the man eventually threatened me for having an illegal research permit and hinted that I could find myself in trouble for my investigation. When I ignored him, he turned his attentions to a CCM supervisor, an African student, and continued his harassment.

nber of Muscovites who were not associated with food
grams expressed similar opinions. Several university
ιs laughed at my interest in studying food assistance.
.__   nner party, three Muscovites who had been friends for
more than twenty years discussed the prevalence of local
soup kitchens and agreed that such aid programs conveyed
misleading information because there was not a widespread
need for them. More intriguingly, however, were the
Muscovite recipients at CCM soup kitchens who argued that
they did not know anyone who was hungry – including
themselves. All respondents confirmed that the majority of
the Russian population was constrained by severe financial
limitations, but nonetheless maintained that material
resources did not adequately represent need or poverty.

Rather, when Muscovites both inside and outside the CCM
soup kitchen community discussed hunger and those who
might be at risk for various forms of food poverty, they
systematically mentioned people who occupied marginal and
tenuous positions in society: specifically, housebound
pensioners and invalids, homeless and mentally ill persons,
and visitors to Moscow. Respondents explained that often
people in these social groups were alone and therefore lacked
the necessary social connections through which they could
gain access to goods and services. In their reports to the
World Council of Churches, representatives from Russian
Orthodox churches that sponsored soup kitchens around
Moscow each noted that their programs served 'poor and
lonely pensioners', 'the least protected social groups
includ[ing] lonely old people, orphans, and the disabled', and
'lonely sick people' (www.rondtb.msk.ru/info/en/food_htm:
Roundtable on 'Education for change and diaconia'. Report by
the Russian Orthodox Church to World Council of Churches).

Social isolation is one of the official prerequisites for
assistance through CCM and other food aid programs. Social
workers and volunteer activists at several regional welfare
offices in Moscow meet monthly to consider letters of
application from local residents who are in need of food
assistance and then to compile lists of eligible recipients for
CCM and other soup kitchens. In their applications,
petitioners describe their material circumstances: for
example, the type of apartment in which they live (communal

or privately owned; number of rooms; type of sanitary facilities; its overall state of repair), their pensions, and any additional sources of income. They also enumerate any extenuating circumstances, such as outstanding debts or the support they provide to other family members. Finally, applicants list living relatives and explain the amount and kind of assistance they receive from each person (i.e., money, living space, food, and so on). In many cases, committee members dismiss applications because petitioners' income levels exceed the imposed limits of approximately 700 to 900 rubles per month. In other cases, committee members who know personal details that applicants have not disclosed – such as live-in relatives or the extra income that those relatives receive from informal employment – turn down applications on the grounds that family members could provide supplemental assistance. Although material resources are important factors, they are not as important as social resources. As respondents have clarified, food poverty is a social, not economic, condition; and it is those persons without social connections who lack access to food and thereby go hungry.

During Soviet times, perhaps the most common strategy that consumers employed to compensate for market shortages and economic uncertainty was the creation of extensive informal networks of friends, relatives, and acquaintances through whom they could locate goods and services (see Ledeneva 1998 and Shlapentokh 1989; cf. Wedel 1986 for Poland and Yan 1996 for China). In some cases, these networks spanned the entire country and even extended across state borders. Researchers who have explored these phenomena in socialist states have repeatedly emphasised the duality of these practices: agents generate social activities to fulfil economic tasks (see, for instance, Ledeneva 1998; Wedel 1986; Yan 1996). Often, as in the case of *blat* (a specific form of networks of influence) in Russia, the circulation of influence over and access to goods through networks is more important and effective than the actual goods themselves (Ledeneva 1998). Thus, social connections have been for many Russians the primary condition for procuring necessary economic resources. Similar patterns have been noted in a study of pensioners in post-unification

East Germany, who have been found to rely on informal networks for social and material support (Scharf 1997).

A Russian Red Cross director who oversees food and other aid programs in the southern region of Moscow explained this connection between the social and the economic in terms of the eligibility requirements for her program:

> We generally take people who are alone. That is the primary criteria because if there is an invalid or pensioner with relatives, of course it is easier for them to survive. When one is completely alone, that is difficult.

Aid workers with another program strategically marketed their services to elderly Russians who lacked extensive social resources. In a program brochure, organisers invited people who were 'over age 65, alone, and in need of social support and defence.' The pamphlet continued with a description of the services the agency provided to accommodate 'the fundamental living problems of single people.'

Marina is representative of CCM recipients in that she has outlived her spouse, children, and friends, and has neither the material nor the social means to support herself. Two other CCM recipients who volunteer as *aktivistki* (activists) for their fellow pensioners note that many CCM recipients and hopeful applicants do not have relatives or friends to help them, and so depend on the soup kitchens for both food and companionship. Several recipients have even expressed concerns that foreign volunteers at the soup kitchens might suffer because they lacked the social capital necessary to find goods and services. By contrast, a woman not directly associated with any food aid programs reported that several years ago, her mother and an elderly neighbour each received an invitation to a soup kitchen in their neighbourhood. Her mother declined the invitation because she lived with her daughter's family and received assistance from them. The neighbour, however, received an adequate pension, but lived alone and without family nearby. He chose to attend the soup kitchen because he had no one else to help him.

CCM soup kitchen recipients support the perception that food poverty is a socially constituted circumstance. Despite the images of hunger and poverty often portrayed in CCM fundraising documents, recipients suggest that concepts, and 'hunger' in particular, do not ac represent their circumstances, even during the 1990s economic crisis. Recipients concede, however, that hungry people might in fact exist in Russia, but maintain that they are most certainly outside the soup kitchen community. Sasha, a long-term CCM recipient and self-proclaimed activist for the elderly, refused to identify herself as hungry, even as she described her severe material resources. She receives a 500-ruble monthly pension with which she pays for food, medicine, and utilities. She also supports her daughter's family because her daughter, an electrical engineer, has not received her salary in six months. Despite her small economic resources, Sasha knows people in various businesses and government offices and procures supplemental goods and services through these connections. She explained that the appellation 'hungry' more appropriately described the circumstances of other neighbourhood residents who lacked these social relations.

As further evidence of the importance of social relations, accusations that one has been abandoned and disconnected from networks are the basis of particularly callous insults among Russian members of the CCM community. When the fourth CCM soup kitchen opened, a new recipient did not follow the serving protocol outlined by the cafeteria manager. After the woman refused to comply with the manager's repeated requests, the worker finally scolded her: 'You are an embarrassment. Your family has dumped you [*vybrosili*] on us.' The recipient insisted that her family connections were secure and cried that the manager had no right to insult her family. On another occasion, a prospective CCM recipient turned down her spot when she was told that she could not take food for several weeks at a time. She explained that she was embarrassed that her neighbours might discover that she was alone and dependent on charitable assistance.

The Sociality of Soup Kitchens

In many ways, CCM participants approach the soup kitchens as more than food distribution points. Instead, the soup kitchens acquire additional significance as lively community-oriented centres. Recipients, volunteers, and cafeteria employees use the soup kitchens as spaces and opportunities to circulate news and gossip; celebrate holidays; and share homemade preserves, pastries, and fresh produce from their summer gardens. In one friendship group, several women frequently bring food from home and distribute it among themselves and several volunteers. In another friendship group, several men sit together and discuss politics. People inquire about each other, share good news, and inform CCM staff when another recipient has fallen ill or has special needs. On occasion soup kitchen directors have even acted as intermediaries for recipients who want to pass on messages and small items to each other. Some recipients come simply to socialise and do not eat.

CCM staff proudly acknowledge that the soup kitchens provide a setting where recipients can socialise with each other and feel that they are members of a community. When the CCM program first began some ten years ago, recipients and volunteers frequently stayed at the soup kitchens after serving hours to play cards, sing, and listen to lectures. One welfare official explicitly linked the connection between material and social resources when he praised the CCM program, among others, for providing 'charitable aid and social support to our members ... . It is very significant support.' A brochure for another domestic aid program advertised that it provided the most important form of assistance – 'moral support for the single person' (author's translation). Similarly, the director for a Jewish soup kitchen in Moscow reflected in a newspaper interview that her staff try to make recipients feel welcome: 'We try to put them at ease by making them feel that this is their home and that we are all in this together' (Ruby 1999).

Today, however, CCM staff and cafeteria employees voice practical concerns about the length of time that recipients spend in the cafeterias. The four soup kitchens only operate for one to two hours each day, and the managers of the four cafeterias request that recipients leave promptly to create space for paying customers. Some of the less subtle techniques that cafeteria employees have employed to convince recipients to leave include putting away the food

and dishes, clearing away trays of food as recipients atte꜡
to eat, and even scolding and shouting at people to leave. The
janitor at one cafeteria takes away volunteers' trays and
shoos them out the door, thus preventing them from serving.
Nevertheless, recipients generally find ways to circumvent
these time limits. One CCM supervisor reports that although
the soup kitchen he directs opens at 9.30am, it is not
uncommon for recipients to congregate in the corridors by 7
am. On pleasant days, people continue their discussions
outside on the benches and railings in front of the soup
kitchens. Meanwhile, volunteers and cafeteria employees
jointly monitor the doors of the dining area before and after
the serving times and check the bathrooms and hallways to
make sure that recipients have left the building.

Muscovites also draw upon their social resources to help
them enter assistance programs. Even after potential
recipients receive official paperwork that verifies their
eligibility and describes their levels of need, placement in
CCM and other soup kitchens is not guaranteed. Recipients
must generally provide proof of residence in a specific district,
typically the neighbourhood in which the soup kitchen is
located. One CCM recipient's request to transfer to another
soup kitchen was denied on the grounds that the new soup
kitchen was not located in the region to which she was
registered to live. Nevertheless, another woman who lives in a
region not covered by the CCM programs was able to
circumvent the rules because of personal connections. Her
apartment is located near the university attended by most of
the African student volunteers. Several years ago she was
befriended by a young African woman who told the soup
kitchen coordinator about her situation as a widower who
lived alone. It was through this connection that the Russian
woman received her place in the soup kitchen. In a more
tragic instance, a CCM recipient who had attended for many
years died after being hit by a car as she left the soup
kitchen. Instead of going through their waiting list of potential
recipients, CCM supervisors agreed to give the woman's spot
to her sister as a means to recognise their family relationship.
In more fortunate circumstances, some soup kitchen regulars
do not have to leave visitors at home. When Zhenya's sister
visits from a town outside Moscow, she attends the soup

kitchen with Zhenya, receives her own meal, and participates in Zhenya's conversation groups. Marina Fyodorovna frequently brings her five-year-old granddaughter; volunteers pay special attention to the girl, play with her, and give her treats. Other recipients take their meals home to share with visiting relatives and friends.

The importance of social relations as the criteria by which people evaluate food poverty underscores the significance of group membership in everyday Russian life. People who are within the soup kitchen system do not see themselves as hungry precisely because they belong to a network. Instead, they perceive the people who live outside the soup kitchen network as those who are hungry. Nevertheless, merely belonging to a social network is not enough to protect people from threats of material scarcity – either real or imagined. In particular, individuals must also demonstrate morally appropriate social behaviour.

A university student in Moscow argued that food aid recipients were alcoholics who had caused their own problems by squandering their apartments and savings on alcohol. A middle-aged professional suggested that the only people who were hungry in Moscow were those who were too lazy too work. Despite the availability of such jobs as selling cigarettes by the metro stations, the woman complained, lazy people found it easy to stand on the street, hold out their hands, and beg, 'Give me money.' These people were embarrassments to Russians who supported themselves, she finished. Similar comments emerged in conversations among Russian members of the CCM church. One congregant, a Muscovite who worked in an American company, confided that she only gave money to invalids who begged. She claimed that other people could find ways to support themselves if they were truly in need of food.

Such comments highlight the ways in which local understandings of social assistance and responsibility to the community are closely intertwined. A sixty-year-old pensioner whose son lived at home explained her efforts to share food and other resources with relatives and friends: 'We all help each other; we are collective (*my kollektivnye*)'. Her best friend, also a pensioner, related her own constrained living situation and the forms of assistance she exchanged with her

brother's family in this way: 'In Russia, we need to he
other.' Thus socially intimate relationships such as fri₁
and acquaintanceship bring with them a sense of oḃ
to help (see Ledeneva 1998 for a discussion of this in the
context of other types of exchange relations in Russia).

Aleksei Mikhailovich is the director of one of Moscow's
regional welfare offices, and he works closely with CCM soup
kitchen supervisors. When describing the various social
programs operating in his district, he spoke of them as forms
of social assistance: 'We administer charitable activities, so
that we help them [i.e., recipients].' He continued by talking
about a sense of duty (*dolg*) to care for the well-being of the
people who lived in his region. Svetlana Grigorievna, the
manager for one of the cafeterias serving CCM soup kitchens,
named the private food charity that she founded 'Our Duty'
(*Nash Dolg*). She explained that she chose this name because
it reflected

> ... the duty of every person to help those who are doing poorly
> ... We have the means first of all to feed people, because the
> government does not have any money, the labour unions do not
> have any money, and therefore the people of good will of our
> country ... can now possibly help those who have found
> themselves in a hopeless situation.

In their own words, CCM recipients support these themes
of collective assistance. Several of them explicitly suggested
that their participation in food aid programs has resulted
from the fact that fellow Russians are not meeting their
obligations to society. Boris, a sixty-year-old invalid and
pensioner, expressed his frustrations in this way:

> I was in the army for three years. I served at [various fronts] and
> now cannot afford to feed myself. Gaidar [ruined the economy].
> Now you feed us. I cannot buy sausages, meat, bread.
> Pensioners do not receive much money. It all goes to Gaidar.
> Chernomyrdin takes it ... . Gazprom takes it from us. I have no
> relations with Gazprom.

Yegor Gaidar was a pro-reform finance minister in the
early 1990s, and Viktor Chernomyrdin was a pro-reform
prime minister during the 1990s. Gazprom is the national gas

company, rumoured to have special relations with various oligarchs and politicians.

On another occasion Boris pointed out a young woman who was leaning against a Mercedes, talking on her cellular telephone. 'Look at the New Russian,' he said, 'They don't feed us.' Similarly, a domestic aid worker blamed Russia's new class of young, middle-class professionals for privileging money and neglecting their parents and grandparents. Another recipient, Oksana, expressed her disappointment more simply. Through her tears at the soup kitchen, she reflected, 'I have spent my whole life defending Moscow. And for what?'

Rethinking Society and Economy

Anthropological discussions of social relations frequently point to exchange practices as a fundamental medium through which interactions occur and social solidarity is alternately constituted and challenged (e.g., Bakhtin 1981; Herrmann 1997; Mauss 1925; Sahlins 1972; Thomas 1991). As Thomas has remarked in his work on trade networks in the southwestern Pacific, 'Exchange relations seem to be the substance of social life ... Exchange is always ... a political process, one in which wider relationships are expressed and negotiated in a personal encounter' (Thomas 1991: 7). As the give-and-take between individuals, exchanges of commodities and gifts are always simultaneously economic and social. This is particularly relevant for Russia, among other formerly socialist states, where exchange relations have long permeated everyday life.

Yet analyses of social relations tend to differentiate the economic from the social by delineating the different resources that social actors manipulate as they situate themselves with regard to other people. Bourdieu's distinctions of economic, cultural, and social capital emphasise the different uses to which social actors put both material and symbolic resources (Bourdieu 1984: 114). To paraphrase Bourdieu, economic capital operates in an economic field, while social capital operates in fields of social interaction (1990: 124). Social scientists have further refined and subdivided the concept of capital to include such aspec as 'material assets', 'skill assets', 'social assets', and 'citizenship assets' (see, for example, Burawoy, Krotov, and Lytkina 2000). By pointing out the limitations of such reductionist perspectives, Smart has redirected analytical attention to the ways in which these variants are mutually explicated and converted (Smart 1993). Not only does this approach retain and emphasise the inherently social aspect of practical activity, but it also clarifies Bourdieu's seemingly paradoxical arguments both for and against an economic/ non-economic dichotomy (compare Bourdieu 1990: 122 with Bourdieu 1990: 124, for instance). Perhaps more important, however, is Smart's emphasis on the strategic instrumentality of capital as the means to recognise and constitute the boundaries between the economic and the social.

Nevertheless, this distinction does not adequately capture the complexities of the social nature of economic activities in Russia. On the one hand, Muscovites convert their material resources into social resources. By sharing food, money, and other goods with relatives, friends, and friends of friends, Muscovites create and maintain networks of individuals with whom they share a collective sense of mutual responsibility. On the other hand, social resources are themselves significant forms of economic capital. The social connections that Muscovites – both inside and outside food aid communities – strategically employ to gain access to material goods acquire a secondary significance as economic resources. Muscovites then use their social resources to compensate for a lack of money or suitable barter goods. In effect, social practices and relations are the features that constitute, regulate, and perpetuate the Russian economy.

Thus, for the case of Russia, food aid is not merely a utilitarian solution to a material problem as it has generally been described in the discourses of foreign observers. Rather, it represents a larger debate over the relation between economy and society. The visions of food shortages and the policies for food aid articulated by non-Russians presume economic models and conditions that are focused on macro-level national and global processes and are otherwise disconnected from the everyday lives of ordinary Russians. As various scholars and analysts have proposed, the dangers of food poverty are closely connected with Russia's transition to a political and economic system that is regulated by impersonal market forces. This perspective conflicts with the practices and views of Russians themselves, whereby consumers emphasise the socially constituted and contested nature of the local economy. In Russia such fundamental economic activities as procuring food are intrinsically dependent on personalising forces of community articulation and verification. Therefore, in contrast with analytical approaches that juxtapose economic and social spheres as corollary but distinct resources, the case of food aid in Russia suggests that the economic and the social are in fact intrinsically and mutually constituted.

Acknowledgements

Funding for this research was provided by the US Department of Education (Title VI), Mellon Foundation, and the Department of Anthropology and the Davis Centre for Russian Studies at Harvard University. Earlier drafts of this manuscript were presented to the Workshop on Postcommunism at the Davis Centre (March 2000) and to the Workshop on 'Culture and Economic Development in Europe' at the European Association of Social Anthropologists meeting in Krakow, Poland (July 2000). I thank Bernie Perley, Máiréad Nic Craith, Ullrich Kockel, and my EASA colleagues for their questions, criticisms, and suggestions for improving this article. I am also grateful to the members of the CCM community for sharing their stories and views with me.

References

Ammons, S. (n.d.), *Description of Christian Church of Moscow Soup Kitchen Ministry*, included in personal correspondence.

Aretxaga, B. (1997), *Shattering Silence: Women, Nationalism, and Political Subjectivity in Northern Ireland*, Princeton.

Babakian, G. (1999), 'Hunger, Bad Health Are Subjects that Russian Children Know Well', in *USA Today*, 4 February, 10D.

Bakhtin, M. (1981), *The Dialogic Imagination*, ed. by M. Holquist, trans. by C. Emerson and M. Holquist, University of Texas Press.

Bourdieu, P. (1990), *The Logic of Practice*, trans. by R. Nice, Stanford.

Bourdieu, P. (1984), *Distinction: A Social Critique of the Judgement of Taste*, trans. R. Nice, Harvard.

Brady, R. (1992), 'The Great Russian Depression of 1992?', in *Business Week* 3262, 47-48.

Brownell, S. (1995), *Training the Body for China: Sports in the Moral Order of the People's Republic*, Chicago.

Burawoy, M., Krotov, P. and Lytkina, T. (2000), 'Involution and Destitution in Capitalist Russia', in *Ethnography* 1 (1), 43-65.

The Chattanooga Times (1997), 'Russians Face Food Shortage', 25 April, A2.

Clinton, W. (1998), 'Statement on the Russia–United States Agreement to Provide Food Aid to Russia', in *Weekly Compilation of Presidential Documents*, 9 November, 34(45), 2250.

Coleman, F. (1998), 'Russia's Future Looks Bleak: Food Shortages, Unrest Not Far Off', in *USA Today*, 10 November, 1B.

Cohen, S. (1998), 'Why Call It Reform?', in *The Nation* 267 (7), 6-7.

Conquest, R. (1986), *The Harvest of Sorrow: Soviet Collectivization and the Terror-Famine*, Oxford.

Davydov, M. (1971), *Bor'ba za Khleb.* Mysl' (Moscow).

Dirks, R. (1980), 'Social Responses During Severe Food Shortages and Famine', in *Current Anthropology* 21 (1), 21-44.

Drèze, J, and Sen, A. (1989), *Hunger and Public Action*, Clarendon.

Economist, The (1998), 'Europe: But Will It Help?', 14 November, 54-55.

Ericson, R. (1995), 'The Russian Economy Since Independence', in Lapidus, 37-77.

Foucault, M. (1990), *The History of Sexuality: An Introduction*, Vol. 1, trans. by R. Hurley, Vintage.

Glasser, I. (1988), *More Than Bread: Ethnography of a Soup Kitchen*, Alabama.

Hastrup, K. (1993), 'Hunger and the Hardness of Facts', in *Man* 28 (4), 727-39.

Herrmann, G. (1997), 'Gift or Commodity: What Changes Hands in the U.S. Garage Sale?', in *American Ethnologist* 24 (4), 910-930.

Johnson's Russia List (1998),Comments by Jerry Hough with Response by Leonid Bershidsky. #2316, 20 August 1998.

Kates, R. (1995), 'Times of Hunger', in *Person, Place and Thing: Interpretive and Empirical Essays in Cultural Geography*, Geosciences Publications, Louisiana State.

Khruschev, N. (1964), 'Report to the USSR Supreme Soviet on Measures for Fulfilling the CPSU Program for Raising the Living Standards of the People, July 13, 1964', in *Soviet Documents* II (33-34), 3-58.

Kingsbury, S., and Fairchild, M. (1935), *Factory Family and Woman in the Soviet Union*, G.P. Putnam's Sons.

Kitanina, T. (1985), *Voina, Khleb i Revoliutsiia*, Nauka.

Kroncher, A. (1979), 'The Economic and Political Aspects of Combatting Grain Losses in the USSR', in *RFE/RL Radio Liberty Research Bulletin*, RL L55/70, 1-2.

Lapidus, G. (ed.) (1995), *The New Russia: Troubled Transformation*, Westview.

Ledeneva, A. (1998), *Russia's Economy of Favours: Blat, Networking and Informal Exchange*, Cambridge.

Lih, L. (1990), *Bread and Authority in Russia, 1914-1921*, California.

Mauss, M. (1925), *The Gift: The Form and Reason for Exchange in Archaic Societies*, trans. by W. Halls, Routledge.

McCauley, M (1991), *Bread and Justice: State and Society in Petrograd, 1917-1922*, Clarendon.

McGuire, M. (1998), 'Living on $10 a month: Plunged into Poverty, Pensioners Try to Survive', in *The Chicago Tribune*, 24 December, 1, 9.

Pipes, R. (1984), *Survival Is Not Enough: Soviet Realities and America's Future*, Simon and Schuster.

Pottier, J. (1999), *Anthropology of Food: The Social Dynamics of Food Security*, Polity.

Prindle, P. (1979), 'Peasant Society and Famine: A Nepalese Example', in *Ethnology* 18 (1): 49-60.

Riches, G. (ed.) (1997), *First World Hunger: Food Security and Welfare Politics*, St. Martin's.

Ries, N. (1997), *Russian Talk: Culture & Conversation during Perestroika*, Cornell.

Ruby, W. (1999), 'Moscow Soup Kitchen Nourishes Pensioners' Spirit as well as Body', in *New Jersey Jewish News*, 1 April, posted on www.njjewishnews.com/issues/4_1_99/mw/feature/text/strory1.html.

Russian Red Cross Society Central Committee (1988), *Belarus, Moldova, Russian Federation, Ukraine: Winter Emergency 1998-1999.* Appeal No. 30/98, 30 September 1998.

Sahlins, M. (1972), *Stone Age Economics*, Aldine Atherton.

Scharf, T. (1997), 'Informal Support for Older People in Post-Unification East Germany: Stability and Change', in *Journal of Cross-Cultural Gerontology* 12, 61-72.

Scheper-Hughes, N. (1992), *Death Without Weeping: The Violence of Everyday Life in Brazil*, California.

Shlapentokh, V. (1989), *Public and Private Life of the Soviet People: Changing Values in Post-Stalin Russia*, Oxford.

Slavin, B. (1998), 'Distribution Dispute Tangles Relief Package for Russia: U.S. Wants to Ensure $885 million Worth of Food Gets to Needy', in *USA Today*, 23 December, 8A.

Smart, A. (1993), 'Gifts, Bribes, and Guanxi: A Reconsideration of Bourdieu's Social Capital', in *Cultural Anthropology* 8 (3), 388-408.

Steele, J. (1998), 'Russia's Abnormal Economy', in *Journal of Commerce*, 14 August. Cited in Johnson's Russia List #2307, 14 August.

Thomas, N. (1991), *Entangled Objects: Exchange, Material Culture, and Colonialism in the Pacific*, Harvard.

Verdery, K. (1996), *What Was Socialism and What Comes Next?* Princeton.

Wedel, J. (1986), *The Private Poland*, Facts on File.

Womack, H. (1998), 'A Rotten, Decaying Nation', in *The Independent*, 17 August. Cited in Johnson's Russia List #2311, 17 August.

Yan, Y. (1996), *The Flow of Gifts: Reciprocity and Social Networks in a Chinese Village*, Stanford.

3 Strategies and Tactics of Economic Survival: De-Industrialisation, Work, and Change in an Alpine Mining Community

Johannes Moser

Eisenerz, an Alpine community in the Upper Styrian region of Austria, lies in a basin formed by surrounding mountains. Especially in winter months, it frequently finds itself isolated from the outside world due to the danger or actual occurrence of avalanches. Considering its peripheral location, it was only by virtue of iron ore that Eisenerz became an industrial city with great regional significance. Iron ore has been extracted in Eisenerz since the Middle Ages, but mining did not become a profession unto itself until modern times, particularly with the industrial revolution. This is not the place to describe in detail all of the expansions and contractions the mining industry in Eisenerz has experienced over the centuries. The city has certainly both lived from mining, and suffered with it. Following World War II, and continuing into the 1960s, the industry experienced a boom, but its positive effects on employment have since been reversed by technological improvements and rationalisation. Employment in mining operations peaked at 4,000 workers in the early 1960s, but has declined steadily since that time.

Since the mid-1980s, the Upper Styrian industrial region has found itself caught in a wave of deindustrialisation. For Eisenerz in particular this trend initially threatened economic and social disaster because the city's peripheral location hampered attempts at economic restructuring. Lloyd Rodwin's claim regarding the fate of declining industrial regions applies directly to this mining community: local institutions could no longer meet the demands of development, and the rate of out-migration exploded (1989: 19). Eisenerz counted 12,435 residents in 1961, but by the year 2001 its population had fallen to 6,455 and its demographic structure showed an imbalance toward older residents. Today, the mine operator, the *Erzberg* company, employs only about 300 people whose work is by no means restricted to mining.

In the years prior to the onset of decline, Eisenerz developed into a 'classic' mining community that exhibits the ideal-typical traits outlined by Martin Bulmer. Such towns are usually geographically isolated, and mining dominates the local economy. Work in the mine is quite exhausting and dangerous, but at the same time produces a special solidarity among workers and serves as a primary source of pride and satisfaction. Finally, the classic mining town exhibits a relatively homogenous social landscape, where those who work together also associate in their free time (Bulmer 1975: 85ff.).

Eisenerzer typically voted for the Social Democratic Party of Austria (SPÖ), and nearly all of the *Erzberg* company employees belonged to the Austrian Federation of Labour Unions. And since the mining enterprise was publicly owned, local union representatives also often held important positions within the company and in local political bodies. These individuals were party to decisions with effects ranging from individual workers' chances for advancement to placement in living quarters, and this to the same degree that they helped with income tax forms and family problems. These political representatives stood at the centre of a social world comparable to a kinship-based system in which they bore responsibility for preserving jobs and ensuring good incomes as well as providing for apartments and workplace safety. In return, they could expect the votes of their clients in the next election.

In the period 1986-87, the mining industry experienced an acceleration of its formerly gradual decline. Labour-intensive underground mining was discontinued entirely, and hundreds of employees were laid off or sent into early retirement. The very survival of the industry now hung in the balance. The people of Eisenerz sought to prevent the termination of underground mining and the possible closure of the company with all means at their disposal. The situation was extremely tense at this juncture, and many people became despondent: the end of underground mining and the drastic reduction of personnel it caused not only threatened residents' economic survival, but also threatened to eradicate the professional identity of the miner, an image that had long defined the local community. This image centred specifically on those who worked in the underground shafts: only they counted as true miners, while workers on the surface were characterised as mere 'quarry labourers' (see Moser and Graf 1997: 43f.).

Stanley Diamond's (1972: 401) description of anthropology as a science for 'the study of men in crisis' applies quite well to my investigation of Eisenerz. Periods of crisis often prove quite revealing because they release new energies and possibilities that extend well beyond the immediate task of 'weathering' a difficult transition. As Hannerz (1995: 70) has observed:

> Over and over again ... humans arrive at the conviction that something in their lives is endangered ... In this moment cultural meanings acquire special significance and become the basis for social and cultural movements and initiatives.

This is precisely what occurred in Eisenerz, where a threatening situation set new forces in motion, which in turn gave rise to a variety of new discourses and stimulated new negotiations of meaning and forms of action, that is, cultural practices. This creativity corresponds precisely to an account of the Cholo in Bolivia (Nash 1993: 311), which also embodies a specifically anthropological perspective:

> In studying such transitional cultures we discover that culture is not only something transmitted from the past to present and future generations. It is the generative base for adapting to conditions as well as for transforming those conditions.

Work and Work Society in Transition

Given the large number of individuals now released from and no longer deemed useful in the labour market, one could presume that the changes underway in Eisenerz would place fundamentally in question not only the meaning of labour but also of the *Arbeitsgesellschaft*. Many of the unemployed in Eisenerz cannot even join the labour reserves for which the economy may again someday have use. Instead, as Birgit Mahnkopf concluded in a different context, they have become essentially superfluous (1997: 56ff.). This may represent one of those instances that Jeremy Rifkin has in mind when he argues that the increasing obsolescence of labour power as a commodity forces people to redefine their relationship to society (1995: 13). For Rifkin, the solution to this problem lies in the creation of a 'third sector' outside the formal economy (ibid.: 183ff.). Ulrich Beck moves in a similar direction when he proposes a new form of public labour that would serve, in his words, as a 'kind of state-sanctioned exit from the labor force' (1999: 128). Yet putting such proposals into practice faces immense difficulties, particularly because they still remain subject to the constraints of the established order and therefore dependent on it. Furthermore, they may contribute to the emergence of an informal and ultimately disadvantaged labour sector comprised mainly of individuals employed in social work and artistic activities.

Others have proposed even more radical solutions: André Gorz, for example, advocates a wholesale exodus from the *Arbeitsgesellschaft* in its present form because productive labour is being eliminated on a massive scale but at the same time is 'still presented as a universal duty, as a binding norm and the necessary basis of our rights and dignity' (2000: 9). Few workers can today point to a product that they themselves have fashioned, Gorz contends, and for that reason, people should reappropriate work by approaching it from a new perspective, namely as what they do rather than what they do or do not have (ibid.: 10). Gorz thus sees the best way out of our present predicament in the form of a social order characterised by a multitude of activities in which everyone is guaranteed minimum income and thereby freed from the constraints of the labour market (ibid.: 102ff. and 113ff.).

Whatever one's opinion of these proposals, a number of structural and cultural obstacles stand in the way of their practical realisation. Adopting the perspective of economic theory, we simply cannot yet envision the complete demise of labour as the central organising principle of society. As the most important source of surplus value, labour remains a pillar of the capitalist system, a fact that even the virtual monetary transactions of the New Economy cannot dislodge. Still, we can detect fundamental transformations in the conditions of production and labour. According to Joachim Hirsch, '[j]ob insecurity and unemployment are basic structural characteristics of this system' (1999: 15). There can be no doubt that massive changes in the economy as a whole and in the structural relations of employment are underway. The specific conditions of globalisation in the world economy, for example, have unleashed developments that appear to restrict the nation-state's traditional sphere of influence. This effect is intensified by the decoupling of production from employment on the one hand, and by monetary and material economic processes on the other' (Zilian 1997: 11). In addition, an economy of symbolic goods has emerged that portends a dramatic change in the traditional economic structures of industrial societies.

Symbolic goods like 'statistics, data, fashion trends, programs, information of all kinds, models of technological development and "knowledge" are becoming ever more important' (Stehr 1994: 340). Such developments place in question many of the founding assumptions of the 'social' market economy as it emerged after World War II in the industrialised west, and especially in Europe. In contrast, flexibility and mobility have become the primary catchwords of the 'New Economy' or 'flexible capitalism', though such slogans often seem less truly descriptive than euphemistic. In fact, according to a number of new studies, these processes forebode increasingly precarious conditions of employment (such as limited contracts and part-time jobs, spurious independence for businesses, or wage-dumping), and thereby not only a fragmentation of the everyday experience of work, but also of work biographies.

While a small group of highly trained individuals may stand to profit from these developments, the mass of working people find themselves subjected to these rather capricious conditions. In the industrialised West, the informal sector shows steady growth, as do the numbers of working poor. Beck speaks in this connection of a 'Brazilianization of the West' (1999: 98). As Hirsch shows, however, from a historical perspective this hardly seems novel, since the 'exploitation of other forms of labor (e.g. housekeeping, agrarian subsistence production)' were already pervasive in the early days of capitalism (Hirsch 1999: 16):

> The actual trend appears in the re-expansion of subsistence production, i.e., in the creation of the infrastructural, natural, and social prerequisites of mass production, including the reproduction of labor power through unpaid or under-paid work.

Displacements such as these intensify conditions of inequality. The effects are especially onerous for women, who often have no choice but to work a 'triple shift' combining formal, informal, and subsistence or household labour (Young 1998: 85).

With respect to culture, these developments unsettle the meanings that were once commonly associated with gainful employment – e.g. constancy, security, routine, experience. In his book, *The Corrosion of Character* (1998), Richard Sennett addressed precisely this issue by investigating the meanings people attach to such upheavals. Surprisingly, recognisable changes at other levels do not necessarily undermine the cultural and personal relevance of work (Moser 1998). I found that work also remains of central importance in Eisenerz: it continues to confer recognition and social status, even when it also operates as an instrument of power and discipline. The continued significance attached to work is felt most powerfully by those workers who, on account of the local mining industry's collapse, have entered the ranks of the long-term unemployed, only to move from there into early retirement. They experience intense feelings of shame because they cannot fulfil their own ideals – above all, to have gainful employment for the duration of their working life. Most discussions and new ideas among residents thus concentrate on how to ensure that their children will enjoy better prospects – i.e., on ways to create new jobs in Eisenerz so that its younger residents will not be forced to leave in order to survive.

Globalisation and Local Community

Migration has 'always' been part of life in Eisenerz: people came to the city to work in the mines, and they departed when the industry declined. A massive flow of out-migration began in the 1960s, specifically among people seeking employment and educational opportunities. Few who left ever returned. Among the adults in my sample, sixty-two percent of their grown children had moved away from Eisenerz; more than a third left to pursue a university degree, while another third sought a higher level of secondary education. The proportion of commuters is also quite high: a full twenty-one percent work outside Eisenerz.

Following those who have moved away from Eisenerz in a 'multi-sited ethnography' (Marcus 1995) or with a kind of mobile field research (Welz 1998) would surely prove quite informative. My central concern here, however, is not primarily those who have departed under the pressure of recent developments – people forced to submit to the dynamics of what Arjun Appadurai calls 'deterritorialization' (1991: 192) – but rather those who have either returned to Eisenerz or have never left. These residents view emigrants as victims of forces that compelled them to leave their 'home place' or *Heimat* – a term which, although it has fallen out of fashion among scholars, still enjoys wide popular use. Eisenerzer lament the plight of these victims and devote much of their energy to developing strategies intended to protect themselves or their children from suffering the same fate.

Like so many other regions and cities, Eisenerz operates in a field of intersecting forces now referred to as the 'global-local', a condition that has served as the focus of numerous recent scholarly studies. Anthony Giddens, for example, has pointed out that 'events in a given place are shaped by processes whose origins lie many kilometers away' (1995: 85). It has become a basic characteristic of late modern society that our way of life is embedded in global processes, even when we ourselves do not travel beyond the bounds of our local community. Locality, Appadurai argues, becomes in this context a fragile social achievement, exhibiting primarily relational and contextual qualities rather than spatial ones (1995: 204). These observations have led scholars such as Martin Albrow (1997; 1998) to question the continued relevance of locality and community as descriptive concepts. Community no longer depends on locality, Albrow contends, and the concept of 'local culture' overlooks phenomena that transcend the supposed integrity of local community, such as migration and various external relationships (1997: 40).

Such conclusions seem to me to be rather premature, particularly when viewed critically from an anthropological perspective. Albrow bases his argument on a closed and static conception of culture long abandoned by most other scholars. Local culture appears in a new light, however, when we approach the concrete locale as an arena in which a number of individual universes of meaning intersect and new meanings are negotiated. In contrast to Albrow, who acknowledges these intersections but denies their broader relevance for the constitution of local culture, we must investigate whether and how these processes occur. As Hannerz explains, in the place where these universes of meaning collide, the global – which began as local in another setting – holds the possibility of becoming 'native'. 'At this intersection', he adds, 'things are forever working themselves out, so that this year's change is next year's continuity' (1996: 28). Here lies the peculiar meaning of local culture: it is idiosyncratic but not autonomous; it remains in some sense bound to a particular locale but also responds to extra-local forces. The decisive fact is that larger forces reverberate at the level of the local. They directly affect people who, even when they sustain a variety of relationships that reach well beyond the local community, still live in a concrete place and share a particular cultural (and local) memory. The economic changes occurring in Eisenerz were provoked by global processes, but they are confronted with forms of 'local knowledge' that can generate idiosyncratic approaches to processes of transformation.

Discourses of Economic Crisis and Recovery in Eisenerz

Rodwin has proposed two options for regions in economic decline – one must either bring the jobs to the people, or the people must go to the jobs (1989: 21). Eisenerz has pursued both options, but with uneven success. One the one hand, the high rate of out-migration reduced some of the pressure on the local labour market that characterised the 1980s. On the other hand, efforts were undertaken to open up new possibilities for the remaining residents.

Modernisation theory sees traditional value orientations as one of the main obstacles to development in such regions. In Eisenerz the reigning perception was no different, a fact that revealed itself in numerous contexts. For example, one effect of the economic crisis lies in the increasing power of the local elite to define the terms used to comprehend the situation; they are regarded as the experts and are thereby empowered to construct authoritative accounts. Discourses concerning the future of the city, about the causes of the economic crisis and possibilities of overcoming it, are thus a natural expression of power relations: as Michel Foucault has revealed, securing power depends on gaining control over discourse (1974: 7). In a manner that echoes Karl Rohe's study of the Ruhr industrial region in Germany, the educated 'bourgeois' class in Eisenerz in former times had no role as bearer and administrator of a specific regional culture, the culture was socially speaking that of the common people (1984: 137), but more recently it has acquired a new form of hegemony, namely in the realm of interpretation. Their accounts often blamed the miners – more precisely their attitudes – for the fact that neither economic transformation, the introduction of new industries, nor the upswing everyone so passionately desired occurred as quickly as hoped. As interviews I conducted with experts attest, expert discourses attributed these failures to a fixation on security prevalent among employees of state-owned enterprises. One assistant mayor, for example, lamented local workers' sense of entitlement and expressed doubt that those in charge – namely the factory councils who at this point actually no longer had a say in much of anything – could make the necessary intellectual adjustments.

One group in particular, owners of local businesses, now find themselves more inclined to voice their concerns in local affairs. This situation stands in marked contrast to earlier, more prosperous times when they profited greatly from high employment rates at the mining company and chose not to involve themselves much in political matters. In assessing the economic crisis, one businessman called for a fundamental shift in attitude among the workers: they would now have to make adjustments after having been spoiled in the past. They were even picked up on their doorstep and brought to work, he explained, then dropped off at the end of the day. Another local entrepreneur offered a similar criticism of the prevailing mentality: not once in their lives had most of the Eisenerzer borne responsibility for others, and for that reason they lacked a broader perspective.

Images of this sort also appear in many studies promoting tourism as Eisenerz's best chance to master the crisis. Here too, the 'mining mentality' appears as an obstruction because, as the standard argument goes, industrial workers cannot warm up to the notion of becoming service workers in touristic establishments (Knoth and Schadt 1991: 71). The responsible parties in Eisenerz, along with those who would like to hold responsibility, have internalised such studies to the extent that they often repeat the scenarios contained in them without referring to their source, presenting them instead as products of their own reflections.

Strategies and Tactics

According to Foucault, control over discourse can establish or reinforce relations of power. Foucault also shows, however, that 'at the core of any relations of power, as a permanent condition of their existence, lie rebellion and the unruly freedoms'. He concludes that there exists 'no relation of power without resistance, without a way out or means of evasion, without possible reversal' (n.d.: 45). In my view, the strategies and tactics I observed in Eisenerz are extremely important both as ways of confronting the economic crisis in Eisenerz and as implicit responses to dominant discourses. I therefore want to suggest that the activities prescribed by local hegemonic discourses by no means represented the most effective measures, and certainly not the only possible ones. In the following, I draw upon the work of Michel de Certeau, whose book, *The Practice of Everyday Life* (1988), portrays the 'activities of consumers', which include a rich repertoire of practices that belies their supposed passivity and conformity.

In his discussion of social practice, de Certeau draws a distinction between tactic and strategy. Strategy, he explains (1988: xix), consists in

> ... the calculus of force-relationships which becomes possible only when a subject of will and power (a proprietor, an enterprise, a city, a scientific institution) can be isolated from an 'environment'.

A strategy requires its 'own' place that can

> ... serve as the basis for generating relations with an exterior distinct from it (competitors, adversaries ...). Political, economic, and scientific rationality has been constructed on this strategic model.

Tactic, on the other hand, is 'a calculus which cannot count on a 'proper' (spatial or institutional localisation), nor thus on a borderline distinguishing the other as a visible totality'. Because it possesses no basis of its own, it must use the place of the other, de Certeau writes, 'where it can capitalize on its advantages, prepares its expansions, and secure independence with respect to circumstances'. For this reason, tactic remains more dependent on time: 'it is always on the watch for opportunities that must be seized on the wing'. 'The weak', he concludes, 'must continually turn to their own ends forces alien to them' (ibid.). In this regard, de Certeau's tactics represent an extension of Pierre Bourdieu's strategic praxis. For Bourdieu, social fields are always fields of conflict; there is a constant battle between those in power and those who seek to acquire that power. The power he associates with forms of 'distinction' can be understood as prime examples of this. A given social field thus contains both 'strategies of preservation' and 'strategies of heresy', where the latter seek to undermine the established order (1993: 107ff.). De Certeau's tactics can also serve as strategies of heresy, but their primary function lies in individual attempts to assert control in an environment shaped by outside forces. As the people of Eisenerz became fully conscious of the economic crisis, one could observe the operation of strategy and tactic in a wide variety of settings.

Strategies

The city of Eisenerz – or its elected political representatives – initially pursued two strategies that proved only marginally successful, mainly because these strategies required the co-operation of multiple parties whose interests did not always coincide. The city's primary overture focused on expanded tourism, specifically in the form of a new winter ski resort. Here, as in many regions of the world facing economic crisis, tourism has come to represent the last glimmer of hope for recovery. The Eisenerzer initially hoped – and still imagine today – that tourism would provide an ample supply of new jobs and serve as the motor of economic revitalisation. The high hopes attached to tourism bear a direct relationship to the widespread fear that if revitalisation does not occur, Eisenerz could someday become a desolate ghost town – a fear inspired by one of the numerous future scenarios proffered by experts.

Local leaders sought an external investment partner for the ski resort project. Although both the federal and state governments had already approved or at least indicated the likelihood of generous assistance, the necessary capital was still lacking. A fitting partner was eventually found in a building contractor who had previously undertaken a number of similar projects elsewhere in Austria. Preparations began with great optimism, but soon a number of obstacles came into view that presented insurmountable difficulties. Building the resort would first require purchasing or leasing land, and many of the local residents who owned the needed parcels immediately saw the possibility of a windfall: selling or leasing their forested lots would bring a much better return than the lumber they usually harvested from them. Other owners expressed no interest whatsoever in selling their land because it had been in their family's possession for generations, which in turn conferred a certain security.

Among them are some of the entrepreneurs who are members of a forest co-operative. As a way to avoid directly opposing the project's advocates, this group pointed to difficulties posed by state environmental requirements. Although nominally in favour of the project, these owners wavered when their own property was in question. The environmental requirements actually would have posed more than a minor hurdle, as cutting down trees in an area plagued by frequent avalanches would have necessitated the construction of protective walls. In the end, the main investor jumped ship in the midst of protracted negotiations, and the ski resort plans, although not entirely abandoned, fell by the wayside.

Parallel to the ski resort project, the city also sought an investor willing to finance a hotel at the local Leopoldsteiner Lake recreational area, whose lake contained water as cold as it was pure. An architectural competition was held and a winner announced, but as always, a deficit of capital stood in the way of its realisation. The hotel was conceived as a model project for a touristic program incorporating seminars and other educational offerings, a concept that had recently taken hold in Eisenerz in the form of summer universities and cultural programs. In this case, the Eisenerzer were moving entirely within the province of late modern economies, in which knowledge has 'increasingly [taken over] the role of the classical factors of production' (Stehr 1994: 11f.). Compared to other goods, knowledge is highly transportable and requires for its application only a few specialists joined by a few others interested in profiting from it. Yet this sort of transformation also requires a specific infrastructure, and Eisenerz lacked the appropriate capital to provide it. As a result, at this point only projects of more modest proportions have been pursued.

Yet another strategy adopted by the city administration – this time in co-operation with the former *Voest-Alpine* company, now the *Erzberg* company – focused on attracting new industries to replace mining. This effort initially proved quite successful: a factory for the production of artificial stone was established, and the mining company's former main workshop was taken over by a large Austrian corporation whose top managers showed evident enthusiasm for local workers' abilities. Despite its initial promise of success, however, the stone factory soon failed due to management problems. Its managers' inept dealings in what was in any case a very difficult market left the company with a marred image that produced catastrophic results. Similarly, it turned out that the corporation that took over the former workshop seemed more interested in state assistance than the enterprise itself. Unlike the stone factory's managers, however, they were more careful to limit their own risks. With the construction of windmills for electrical power generation and the production of steel and other metal containers as well as engines for Formula 1 racing cars, they had chosen a high-risk course for the firm, but after the subsidies were exhausted, they immediately deserted the company.

Only a glass factory opened under the auspices of *Voest Alpine* and later sold to a British consortium was able to establish itself firmly in its market. The company's unusually low wages and benefits, along with its decidedly flexible approach to policies on work hours and overtime, did not find ready acceptance in the former industrial stronghold of Eisenerz. Extreme tensions between the firm and the labour union ensued. However, the strategy of compensating for material deficiencies with continuous work proved successful.

This firm's success story offers a powerful example of how the New Economy operates. An enterprise is established in a structurally weak region with the help of government aid, and it operates primarily as a sub-contractor for a major industry (the firm's main product is automobile windscreens). The contracting firm pushes down prices, which directly affects the sub-contractor's wages and working conditions. But since production can always be moved elsewhere, resistance is useless. At the time of writing, even this model case has fallen victim to the restructuring tendencies of 'flexible capitalism' and is about to close down, with a loss of over one hundred jobs. According to employees, the Eisenerz branch has been consistently profitable, but its profits have been siphoned off to support the establishment of new branch plants in Eastern European countries.

In comparison to the efforts of the city administration, the strategies pursued by the *Erzberg* company have enjoyed greater success. Under the leadership of its now retired Mine Director, the company underwent extensive restructuring.

The mining of iron ore now constitutes only one section of the firm alongside a number of service operations including blasting and tunnel construction, other services offered to mining companies, and a repair workshop. The company has been able to maintain relatively good wages and benefits in these sections.

The strategies described up to this point move either within the field of industrial activities or in the sector I have categorised as recreation and tourism. These strategies are set in motion by actors, or rather 'institutions', that command their own place in the sense introduced by de Certeau. That is, they possess their own capacities for realising their particular form of rationality. Yet as we have seen, this by no means guarantees success. As Bourdieu suggests, there are other actors at work in these fields, actors who compete for economic and possibly symbolic dominance. And alongside these actors we find initiators whose activities do not seem to fall readily into the category of strategy or tactic. It is instead, I suggest, the 'tactics of practitioners' that institutions adopt and fashion into strategies.

Examples of the 'Tactics of Practitioners'

The most striking example of this appears in the section of the *Erzberg* company devoted to recreation. The firm re-opened parts of the mine closed in 1986, outfitting them for display to visitors. A huge *Haulpak* mining truck modified to carry passengers brings guests to various sections of the former mining operation. They can then board a train that carries them into the mine itself, where they take a tour under the guidance of a mining specialist. A total of 100,000 people per year take advantage of this opportunity. This venture has proven quite profitable, which in the area of museum activity (understood in its broadest sense) is quite rare. This project did not, however, begin as a strategy of the *Erzberg* firm itself; quite to the contrary, its employees first hit upon the idea and initially faced a formidable task in convincing the company's managers that it might work. What first began as a visitors' mine was subsequently expanded into a more encompassing recreational facility. In addition to the mine tours and the trips on the '*Hauly*' truck, the *Erzberg* company now sponsors open-air concerts with national and international music talents as well as motor sport events. Yet however successful this project appears, it still remains subject to the demands of the late modern economy. Since the visitors' mine and its recreational offerings are open for only six months, between May and October, most of its employees are jobless for the remaining half of the year. They also work under limited contracts and thus suffer many of the disadvantages associated with precarious employment conditions. The firm's female employees are not, however, entirely dissatisfied with this situation, since positions for women in Eisenerz have always been scarce. Many women also welcome six months of unemployment because it allows them more time with their children or for other activities, and since most of their male partners still earn an income during this period, this does not threaten the economic survival of the household.

Another example of how tactics become strategies appears in the schools of Eisenerz. In addition to its schools (which include a basic primary and secondary school, a general secondary school, and a polytechnical school), Eisenerz also has a college preparatory *Gymnasium*, a business academy, and the Adult and Youth Education Centre (AYEC) that grew out of *Voest Alpine's* former instructional workshop. All of these schools have suffered a decline in attendance due to the continuing decrease in Eisenerz's population. Ideas for addressing this problem proposed by teachers were eagerly embraced by school administrators, since they shared a common interest in preserving existing teacher positions. Thus, in order to avoid the painful discussion that would ensue if it became necessary for some teachers to give up their positions or be transferred to a school outside Eisenerz, these actors developed a broad new palette of experimental school offerings and educational concentrations intended to ensure the long-term preservation of teaching jobs and survival of the schools themselves. The new Nordic Training Centre represents the most impressive of these measures. Promising young athletes in winter events like the ski jump, cross-country skiing, and the Nordic combination come to the centre to focus on athletic training while completing their secondary education or an apprenticeship. Similarly, the

Sport High School offers athletic training, in preparation for later specialisation in Nordic events, to pupils aged between ten and fourteen years, although it also offers a concentration on volleyball. Whether one pursues this depends, of course, on the preferences of the 'practitioner'.

Eisenerz's new educational offerings do not end there. The Gymnasium and business academy have joined with the AYEC in a co-operative program that allows pupils to learn a skilled trade alongside their academic or business training. The AYEC also operates as a retraining centre for the unemployed, who can take a wide array of courses in areas ranging from job application skills and computer applications to specialised training in computer-aided design (CAD). Measures such as these serve above all to ensure the continued existence of the schools, since they also attract pupils from outside the region. Particularly the Sport High School and Nordic Training Centre draw pupils from all parts of Austria. However clever and successful this strategy derived from tactic has been, it has actually helped 'only' those teachers who already worked under a guaranteed contract. Young teachers have, in contrast, gained much less. The case of Gerlinde Gruber offers a vivid example: she has not been able to find a teaching position since the birth of her daughter some years ago, and must now find other ways to survive as a single mother.

Tactics

At this juncture I would like to shift my focus to those initiatives that can be primarily understood as tactics, although in practice the line between tactic and strategy sometimes proves quite fluid. As the aforementioned plans for a seminar hotel and the summer universities show, a variety of actors in Eisenerz have set their sights on the sector of knowledge production and transmission, which broadly speaking falls within a field whose representatives are today characterised as 'symbolic analysts' (Oberbeck 1997) or 'knowledge workers' (Stehr 1994). The building that formerly housed the *Voest Alpine* central administration, the *Amtshaus*, is now occupied by a number of initiatives working in this sector. The *Styrian Iron Road Association*, for example, is a group that has developed cultural activities and tourism in co-operation with other communities whose prosperity used to rely on iron ore mining or processing. In this case, the use of local (human) resources plays a significant role to the degree that one seeks to avoid transplanting external schemes, which frequently occurred in this region, choosing instead to involve local people in the planning process. The same building also houses the project *@ftermining*, a program headed by a young intellectual that receives support from the European Union as well as other institutions. The project, which she devised in collaboration with local residents and works in co-operation with regions in Finland and Sweden similarly affected by deindustrialisation, seeks to develop conceptions of a future 'after mining'. Taking advantage of the possibilities presented by new media, they worked on an international level to create joint web pages that showcase these regions and their potential for development. At the local level, the organisation offered courses for skill enhancement, developed employment programs, and sought to establish an institute that would offer training in tourism-related professions. Yet another resident of the *Amtshaus* is a geological research institute specialising in the history of smeltery. The institute, which has also created new jobs, owes its existence to the initiative of a highly motivated engineer, whose passionate pursuit of a hobby (locating early sites of metal processing) eventually led to the foundation of an institute. One thing common to all of these initiatives is that, however creative their ideas and efforts may be, they remain dependent on the financial support of the public household or the European Union.

Yet another idea was conceived and set in motion by a former miner. On the mining company grounds on the Erzberg, he established a workshop where the general public could try its hand with the tools of the blacksmith and ironworker. The workshop is now included on the standard itinerary for most tourists visiting Eisenerz. It offers the former miner and his participating colleagues the opportunity to further pursue a profession that had long brought them fulfilment.

A further initiative was the brainchild of a couple with whom I became personally acquainted, Marianne and Jürgen, who grew up in Eisenerz but now live and work in Vienna. Marianne was the driving force behind this endeavour. After completing her training as a specialist in tourism and hospitality, she worked in a number of hotels, then some years ago she became the right-hand associate for the owner of a hotel chain operating in several countries in central Europe, an enterprise in which she also holds a financial stake. With the help of Jürgen, who works as an engineer in an international electronics firm, Marianne convinced her boss to follow their lead by investing in a kiosk located at the visitors' mine in Eisenerz. The kiosk, which they lease from the *Erzberg* company, is located in the building from which tours of the *Erzberg* and visitors' mine depart. At first the kiosk offered souvenirs, beverages, candy, and snacks, but its proprietors have in the meantime expanded their operations. They now prepare meals for all of the 'busloads' of tourists. As Marianne recently explained, something that actually began as a private pursuit inspired in part by a certain affection for her hometown quickly grew into a legitimate business that turns a substantial profit.

In much the same way as Marianne and Jürgen started a successful enterprise, a number of local people have begun to undertake new initiatives such as the letting of rooms and apartments to visitors, thereby filling a gap in the market caused by the continued absence of large hotels and other accommodation. Because the area offers ideal opportunities for hiking and cross-country skiing as well as other new offerings, Eisenerz has become a choice destination for those who prefer 'environmentally sensitive tourism'. Christian and Josefine Berger have discovered ways to profit from this. Christian is a trained mechanic who worked repairing vehicles for the *Erzberg* company until he was caught by the wave of layoffs in the 1980s. Christian and his wife, who for many years did the accounting and secretarial work for her father's bakery, opened a locksmith shop even while he was still employed at *Erzberg* in order to give themselves an extra leg to stand on. In addition, Mrs. Berger hit upon the idea of opening a bed-and-breakfast. She was able to get the enterprise off the ground in a short time, and it has enjoyed great success. Mrs Berger provides a good example of how new conditions have to some extent undermined the old gender regime characteristic of traditional industrial society. While running a bed-and-breakfast does fit the 'classic' model of female activity in a touristic region (men generally pursue other activities), Mrs. Berger does not merely operate the pension by herself for supplementary income. Rather, she runs it as an independent enterprise – she has hired low-wage workers paid on an hourly basis to do the cleaning, and she knows quite well how to set priorities in other realms. The standard reproductive labour of the household, for example, must simply wait when more important tasks call. At first she found herself unable to 'tear herself away' from the duty of regularly preparing a complete meal for her husband, but now he often either cooks something for himself, or they go out to a restaurant.

Here, at the level of the everyday, two aspects of the discussion concerning gender regimes become clear. First, in order to fulfil their own occupational duties, women with higher qualifications or in positions of responsibility find it necessary to employ other women who either possess fewer skills or have been forced to accept low-wage employment. Second, even if gender inequalities do not thereby disappear, these women no longer allow themselves to be forced into 'the kitchen' (Young 1998: 84, 87) quite so easily.

I have thus far enumerated a number of examples of the ways local residents have responded successfully to the difficult economic situation in Eisenerz. At the same time, I wish by no means to suggest that everyone has enjoyed equal success. The unemployed teacher Gerlinde Gruber and the part-time workers at the visitors' mine illustrate this quite powerfully. Still another downside of an otherwise successful model appears in Michaela Murschetz, a single mother who, after the untimely death of her father, dropped out of school and since then has managed to find jobs that offer only the most precarious of employment conditions. If she did not have a post as a kind of building superintendent, for which she receives meagre compensation as well as a rent-free apartment, she would not be able to survive financially. Working as a housekeeper paid on an hourly basis – for individuals like Mrs Berger – is her only other source of income. Michaela's case reveals how a variety of factors can work to exclude someone from the regular economy. As a single mother, she lacked a partner who would otherwise contribute to the family income; because she had to care for her daughter, she could not accept a full-time position; and since she has no diploma or certificate, she finds herself trapped in unskilled jobs – in this case housekeeping – where advancement is practically impossible. As a result, she lacks both the self-confidence and the symbolic capital of social networks necessary to improve her situation. Regardless of how much effort she invests or strain she endures, she can do little against these mechanisms of exclusion. And failed attempts to improve one's lot usually remain hidden. Who likes to tell the tales of defeat? Instead, one pursues new possibilities or 'wriggles' one's way through and declares oneself satisfied. If Appadurai's observation is correct, namely that fantasy and imagination have become essential tools for the construction of social life and identity (1991: 198ff.), then it should come as no surprise that the less satisfactory parts of our biographies tend to fade from the overall picture.

Conclusion

An important element common to the activities outlined here is that they did not originate 'from above', but rather through the initiative of individuals in Eisenerz whose engagement eventually received public attention as well as recognition from diverse institutions. In a manner very much in line with de Certeau's discussion, these actors have occupied new locations and spaces, used their circumstances to their advantage, and launched new initiatives. Perhaps not entirely commensurate with de Certeau's account, however, are those tactics that were transformed into strategies – i.e., where particular institutions discovered emerging tactics and judged them worthy of more serious attention. In such cases, tactics acquire a location, strategies are then developed, and new concepts devised. The tactics nevertheless originate in the creative minds of people in the region, whose endogenous potential for development is often underestimated. In this light, my research confirms what Georg Elwert has insisted with reference to studies in economic anthropology: the assumed stagnating effects of traditionalism can seldom be established scientifically. Instead, research 'shows the endogenous dynamics of change and strategic, optimising behaviour rather than cumbersome traditionalism' (Elwert 1984: 381). Moreover, it is essential to recognise that the initiatives described here draw upon traditional funds of knowledge and understanding that actors have adapted to new challenges. Although it may not occur in every case, this process generally produces new structures that can endure over the long term and may help actors to circumvent precarious and uncertain situations in the future. This has occurred, for example, in the activities linked to the cultural heritage of mining – the visitors' mine, the blacksmith workshop, the *Styrian Iron Road Association*, the geological research institute, and the *@ftermining* project, along with those initiatives that reach beyond that heritage, such as the glass factory, the private tourist accommodations, and many other enterprises. For many projects, the possession of various forms of capital by those involved proved decisive in their success or failure. Economic capital actually proved rather less important in this regard than the symbolic capital of social networks – a form of capital that opens doors, allows access to various forms of assistance, and makes it possible for a wide array of new ideas to be heard. For these purposes, the old political channels offered by the unions and the Social Democratic Party have proven quite helpful, which suggests that these groups may have regained some of their old strength following the low point they experienced in the mid-1980s.

In the foregoing account, the central issue is not who has emerged as the winners and losers in the course of these developments. Rather, I have sought a perspective that relativises such judgments. Jeremy Rifkin has claimed, for example, that the 'symbolic analysts' and knowledge workers with high levels of training emerge as winners in the context of current economic transformations (1995: 127ff.). Many other studies recapitulate this distinction between winners and losers. Among the winners we usually find the mobile, transnational actors who possess the right skills and are able to transport and profitably apply them anywhere in the world. The losers, on the other hand, are the actors who remain settled in one place, have less education, and show less openness toward increased mobility. In a critical analysis of postmodern discourses of identity and territoriality, Orvar Löfgren asked some years ago precisely what types of people the standard postmodern metaphors actually describe and concluded that they generally refer to middle-class men (1995: 352). Expanding upon some of Bourdieu's critical remarks, I suggest that we anthropologists must remain intensely aware of the fact that our own position in this world can inspire peculiar evaluations of it. In Eisenerz and a number of other contexts I learned that who counts as winners and losers can vary greatly. The people of Eisenerz have developed tactics and strategies that clearly reflect economic transformations at the global level, but these activities also serve to secure their local sense of belonging. When mobility means acquiring an education or going on vacation, they view it as quite desirable, and flexibility acquires significance for them only insofar as it supports their own endeavours. Unlike the scholars cited above, they see the losers in those people whose survival has come to depend on permanent mobility or nomadism and are therefore deprived of any real place of belonging, in spatial as well as other senses. These perceptions represent a reaction to global economic changes. The people of Eisenerz seek creative solutions to the problems posed by these changes in their own concrete locale and for their specific circumstances, solutions that make use of traditional knowledge in order to meet the challenges of a late modern post-industrial society.

Translated by Jason C. James (San Diego/California)

References

Albrow, M. (1997), 'Traveling Beyond Local Cultures: Socioscapes in a Global City', in Eade, 37-55.

Albrow, M. (1998), 'Auf dem Weg zu einer globalen Gesellschaft?', in Beck, 411-34.

Appadurai, A. (1991), 'Global Ethnoscapes: Notes and Queries for a Transnational Anthropology', in Fox, 191-210.

Appadurai, A. (1995), 'The Production of Locality', in Fardon, 204-25.

Beck, U. (ed.) (1998), *Perspektiven der Weltgesellschaft*, Suhrkamp.

Beck, U. (1999), *Schöne neue Arbeitswelt. Vision: Weltbürgerschaft*, Campus.

58   *Culture and Economy*

Bourdieu, P. (1983), *Die feinen Unterschiede: Kritik der gesellschaftlichen Urteilskraft*, Suhrkamp.

Bourdieu, P. (1992), *Rede und Antwort*, Suhrkamp.

Bourdieu, P. (1993), *Soziologische Fragen*, Suhrkamp.

Bruckner, P. (1996), *Ich leide, also bin ich. Die Krankheit der Moderne. Eine Streitschrift*, Quadriga.

Bulmer, M. (1975), 'Sociological Models of the Mining Community', in *Sociological Review* 23 (1), 61-92.

de Certeau, M. (1984), *The Practice of Everyday Life*, University of California Press.

Diamond, S. (1972), 'Anthropology in Question', in Hymes, 401-429.

Eade, J. (ed.) (1997), *Living in the Global City: Globalization as a Local Process*, Routledge.

Elwert, G. (1984), 'Die Verflechtung von Produktionen: Nachgedanken zur Wirtschaftsanthropologie', in *Kölner Zeitschrift für Soziologie und Sozialpsychologie* (Special Issue No. 26), 379-402.

Fardon, R. (ed.) (1995), *Counterworks: Managing the Diversity of Knowledge*, Routledge.

Fehrmann, E. (ed.) (1997), *Turbo-Kapitalismus: Gesellschaft am Übergang ins 21. Jahrhundert*, VSA-Verlag.

Foucault, M. (n.d.), 'Wie wird Macht ausgeübt', in Foucault and Seitter, 29-47.

Foucault, M. (1974), *Die Ordnung des Diskurses*, Hanser.

Foucault, M. and Seitter, W. (n.d.), *Das Spektrum der Genealogie*, Philo.

Fox, R. (ed.) (1991), *Recapturing Anthropology: Working in the Present*, School of American Research.

Giddens, A. (1995), *Konsequenzen der Moderne*, Suhrkamp.

Gorz, A. (2000), *Arbeit zwischen Misere und Utopie*, Suhrkamp.

Hannerz, U. (1995), 'Kultur in einer vernetzten Welt: Zur Revision eines ethnologischen Begriffes', in Kaschuba, 64-84.

Hannerz, U. (1996), *Transnational Connections: Culture, People, Places*, Routledge.

Hirsch, J. (1999), 'Geht die Arbeit wirklich aus? Der Fordismus ist am Ende, die informelle Ökonomie kommt in dieMetropolen', in *Jungle World* 24 (9 June), 15-8.

Hymes, D. (ed.) (1972), *Reinventing Anthropology*, Pantheon Books.

Kaschuba, W. (ed.) (1995), *Kulturen - Identitäten - Diskurse: Perspektiven Europäischer Ethnologie* (zeithorizonte, vol. 1), Akademie Verlag.

Knoth, E. and Schadt, G. (1991), *Was kommt nach dem Erzberg? Szenarien zur Ortsentwicklung von Eisenerz*, Kommunalwissenschaftliches Dokumentationszentrum.

Lipp, W. (ed.) (1984), *Industriegesellschaft und Regionalkultur: Untersuchungen für Europa*, Heymann.

Löfgren, O. (1995), 'Leben im Transit? Identitäten und Territorialitäten in historischer Perspektive', in *Historische Anthropologie* 3 (3), 349-63.

Lüdtke, A. (1993), *Eigen-Sinn: Fabrikalltag, Arbeitererfahrungen und Politik vom Kaiserreich bis in den Faschismus*, Ergebnisse.

Mahnkopf, B. (1997), 'Die Globalisierung der Ökonomie als soziale Pathologie: Über Probleme der politischen Regulierung von Arbeit in einer interdependenten Welt', in Zilian and Flecker, 49-83.

Marcus, G. (1995), 'Ethnography in/of the World System: The Emergence of Multi-Sited Ethnography', in *Annual Review of Anthropology* 24, 95-117.

Moser, J. (1993), *'Jeder, der will, kann arbeiten': Die kulturelle Bedeutung von Arbeit und Arbeitslosigkeit*, Europa.

Moser, J. (ed.) (1997), *Eisenerz: Eine Bergbaugemeinde im Wandel* (Notizen 57), Institut für Kulturanthropologie und Europäische Ethnologie der Universität Frankfurt am Main.

Moser, J. (1998), 'The Cultural Meaning of Work in Postindustrial Societies', in *Ethnologia Europaea* 28 (1): 55-66.

Moser, J. and Graf, M. (1997), 'Vom zentralen Faktor zurMarginalität? Bergmannsarbeit und Bergarbeiterleben in ihrer Bedeutung für Eisenerz', in Moser, 27-71.

Nash, J. (1993), *We Eat the Mines and the Mines Eat Us: Dependency and Exploitation in Bolivian Tin Mines*, Columbia.

Neckel, S. (1991), *Status und Scham: Zur symbolischen Reproduktion sozialer Ungleichheit* (Theorie und Gesellschaft 21), Campus.

Oberbeck, H. (1997), 'Die Entwicklung der Arbeit in der Dienstleistungsgesellschaft', in Fehrmann, 133-54.

Orwell, G. (1982), *Der Weg nach Wigan Pier*, Diogenes.

Parker, T. (1986), *Red Hill: A Mining Community*, Heinemann.

Pitt-Rivers, J. (1968), 'Pseudo-Kinship', in *International Encyclopedia of the Social Sciences*, vol. 8, MacMillan/Free Press, 408-13.

Rodwin, L. (1989), 'Deindustrialization and Regional Economic Transformation', in Rodwin and Sazanami, 3-25.

Rodwin, L. and Sazanami, H. (eds) (1989), *Deindustrialization and Regional Economic Transformation: The Experience of the United States*, Unwin Hyman.

Rohe, K. (1984), 'Regionalkultur, regionale Kultur und Regionalismus im Ruhrgebiet: Empirische Sachverhalte und theoretische Überlegungen', in Lipp, 123-53.

Sennett, R. (1998), *The Corrosion of Character*, W.W.Norton.

Sennett, R. and Cobb, J. (1977), *The Hidden Injuries of Class*, Cambridge.

Stehr, N. (1994), *Arbeit, Eigentum und Wissen: Zur Theorie von Wissensgesellschaften*, Suhrkamp.

Stötzel, R. (ed) (1998), *Ungleichheit als Projekt: Globalisierung – Standort – Neoliberalismus*, BdWI-Verlag.

Welz, G. (1998), 'Moving Targets: Feldforschung unter Mobilitätsdruck', in *Zeitschrift für Volkskunde* 94 (II), 177-94.

Young, B. (1998), 'Globalisierung und Genderregime', in Stötzel et al., 77-88.

Zilian, H. (1997), 'Einleitung: Pathologien, Paradoxien, Eulenspiegeleien – Arbeitswelt zwischen Knappheit und Ideologie', in Zilian and Flecker, 8-31.

Zilian, H. and Flecker, J. (eds) (1997), *Pathologien und Paradoxien der Arbeitswelt*, Forum Sozialforschung.

4 Social Markets and the Meaning of Work in Eastern Germany

Angela Jancius

The micro-politics of 'social markets' in post-Cold War Europe is the theme of this chapter. In eastern Germany, a region with an official unemployment rate of 17.5%, unemployment statistics are a subject of constant debate, especially because they do not count participants in training or work-creation programs. On several occasions, the national work-creation program, *ABM*, was expanded just prior to elections, with the effect of lowering the official unemployment rate. People here make an interesting distinction when they talk about work. They make reference to a 'competitive' labour market, and contrast this with a federally subsidised work sphere, the *zweiter Arbeitsmarkt* (second labour market). At the Leipzig Unemployment Office, social workers will tell you that one in four of the jobs listed in their database fall into this category. These are not real jobs and this is not the real labour market either, they will explain. In the following discussion, I retain the German phrase, *zweiter Arbeitsmarkt*, because the literal translation, 'second labour market,' might remind readers of a similarly sounding term, 'second economy'. In socialist countries, the term 'second economy' has been used to describe underground and informal economic activities. This use of the term is not related to the concept of a *zweiter Arbeitsmarkt*.

Debates about the *zweiter Arbeitsmarkt* in Germany have become symbolic of the widespread uncertainty people feel towards the direction of labour and welfare reform since reunification. During socialism, welfare structures had been interlinked with workplace collectives, in a regime of full-employment. In reunified Germany the 'social market economy', which incorporates a safety net at its base, is generally seen as an improvement on *laissez faire* capitalism. Unlike socialism, the social market economy model sets clear boundaries between the production and redistribution of wealth. If labour markets were not kept separate from social welfare, it is believed, the 'invisible hand' would not function. Since the early 1990s, economic anthropology has moved more towards the study of how people conceive of market systems (Dilley 1992; Carrier 1997). In the example I present here, critics of the *zweiter Arbeitsmarkt* say this policy has crossed the line, dangerously blurring the distinction between production and redistribution. Proponents of the idea claim the state has a duty to support their 'right to work'.

The Birth of a New Sphere of Labour

The definition of the *zweiter Arbeitsmarkt* is dependent on the belief that an *erster Arbeitsmarkt* (first labour market) exists: this labour market is the 'real' one, and abides by the laws of supply and demand. The *zweiter Arbeitsmarkt* takes on the role of social welfare, to become a sector for people who need help keeping or obtaining work. The roots of this distinction trace back to West Germany in the late 1960s. During this prosperous time, the unemployment rate was less than 1%, and *Gastarbeiter* (guest workers) were being recruited from the Mediterranean. Worried that the good fortune of the post-War period might not last, the government passed the Law for Promoting Stability and Growth in 1967. Its counter-cyclical measures aimed to support and stabilise full-employment (meaning an unemployment rate of less than 0.9%). This Keynesian policy was followed with the Labour Promotion Act (*Arbeitsförderungsgesetz*, or *AFG*) of 1969, which provided a legal framework for 'active' labour policy.

Such a perceived equilibrium of 'full-employment' has only been a social goal since the late nineteenth century, and then only within the context of industrialisation (Polanyi 1944). This conceptual shift formed a pivotal base for the way national economies, social security systems, households and daily lives were structured after World War II. In the 1960s, both East and West Germany aspired for and claimed to have achieved full-employment, but defined the idea differently. The German Democratic Republic (GDR) guaranteed a 'right to work' in its constitution and made the 'asocial' behaviour of refusing employment a punishable crime. Marx's belief that the liberation of women would be achieved through their participation in the labour market (Engels 1940) became practice, and by the 1980s more than 90% of women were employed. West Germany's social welfare system, in contrast, supported a male breadwinner model, and at the time of reunification only half of working-age women had joined the labour market (see Borneman 1992: 58-9).

The economic crisis of 1973 brought an end to 'full-employment' in West Germany. Unemployment climbed above one million in 1975, and doubled again by 1982, reaching 7.5%. There was a growing awareness of the speed with which technological change transforms economies and displaces workers (Bell 1973; Braverman 1974). In 1982, the German Evangelical Church published a book on unemployment and social ethics that considered possible applications of the 1969 Labour Promotion Act. The market's cyclical structure would always displace some workers, they reasoned, and therefore the government should create a space for people who were more vulnerable to long-term unemployment. They referred to this as the '*zweiter Arbeitsmarkt*'. It was election time, and the Social Democrats picked up the term in their campaign, proposing a nation-wide *zweiter Arbeitsmarkt* and lauding Hamburg's experiment with government-subsidised jobs, so-called *ABM* (*Arbeitsbeschaffungsmaßnahmen*). Ambiguous from the beginning, the idea of the *zweiter Arbeitsmarkt* gained definition through its use in regional unemployment policies. Those who rejected the concept placed it in parentheses, referring to a 'so-called *zweiter Arbeitsmarkt*'. Members of the Evangelical Church claimed they had wanted a work sphere for people with physical handicaps and learning disabilities – not one that battled unemployment in general (Steinjan 1986). The labour unions saw *ABM* as a low-wage sector threatening job security and disguisedly introducing 'flexibility' to German markets. They complained that its participants were not counted in unemployment statistics (König 1987).

Municipal governments welcomed the federal funding, though, and by the mid-eighties West Germany had more than 100,000 *ABM* workers (Erlich 1997: 54-5). Supporters of the zweiter Arbeitsmarkt interpreted its function in different ways. All agreed that 'useful' (*sinnvoll*) activities should be supported (from gardening to university posts, to retraining firms in the Saarland), and that these should not compete with the 'real' labour market. But should projects be designed to prepare participants for the workforce? Taking seriously the 'end of work' thesis (Rifkin 1995), programs in Nürnberg and Hamburg were set up under the rubric of 'alternative economy'. Premised upon the belief that the official labour market was shrinking due to technological change, these low-tech, ecological projects were designed not to help prepare participants for the regular labour market, but rather simply to give them something to do.

The 'zweiter Arbeitsmarkt' Comes to Leipzig

As one could imagine, this ambiguous economic sphere takes on new dimensions in the context of German reunification. The remainder of this article focuses on enactments of the zweiter Arbeitsmarkt in Leipzig. It is based upon material gathered from a two-year (1998-99, 2000-01), multiple-site field study of local unemployment politics. I observe three political phases:

- In the early nineties this fuzzy labour sphere is utilised as a short-term tool for the economic 'transition'.

- With protests against unemployment mounting, political rhetoric reinterprets the *zweiter Arbeitsmarkt* as something uniquely beneficial for regional economic development in the East.

- No longer considered innovative, in the late-nineties the zweiter Arbeitsmarkt is seen to perpetuate the work culture of socialism. Policy-makers now focus on 'de-centralising' projects.

For most inhabitants of eastern Germany, this decade of reinterpretations has meant that the rules of the market are often contradictory, sometimes even evasive.

Phase One: 'Getting Them off the Street'

During the period of the GDR, most of Leipzig's half-million residents had worked in textile and machine construction, in the chemical industry, and in the lignite mines on the city's southern belt. Leipzig had also been the 'window to the East' for international trade fairs. After reunification, the trade fair flailed, the lignite mines closed, and within three years more than 100,000 industrial jobs disappeared (Leipzig Office of Employment 1995). During the *Wende* (the turnaround), one third of the city's working-age population was looking for a job or in retraining. An engineering instructor described the end of the 1990 school year, when young people no longer in apprenticeships crowded the already filled, newly established Unemployment Office – housed at the time (as if to symbolise a changed world order) in the old district headquarters of the Ministry of State Security. The man spoke of long evenings in a chaos of paperwork, aligning East and West German occupations and devising 're-training' programs: 'I thought to myself,' he said, 'we've got to at least get them off the street.'

The *zweiter Arbeitsmarkt* became the policy tool for 'getting them off of the street'. Planners envisaged it as a 'transitional' sphere, into which sections of the labour force could be temporarily shifted while the regional economy was being restructured. Niches were earmarked for future Leipzig labour markets – services, banking, trade fairs, mechanical engineering, and the media. Anthropologists working in post-socialist Eastern Europe have criticised this evolutionist perspective of 'transition' theory (Berdahl 2000; Burawoy and Verdery 1999; Hann 1994). The *zweiter Arbeitsmarkt* was to offer the city's displaced workers a space to conduct 'useful' activities until the new labour markets had matured. Short-term *ABM* positions and retraining programs were a base for these. There is also a so-called *SAM* program (*Strukturan-passungsmaßnahmen*), similar to *ABM*, created specifically for structural development in the New Federal States. For the sake of simplification, I make reference in this text mainly to the *ABM* program.

At its height in 1992, the federal government supported one-half million *ABM* positions, three-quarters of which were in the New Federal States. A complex network of projects sprang up, such as the *ABS* (Labour Promotion and Structural Development) enterprises set up during the privatisation of state-owned factories. Former employees of these factories were pooled into these 'legal entities', where they could maintain their old salaries while laying their factories to rest (see Wieschiolek 2000), trying to create spin-off industries, retraining themselves, or remaining in a reserve pool. The City of Leipzig, in a unique initiative, built a municipal work-creation firm, called *bfb – Betrieb für Beschäftigungs- förderung* (firm for activity/work support). The plan was that, if the 'transition' went smoothly, by the mid-nineties work-creation programs would be lowered to western German levels and ABS enterprises would dissolve into the private sector.

In principle, the *zweiter Arbeitsmarkt* should lead to, but never compete with, the commercial sector – this regulation had been applied in West Germany to a small, supposedly 'less competitive,' segment of the population. But in eastern Germany, where subsidised jobs now made up one quarter of available positions, the rule of non-competition caused new problems. Men and women who had imagined, and prepared for, work in capitalist markets found themselves instead in a limbo of 'useful,' but not 'productive', labour. The stigma associated with programs for a 'low-skilled' work force had been transferred into a broader context. Unemployed East Germans fended off any accusations of laziness and state dependency, often made by conservatives from Old Federal States. However, it was not lack of skill or desire, in fact, that best characterised *zweiter Arbeitsmarkt* participants. It was their belonging to groups discriminated against in periods of high unemployment – recent immigrants, women, young adults, and older workers. More often turned down for regular employment, these groups were quickly over-represented at the *bfb*.

Meanwhile, it was difficult to organise a secondary work sphere when restructured markets showed no clear direction for growth. As one person put it:

[*ABM*] is supposed to make people fit for the so-called first labour market', a woman complained to me, 'only ... you can make them as fit as you'd like. There's no work out there, in that first labour market'.

There were reasons to support the *zweiter Arbeitsmarkt*, and these appeared to overshadow difficulties in the early years of reunification. This sector provided work, after all, and pay cheques had government backing – something valued in a region where the bankruptcy rate of new businesses was very high and people were often not paid on time. For the majority of Leipzig's unemployed, the *zweiter Arbeitsmarkt* was preferable to no work at all. In September 1996, as *ABM* funding cuts drew nearer, some 250,000 protesters mobilised in six different cities. Reminiscent of and drawing strength from the rebellious Monday demonstrations, some 35,000 people gathered in Leipzig's Johannapark, demanding work places. The GDR's constitution had guaranteed a 'right to work', and many interpreted a similar promise in the Federal Republic's constitutional law. Germany's largest Trade Union Association, the *DGB*, now stood firmly behind *ABM* jobs – the government should encourage work, and not neo-liberal budget cuts. Or had it forgotten the state's obligation to support full-employment? Heeding to protests, federal work-support funds were extended. From this point onward the question of how to make the 'first' labour market grow and 'second' one shrink has been the echoing *Leitmotiv* of national politics, and a source for cynicism among the jobless.

Phase Two: The Rubber-Boots Brigade

Over the next two years eastern Germany's allotted *ABM* quota rollercoastered up and down, appearing in regional programs in different forms. Leipzig's work-creation firm, *bfb*, was suddenly discovered in 1997, and lauded by the press as an example for other cities (*Kölner Stadtanzeiger* 1998; *die tageszeitung* 1997; *Der Spiegel* 1998; *Süddeutsche Zeitung* 1997; *Die Zeit* 1997). Such models were desperately sought in a year when the national unemployment rate, concentrated in

the East, had climbed to a post-War record of 4.7 mill
this point, a charismatic figure enters our story.

Matthias von Hermanni, who had previously been involved
in 'alternative economy' programs in Hamburg, was the
founding director and inspiration of *bfb*. He had managed to
reduce Leipzig's welfare rate to the lowest in the country by
enforcing a little-known law (§19 BSHG) that enabled
municipalities to revoke benefits from welfare recipients who
refused a viable work offer. Newspapers across the country
quoted von Hermanni as he claimed, 'I've got work here for
everyone, absolutely everyone'. I first visited the *bfb* in the
autumn of 1998. With about 8,000 workers, it had become
the largest employer in all of Saxony. I knew some people
called it a model for new welfare politics, and others lamented
that it was a relic of socialism: a state-owned work collective,
affectionately nick-named 'the rubber boots brigade' (*die
Gummistiefel-Brigade*) – what else could it be? On the edge of
the city, a second headquarters of the secret police had been
transformed into a work-creation village comprising a wood-
cutting shop, a printing press and newspaper, horse stables,
and a machinery workshop. In other locations, *bfb* workers
maintained a glass recycling centre and botanical gardens,
and renovated a camping resort and several farm grounds
that dated back to the seventeenth century.

Von Hermanni was able to popularise the *zweiter Arbeitsmarkt* by combining two very different political interests. His
use of a 'good poor, bad poor' work ethic (whose roots trace
back to Martin Luther in this very region) advertised a 'right
to work' and thereby won strong support from the SED's
successor, the Party of Democratic Socialism (PDS). Cutting
welfare costs and using *ABM* and welfare recipients as a
cheap municipal labour force, on the other hand, seemed
wonderful to the Christian Democrats. 'Politicians in the West
– the Green Party, the SPD – would call it forced labour', one
supporter of CDU Bayern told me, 'but what they're doing in
Leipzig, it's creative.' What bothered me in this creativity were
the undertones of social Darwinism. These stemmed from the
director's conviction that the formal labour market was
shrinking, and a non-competitive sphere would grow to serve
as a kind of resting ground for all those who could not keep
up in a world of global, competitive markets and flexible

specialisation. These arguments had become popular partly through the outspoken sociologist, Ulrich Beck. For his part, von Hermanni promoted this philosophy in *bfb* orientation programs and in the local press.

Phase Three: A Full Circle

In 1999, Leipzig's Handworker's Union declared war on Matthias von Hermanni and his 'rubber-boot brigades.' The Union attacked the *bfb*'s ecological slaughterhouse, saying it competed with the commercial sector. It had the capacity to prepare twenty-five pigs, five cows, and fifteen sheep or goats for slaughter each day – with the support of taxpayers! This kind of planned market politics would ruin the city's fledgling small businesses. Many began to about worry about what the *bfb* would grow into after the municipal properties had been renovated. Tensions mounted and political parties joined the debate. In a regional scandal von Hermanni was accused of using city money to rent construction equipment for building his home. In November, he was suspended from duties, and even thrown in jail for a time. Five thousand *bfb* supporters blocked the road in front of city hall and demonstrated for his release. In a rally they declared: 'von Hermanni is innocent! The city can't destroy the second job market, what will happen to *bfb*?' In the following months the *bfb* came under new management, and was decreased in size until ultimately, in February 2002, the work-creation firm's closure was announced.

Municipal and federal labour policies in Germany have become critical of what is now called the 'normal' or 'traditional' *ABM* program. A new variant of the policy is supported, called 'contract' *ABM*. In this model federally subsidised, short-term jobs are offered to private commercial enterprises that fulfil certain criteria. With these revisions it is argued that the state's commitment to social welfare can be maintained without creating competition with the 'productive' sector – the commercial sphere. In Leipzig, 'traditional' *ABM* is still supported, but now only for 'non-profit' sector positions. Currently, care for elderly and disabled people and counselling services are heavily dependent upon short-term,

ABM positions. Officials at the Chamber of Commerce (who now have veto power over *zweiter Arbeitsmarkt* applications) feel the business community should allow non-profit sector *ABM* jobs. Two East German businessmen spoke critically with me about the brutality of markets like those in the US, which 'run on their own'. They were very critical of the *zweiter Arbeitsmarkt*, however, and ideally would like it to disappear, suggesting that at least it ought to be carefully regulated – the 'grey markets' of post-socialism endanger small business growth, and it is this vicious circle that causes the region's high unemployment.

West German work-creation programs of the early 1980s had supported social equality through a classic post-War model of full employment. These policies contrasted with the way many countries were responding to the economic crisis of the 1970s. In Great Britain and the United States, rising unemployment and social welfare costs were resolved through structuring of low-wage labour sectors, decreased benefits, and 'Third Sector' activities. Another fuzzy labour sphere, the 'Third' sector is associated with 'non-profit' and 'voluntary' work and the idea of 'civil society'. It became extremely popular in Eastern Europe after 1989 – but not in reunified Germany, where a social market model continued to strongly oppose deregulation at the expense of social welfare, and where the government had the finances to back such ideals.

But since the late 1990s the 'Third' sector is experiencing a delayed popularity in Germany, as a model that could heal what now appears to be a completely out-of-control *zweiter Arbeitsmarkt*. Work-creation politics in Leipzig reveal a small discursive part of a larger ongoing debate. It is about how to balance production with the redistribution of local and global wealth, and about whether markets can be 'social'.

Acknowledgements

I am grateful for the generous support of the Alexander von Humboldt Foundation and Michigan State University. I would also like to thank the research staff of the Max Planck Institute for Social Anthropology (Halle/Saale) for their hospitality. Finally, I am especially indebted to the many men and women in Leipzig, who offered their time, knowledge, and enthusiasm.

References

Bell, D. (1973), *The Coming of Post-Industrial Society*, Basic Books.

Berdahl, D. (2000), 'Introduction: An Anthropology of Postsocialism', in Berdahl et al., 1-13.

Berdahl, D. Bunzl, M. and Lampland, M. (eds) (2000), *Altering States: Ethnographies of Transition in Eastern Europe and the Former Soviet Union*, University of Michigan Press.

Borneman, J. (1992), *Belonging in the Two Berlins: Kin, State, Nation*, Cambridge.

Braverman, H. (1974), *Labor and Monopoly Capital*, Monthly Review.

Burowoy, M. and Verdery, K. (1999), 'Introduction', in Burowoy and Verdery, 1-17.

Burawoy, M. and Verdery, K. (eds) (1999), *Uncertain Transition: Ethnographies of Change in the Postsocialist World*, Rowman and Littlefield.

Carrier, J. (ed.) (1997), *Meanings of the Market. The Free Market in Western Culture*, Berg.

City of Leipzig (1996), *Statistical Yearbook.* Leipzig Bureau of Statistics.

Dilley, R. (1992), 'Contesting Markets', in Dilley, 1-34.

Dilley, R. (ed.) (1992), *Contesting Markets: Analyses of Ideology, Discourse, and Practice*, Edinburgh.

Ehrlich, V. (1997), *Arbeitslosigkeit und zweiter Arbeitsmarkt. Theoretische Grundlagen, Probleme und Erfahrungen*, Peter Lang.

Engels, F. (1940), *The Origins of the Family, Private Property, and the State.* Lawrence and Wishart.

Götz, I. and Wittel, A. (eds) (2000), *Arbeitskulturen im Umbruch. Zur Ethnographie von Arbeit und Organisation*, Waxman.

Hann, C. (1994), 'After Communism: reflections on Eastern European anthropology and the "transition"', in *Social Anthropology* 2 (3), 229-49.

Kölner Stadtanzeiger 1998. 'Das Kombinat der Billiglöhner. Sie bauen Spielplätze und restaurieren Höfe: Sachsens größtes Unternehmen beschäftigt nur Sozialhilfeempfänger und Arbeitslose', 20 February, 3.

König, D. (1987), '*ABM* oder Recht auf Arbeit?', in König et al., 13-17.

König, D., Krüger, H. and Schröder, U. (eds) (1987), *'Eine Zeitlang gehöre ich dazu.' ABM und zweiter Arbeitsmarkt*, VSA.

Polanyi, K. (1944), *The Great Transformation*, Rinehart.

Rifkin, J. (1995), *The End of Work: The Decline of the Global Labor Force and the Dawn of the Post-Market Era*, G.P. Putnam's Sons.

Der Spiegel (1998), 'Allein hätte ich es nicht geschafft', No. 3, 56-9.

Steinjan, W. (1986), *Zweiter Arbeitsmarkt. Möglichkeiten und Grenzen*, Deutscher Instituts-Verlag.

Süddeutsche Zeitung (1997), 'Job statt Sozialhilfe. Die Stadt Leipzig ist einer der größten Arbeitgeber im Osten', 11 July.

Die tageszeitung (1997), 'Nur mit Schippe zum Sozialamt', 22 October, 1.

Wieschiolek, H. (2000), 'Sozialismus als Orientierungssystem', in Götz and Wittel, 75-88.

Die Zeit (1997), 'Das soziale Imperium', 24 October, 39.

5 Constructing Shareholders: Images of Individual Investors in Stockholm

Mónica Lindh De Montoya

Throughout the industrialised West, individual investment in national and international stock markets is rapidly increasing as people turn to buying stocks and funds as a way of increasing their capital and saving for the future. The incorporation of people who formerly saved in other ways into this more volatile financial marketplace makes the growth of global finance a phenomenon that affects many individuals on a personal plane today.

Once primarily of importance only to members of the financial community, daily news about the international business climate, the fate of established global companies and innovative start-ups, and the measures taken by regulatory agencies have become subjects of interest to the general public. Stock markets are receiving wide media attention through an increase in financial publications, greater television news coverage of both national and international financial events such as mergers, bankruptcies, antitrust rulings, technological innovations, and of course, the day-to-day odysseys of the markets around the world. Outstanding, as well as notorious market actors repeatedly surface in the news headlines. There was, for example, the case of trader Nick Leeson, who sank *Barings Bank* a few years ago, and more recently, the *Microsoft* antitrust trial and the collapse of *Enron*.

Sweden, a very high percentage of the population – now according to a poll conducted by Swedish pollster *Temo* at the end of 2000 – save in stocks or mutual funds, or in both. In part, this elevated rate of investment is due to national pension plan reform that, at the end of 2000, encouraged salaried workers to chose up to six funds (from over 400) for the placement of a percentage of their state pension savings. However, Sweden had a high number of investors even prior to the introduction of the reform – about 60% of the population, according to figures from the end of 1999. Little is known about the motivations of these 'ordinary people' (as opposed to institutional investors) whose money, pay cheque after pay cheque, flows into stock holdings, and into the enormous funds whose investment strategies have an impact on the global economy. The increasing growth of stock investment in Sweden throughout the last decade leads me to ask how Swedes think about this newly popular way of investing earnings. How do they conceptualise the stock market? The general assumption appears to be that all investors think and act the same; that they are all 'rational economic men' trying to make the most of scarce resources. But if so, how do they go about acting 'rationally', how do they use information, establish goals, and make investment decisions?

Within the social sciences there has recently been some attention to actors in financial markets; for example, Ellen Hertz (1998) has documented local peoples' reactions to the Shanghai stock market during an early period of its history, and sociologist Mitchell Abolafia (1996) has written about the strategies and ethics of bond traders on Wall Street. More generally, Carrier (1997a) has edited a volume on the meaning of the market in different contexts, and Callon (1998) has also edited an interesting book that portrays a variety of markets and examines particular market-related phenomena, such as accounting and marketing. But for the most part, anthropologists have left the modern marketplace to the economic sociologists and the economists themselves. I think that anthropologists can contribute to this field, however, and in this chapter I will make a few remarks based on a study in progress of individual investors in the Swedish stock market.

Economists appear increasingly willing to concede that the model of 'rational economic man' is questionable, and that a cultural perspective is relevant to the study of economic activity. My research departs from the point of view that although globalisation ties economies and societies together (Hannerz 1992, 1996; Sassen 1996, 1998) peoples' views of the market and action within it are culturally situated and thus vary with time and place. Carrier (1997b) has suggested that the concept of 'the market' is something like a language, an assemblage of ideas and meanings that have a wide resonance, and I agree with this. But these meanings are filtered through local cultures, through particular national histories and economic experiences; and consequently peoples' models of the market (Gudeman 1986; Gudeman and Rivera 1990) and how it operates must vary. In what specific ways, then, does culture affect peoples' perceptions of financial markets, and their actions within them?

Economic Change and the Swedish Stock Market

Sweden has long been an actor in financial markets, partly due to its industrial base of well-established, multinational listed companies including *Ericsson, Asea Brown Boveri (ABB) Volvo, Electrolux* and *Astra-Zeneca.* More recently, the Swedish stock market has also been characterised by an increasing number of high-tech companies oriented around the growth of the Internet, the fate of which are of great interest to Swedish investors. In the last decade, reporting on the financial market has expanded, and even the evening tabloids now offer stock-picking sections one evening a week. Monthly magazines dedicated to 'managing personal wealth' have appeared, and the media contain a wealth of information about and analyses of the new Swedish Internet and communications companies, foreign markets, and the probable future of Ericsson, the largest and most influential company on the Stockholm Stock Exchange.

Socio-political changes are taking place simultaneously with this expansion of 'the market' in peoples' lives. In the early 1990s Sweden suffered a considerable economic crisis, with high unemployment and a large fiscal deficit, and part of the cure for the predicament involved the downsizing of the public sector. Many public employees laid off at this time were encouraged to start their own companies offering the same services, or began to work for 'flexible labour' companies who hire out employees, such as the agency *Manpower*. Private companies now compete for contracts to deliver many of the services – transportation, care of the elderly, and certain medical services that the state used to regard as its own responsibility. A number of public services have been completely privatised; others have been curtailed or have become more expensive for the user, something quite noticeable in dental services, for example. On the other hand, other services such as telecommunications have decreased dramatically in cost with the demise of state monopolies. This trend towards private alternatives along with – or in place of – public services is often framed rhetorically in terms of returning the freedom of choice to citizens, as widening possibilities, and as making people responsible for their own futures. Thus the market is both held up as an opportunity for personal enrichment (such as in the case of the pension plan reform) and increasingly recommended and instituted as a model for the organisation of daily social life.

Consequently Swedes are gradually moving from communal solutions to more private ones, a transition that involves coming to a new general consensus about how individual and communal responsibilities should be formulated. The medial attention given to the country's situation in the global financial market, and widening participation of the population in this arena can be seen as a reflection of this greater social discourse, and is also something that, in its turn, influences the conversation.

It is important to note that increased stock market participation is enmeshed in a matrix of economic and technological developments that are affecting financial markets worldwide. In Sweden, the currently very low interest rates make regular bank savings accounts unattractive, and for some years banks have been active in encouraging their clients to save in funds instead. As one woman in her late thirties who saved in funds expressed it, she'd really prefer a savings account, but with only one or two percent annual interest, it was no longer a viable choice. Other stock

investors I spoke to were enticed by the impressive ga
made by certain funds and stocks, and wanted to particip
in these profits. Not infrequently, mutual fund investors who
feel they should take a more active role in their investment
activities begin to invest directly in stocks.

Investors are aided and attracted by technological
advances. Powerful personal computers have become
relatively inexpensive, and today it is easy to obtain efficient
and inexpensive Internet trading accounts, and real-time
stock quotes at relatively low prices. Accounts with Internet
stockbrokers are rising rapidly; an article in a Stockholm
morning newspaper (*Svenska Dagbladet*, 10 October, 1999)
noted that such accounts were then increasing by 1,000 per
day, and providers were having a difficult time keeping up
with the demand. Internet data transfers and easy-to-use
software for the technical analysis of stocks also provide tools
for individual investors, making it possible for novices to
track stock performance in sophisticated ways. Information is
everywhere, in the traditional media and on the Internet, and
information is not only available about the local market, but
also about markets abroad, and access to foreign markets is
becoming easier. A new Swedish company has just launched
an on-line service for buying stocks in emerging markets,
including a real-time stock quote service; another company
offers IPOs – initial public offerings, usually managed by
banks over the Internet. Thus there are many new
opportunities for investors; in the scope of stocks and funds
offered, the depth of information available, and the ways in
which investments can be managed.

It may not be surprising, then, that a number of people I
interviewed described their participation in the stock market
as something they needed to do because they felt socially or
psychologically isolated otherwise. I asked a number of the
participants in the classes offered by *Aktiespararna,* the
Swedish shareholders' organisation, why they invested the
time and effort to take a costly course on stock investment. A
frequent reply was that they felt they had to learn more about
the market in order to participate in social conversation
about stocks, both among friends and at work. General
knowledge about the financial market has gradually become
part of any educated person's social repertoire. Stocks and

funds are discussed in workplaces, and in a few, particularly those in the technology and communications sector, some people watch their portfolios daily on their computers, and may even trade stocks while on the job. Several people who had their own one-man companies, such as, for example, consultants and accountants, indicated that they had become involved in the stock market partly because they worked from home and were able to keep in touch with what was going on in the marketplace during the day.

This proliferation of attention to financial markets is also making those with more traditional jobs feel that they need a new level of competence in managing their own financial affairs. Peoples' private economies no longer only involve administrating one's income well enough to pay all the bills through the end of the month, paying taxes and putting away something in a savings account. It now includes choosing funds for long and short term savings, funds for the children, and sometimes, managing a stock portfolio, perhaps an inherited one.

Constructing Needs and Knowledge

Here, then, I am approaching the idea of needs, which Appelbaum (1998) tackled in an interesting article on marketing and consumer behaviour, noting that needs are produced in the communication between marketers and consumers, that they are partners in the marketing process. In this connection it is interesting to look at some Swedish banks' fund advertising, to see how they appeal to ideas Swedes hold about needs. Funds are very abstract economic constructions; and advertising, or representation of the funds, usually strives to embed them somehow within the familiar social world of the prospective investor.

In a typical advertisement for Swedish funds at one of Sweden's four major banks in the autumn of 1998, there were representations of a pleasant old age, in smiling white-haired pensioners (in one case buying postcards in the sun); the needs of children – vacations and computers – and basic consumer luxuries, the sports car, and the traditional red-painted, lakeside summerhouse flying the flag. These all

represent unambiguous, generalised desires, within the
of the average Swedish worker, and also suppo
obtainable through investment and the dynamic grow
capital, as displayed in the inevitable graph in which the
arrow points upwards (sometimes, without numbers, it is
simply the representation of a graph). Particular images, here
the family through generations and the traditional country
summer home with the flag, are used to make the act of
investing concrete, and to signify it as responsible action. The
unfamiliar and uncertain – placing savings in a financial
instrument subject to brusque gains and losses – is offset by
the unequivocal and everyday, with the added reassurance of
the flag. Another advertisement from the same bank
promoting investment in European funds portrays ideas
about unity through a multiplicity of European flags, and
solidity through attractive portrayals of the well-known
products of international companies: tires, mobile phones.

Expectation is a big part of investment; and not only
expectations in regard to the economic futures of particular
companies, industrial sectors, and regions of the world, but
also personal expectations for the future. Ideas about the
kind of life one wants to live as one ages, goals for ones'
children, and the role one wants one's country to have in
Europe's economic future can be equally salient when one
makes financial decisions. These kinds of expectations are
not made explicit in the information about a stock or fund,
where it is the financial expectations of the potential
investment that are in focus. They lie concealed in the
images, not in the figures; decoys placed beyond the realm of
rational thought. Other banks market other expectations
through their advertisements – one had discreet pictures of
spices on some pages of their fund information brochure one
year, implying, presumably, that these funds would spice up
their customers' economic horizons. The following year, their
brochure was very sober, on glossy white paper with no
images at all, giving a very businesslike impression. Suddenly
mutual fund investment had become a more rational and
serious business.

The advertising that appeared to entice people to invest the
pension plan money allotted to them in the funds run by
various banks and insurance companies in the end of 2000

was also telling. The most dramatic advertisement, perhaps, were two huge images covering the surface of two entire high-rise buildings in different parts of town. One featured a woman in her thirties reflecting over a cup of coffee: 'I can't resist Folksam funds because of their low fees'. The other was a hazy image taken from above of a blond older woman and child – presumably grandmother and grandchild – dancing on a red and white tiled floor, with only the name of the company inscribed above. These are only two of many possible examples of advertising where companies, rather than approaching investors on a logical and rational level, tried to appeal to the emotional, to insecurities or hopes for the future. In many ways selling funds appears to be similar to selling cars.

The concept of ethical funds, or ethical investing, is also worth mentioning. Through ethical funds one can, for example, give a part of one's annual profits to selected charities, or focus on supporting companies in particular branches, such as new medical technology. Here one is not only addressing one's own, but also others' needs. Another aspect of ethical investing is about making sure that one does not contribute to harmful enterprises, such as the weapons industry or tobacco companies. An interesting campaign for a company that sells ethical funds uses the image of the devil, a dour middle-aged man dressed in black with two stubby little horns on his head. 'What, no tobacco stock? How cowardly'. he taunts investors in one large ad. By placing ones money in this company's funds, then, one overcomes the selfish, ambiguous side of investing by doing it in a socially responsible way.

In the myriad of advertisements, medial information, and advice from bankers, family and friends, and in the face of needs and wants, hopes and expectations, how do investors find their way? As Gyllenram (1998) notes in his book on stock market psychology, people approach investment from very diverse personal economic situations and ambitions. And in the same way that banks and companies selling funds seek to lodge their messages in the social worlds of potential investors, it appears that investors embed their choices in their own more specific situations. This should not be surprising; Granovetter (1985) has pointed out how economic

behaviour in modern societies is embedded in structures of
social relations.

Among the investors I spoke with, I frequently found
evidence that people tend to invest in things they know
about. A hospital administrator bought shares in companies
offering medical care services, an *IBM* employee invested in
companies that he had business dealings with at work and
felt were responsible business partners; a manufacturer of
dental equipment bought stock in firms that develop new
dental technology. And in general, people commonly own
stock, or are offered options in the companies they work for,
and invest in companies whose products they enjoy or
admire. But there are other ways of embedding choices. One
Swedish investor of Polish origin only bought stock in Polish
companies, and a Swedish immigrant in the US, faced with
the all the companies on the US exchanges, started out by
buying 'good solid Swedish companies'.

Another way to give foundation to one's choices is through
the study of particular stocks. Some people who use technical
analysis look for companies that act in relatively predictable
ways, and buy and sell those companies, acting on the
signals they read in the charts or the 'feeling' or intuition they
gain after following the company intently over a long period of
time. Really, fundamental investing is based on similar
mechanisms; here, the buyer examines the history and
economic statistics of the company, or 'fundamentals', and
deduces its prospects for the future – a process some
investors call 'doing one's homework'. The work involved in
such company studies seems to make people more inclined to
invest in them: I found that sometimes members of stock-
investing clubs bought their first stocks independently soon
after the club decided against buying a stock that they had
researched and liked. Thus people find 'good stocks' and
'strong companies' among those in which they in fact have
some non-economic investment or stake, a fact which may
also explain peoples' reluctance to sell stocks even when they
begin to lose money-they have more than a merely economic
interest in them.

One might say that with all the theory and rhetoric that is
produced about financial markets there is something in the
ether for everybody, and that investing might well be

considered a matter of picking out a personally appealing way of justifying what is basically an emotional decision. Yes, but that is not the way people think about it. Everyone I interviewed took their investing seriously in that they felt it was important to search for information, and make the 'right' decision, and the decision that was 'right for them'. And they also reflected on their act of investment in its relation to the society as a whole.

Shaping the Market and the Community

In the Swedish media, the growth in stock investment is portrayed from a wide range of standpoints, all of which find some resonance within Swedish society. Depending on the author and the circumstances, investors are described as taking risks and contributing to the national economy by investing in local companies, or as usurping the profits that rightfully belong to the workers. They are investing hard-earned savings in exciting new ideas, or simply speculating in greed and in the crowd mentality. They are the vanguard of the future, or the misguided victims of rapacious market players who manipulate economic processes. They are taking responsibility for their economic situation, are 'following the crowd', or have 'sold out'. How do these ideas fit in with the growth of stock market investing?

With slightly over eight million inhabitants, Sweden is a small country, but has a sizable industrial base with a number of internationally well-known companies such as those I mentioned earlier. There is a strong national pride in the cutting-edge technological advances in these companies and their worldwide success, achievements that have also provided, via taxation, part of the economic base for the extensive public welfare programs that were introduced in Sweden, beginning in the 1960s and 1970s. Most Swedes who invest in stocks buy shares in Swedish companies, and particularly members of the older generation see their shareholding as a way of supporting national industries, and therewith the economy in general. People over fifty often described their investment activities as a manifestation of social responsibility, a way of benefiting not only themselves, but also society as a whole. While younger investors are more likely to speak of their investment activities as their own individual endeavours, they are equally interested in Swedish companies, particularly telecommunications and technology stocks, and are excited by the recent boom in new Internet-related companies – perhaps in the same way older people still like companies that were new and exciting when they were young.

Swedish investors have a large and active stockholders association, called *Aktiespararna*, which has for many years played a role in fomenting individual investment. The association's goal is to create the best possible environment for stock investors, and they emphasise fundamental investing and education in the belief that people should know enough about the market to be able to make their own informed decisions. The organisation has put together some simple advice for beginning investors, which they call their 'golden rules'. Shareholders are informed that they should invest gradually, in order to obtain a reasonable average price for a stock, and to hold their stocks over a long term; they are advised to diversify into different branches, to be careful with investing borrowed money, and to know what they buy; that is, to inform themselves about the future prospects of the companies whose stock they buy. They are also encouraged to devise a strategy for their investment activities. The association, then, profiles itself along the lines of the dedicated, long-term investor, as opposed to those who are inclined to 'play' the stock market, trying to make a quick profit by buying and selling stocks frequently (weekly, daily, hourly) and choosing those that are moving the fastest in the market. While *Aktiespararna* do not condemn such speculative stock trading, neither do they discuss it.

Aktiespararna has been instrumental in stopping certain mergers or deals that they felt were detrimental to Swedish investors – and to the Swedish economy – such as the Renault-Volvo merger a few years ago, and they vigorously opposed the recent merger between Astra and British Zeneca. By keeping a high public profile, the organisation puts focus on the role and rights of the small investor in the marketplace, which might otherwise be overlooked amid the medial attention directed at the larger market actors. They claim that investing in stocks has become a peoples' movement in Sweden; and in characterising their activities this way – as part of a peoples' movement – they seek resonance with a concept that is regarded as positive, in Sweden with its long history of social democracy. They make populist an activity that is usually seen as being very individualistic, and seldom identified with the idea of community action.

It is the individualistic aspects of investing that tend to be emphasised in the press, when individual investors are discussed. Perhaps this is because people who quit their jobs in order to day-trade, or who have made sudden fortunes in the markets make better stories than those who, year after year, gradually build their capital by following the 'golden rules'. Thus those who have departed from the routines associated with the working community more readily come to represent the possibilities offered by a serious engagement with the stock market. Yet the vast majority of stock investors in Sweden are fundamental investors, who hold on to their stocks (Temo 2001).

Other Swedes, however, react against the widening of market discourse and what they perceive as disengagement by the state in its responsibility towards its citizens. In the autumn of 1998, and again in 1999, demonstrations 'Against the Dictatorship of the Market' were held in central Stockholm. A network of quite varied organisations, from syndicalists to women's groups, radical vegetarians to workers unions, environmental activists to representatives from established political parties of the left met in the centre of the city to march to the stock exchange, outside of which a theatre group performed and speeches were held. Some speeches criticised the stock market as a legalised casino that appropriated profits that rightfully belonged to the workers. Others condemned the 'slaughter' of social welfare, the privatisation of state-owned housing, and particularly, the greed of shareholders – the capitalists – who, in their single-minded focus on profits, rationalise industrial production to the detriment of employees. For these demonstrators, participation in the stock market is the antithesis of social responsibility.

The rallies gathered about 2,000 protesters; not a very large gathering one might think, but significant in the number of groups and organisations – both fringe and mainstream – that participated. 'We are the pioneers', one speaker intoned as he surveyed the multiform assembly at the first demonstration. 'In a few years, we will have inspired millions of people'. Although this seemed like a gross exaggeration at the time, the creation in France less than a year later of the global action group *Attac*, whose ambition is to bring about a more humane market, and the more conspicuous gatherings that have since taken place in, for example, Seattle, Davos, Prague, Washington and Quebec, show that the sentiments that were manifested in these early rallies are relatively widespread. Undoubtedly many people who would not get involved in a rally nonetheless sympathise with the idea of somehow creating a more humane market. In January 2001, the Stockholm branch of *Attac* was formed, and March of the same year saw parliamentary hearings on the potential consequences of the implementation of a Tobin tax, a tax on speculative capital movements first suggested by economist James Tobin, the implementation of which is one of *Attac's* main goals.

The protest against the 'dictatorship of the market' is grounded in Swedish political culture, which has had employment, and the 'right to a job' as a central discourse for many years. A national discussion about the dangers of unemployment has come to the conclusion that a meaningful job is not only necessary for a person's economic well-being, but also for a successful social life and good mental health. Ideas about job security, social benefits and full employment have been prominent themes in Swedish political life, particularly during the 1990s, when unemployment statistics in the country rose and long remained at politically unacceptable levels. Several prominent Swedish companies have moved their headquarters abroad, or merged with foreign companies, and national industries have repeatedly faced competition from emerging markets: the textile industry, shipbuilding, steel, and paper industries have all had to compete in the global arena during the last decades.

The relationships between company profits, stock prices, market competition and the productive work of people are complicated and do not necessarily make 'common sense'. When companies restructure in a crisis and eliminate jobs their share prices often rise as a reflection of their improved competitiveness, a fact that makes critics feel that 'the market' – read stockholders – profit from others' misery. Quite often restructuring means ceasing production at a site; and when a town loses its main employer problems quickly multiply. Local property prices fall, also making it difficult for people to relocate; and families lose much more than their jobs: homes, expectations, and because of dependence on unemployment and welfare, many feel they lose their dignity. Such processes have been very much in the public eye throughout the 1980s and early 1990s, and make the elimination of jobs a very sensitive issue.

These ambiguities are troubling for many Swedish investors, even if they do not keep them out of the stock market. Frequently people's comments reflect the unpleasant misgiving that their good fortune with a particular stock is someone else's misfortune. Global issues like the destruction of the environment and child labour also have resonance when people speak about the financial marketplace. One fund investor commented that she only had started to save in a mutual fund because her local bank so strongly suggested it, and that she now wondered what mischief her money was up to, as it circulated around the globe. Such worries, most common among fund investors, are probably fleeting for most, but their existence speaks to a perception of the market as something sinister, not to be trusted. It is interesting to note that stock investors seldom voice such concerns – perhaps because they actively choose the stocks they invest in, and therefore know where their money is.

Conclusion

Peoples' reflections concerning the stock market and their actions within it are oriented not only by the rationality that seeks to maximise profit above all, but equally by a complex web of social factors. There is the desire to participate, somehow, in a potentially profitable new venture, and to obtain the social skills that come with this participation.

Banks and fund companies play on this need for inclusio
well as on other social configurations, such as the r
generated by ageing, family responsibilities, and the
individual's desire for excitement and a sense of taking
charge of his economic future. These, in turn, mesh with the
processes of the state, as it deregulates and cuts down on
commitments to, and investments in community. The many
actors in the financial arena – from banks to analysts to
hardware and software vendors – all seek to entice or
persuade the individual to deposit all or part of his money in
their hands, and use the techniques developed within
advertising to do so, playing on a myriad of emotions and
needs, and drawing on the knowledge produced by the
financial community itself. The individual, seeking solutions,
searches for information, and embeds financial decisions in
some kind of logical framework that tends to have more to do
with his or her own highly particular economic resources and
personal world of knowledge than with logical constructions
of the investment experts.

If *Aktiespararna* reflect the idea that investment in the
stock market is a popular and responsible social movement,
but demonstrators regard it as an individualistic activity that
threatens society, what might be the truth about the matter?
Reactions towards the expansion of the market are embedded
in Swedes' conceptions of their society and the appropriate
roles of citizen and state. As the market gains terrain new
concerns are arising, focusing on the morality of the financial
market and the role of the state. Recently, researchers like
the Swedish ethnologist Lindqvist (1999) have discussed the
current financial transformations as related to a postmodern
paradigm, involving fundamental changes in peoples' values
regarding work and savings. Lindqvist notes that money is no
longer accumulated for future needs in a bank account, but
'placed' in financial instruments, in the expectation that it
will multiply miraculously; and he deduces that economic
value is no longer seen as primarily being created through
work, but rather through financial activities and transactions.
The road to well-being no longer goes via work and savings,
but via an ability to decipher what is brewing in the
financial markets, predict future movements, and invest
cleverly; and it is up to the individual to navigate among the

many alternatives and opinions offered up by the actors in the financial marketplace. The connection between productive work and economic well-being is thus being lost.

Lindqvist's ideas are interesting, and would be shared by the participants in the network against the dictatorship of the market, and by other Swedes who, although they are convinced that the stock market is here to stay, feel that it must be firmly reined in by the state. As I noted earlier, fund investors are not infrequently ambivalent about their holdings. But the people who invest directly in stocks usually see a concrete connection between their economic profits or losses and work, for they are dependent on the success of work carried out in innovative and competitive companies. Over time, rising returns on stock investments reflect the return on work well done, in a marketplace that is ever changing, demanding constant attention and creativity. Work is still a central part of economic value's equation, but one might say that there are now new ways of writing the equation, and this is something not accepted by all.

What one does see reflected in discussions of increasing individual participation in financial markets are concerns about the balance between the interests of the individual and those of the community. When does stock investment become disloyal and detrimental to peoples' perception of their needs for salaried work? When does it threaten the ability of the state to make decisions in favour of communal needs? What kinds of services should be controlled by the state, which economic activities and products are good or bad for society, and how should they be regulated? As individuals begin to play new roles in national and international markets through their investment activities, ideas about the nature of economic activity are in flux, and this causes anxiety – especially among those who, for whatever reason, do not or cannot participate in these new economic arenas. One might consider phenomena such as demonstrations and anti-market rhetoric, pension fund accounts, the perspectives offered by stockholders' associations and the daily medial interpretation of, and meditations on, markets' ups and downs – and their consequences – as the outward manifestations of an ongoing debate society is conducting with itself, concerning the merits of this type of wealth creation. When the verdict comes in, stock markets will either be rejected, or taken for granted by most as a 'natural' and 'necessary' part of any society.

Acknowledgements

This study is part of a larger research program in the Department of Anthropology at Stockholm University, focusing on cultural models of the market. I would like to thank the Tercentenary Foundation of the Bank of Sweden and Handelsbankens Forskningsfonder for their financial support. This chapter is based on interviews with fifty individual investors and members of the financial community, carried out in 1998 and 1999.

References

Abolafia, M. (1996), *Making Markets: Opportunism and Restraint on Wall Street*, Harvard.
Appelbaum, K. (1998), 'The Sweetness of Salvation: Consumer Marketing and the Liberal-Bourgeois Theory of Needs', in *Current Anthropology* 39 (3), 323-49.
Callon, M. (ed.) (1998), *The Laws of the Markets*, Blackwell.
Carrier, J. (ed.) (1997a), *Meanings of the Market: The Free Market in Western Culture*, Berg.
Carrier, J. (1997b), 'Introduction', in Carrier, 1-67.
Granovetter, M. (1985), 'Economic action and social structure. The problem of embeddedness', in *American Journal of Sociology* 91 (3), 481-510.
Gudeman, S. (1986), *Economics as Culture: Models and Metaphors of Livelihood*, Routledge and Kegan Paul.
Gudeman, S. and Rivera, A. (1990), *Conversations in Colombia. The domestic economy in life and text*, Cambridge.
Gyllenram, C. (1998), *Aktiemarknadens psykologi, eller Vad styr upp- och nedgångarna på börsen?* Rabén Prisma.
Hannerz, U. (1992), *Cultural Complexity. Studies in the Social Organization of Meaning*, Columbia.
Hannerz, U. (1996), *Transnational Connections: Culture, People, Places.* Routledge.
Hertz, E. (1998), *The Trading Crowd: An Ethnography of the Shanghai Stock Market*, Cambridge.
Lindqvist, M. (1999), 'Igår var vi slösare. Idag är vi sparare. Etnologiska reflektioner kring en privatekonomisk mässa', in *Kulturella Perspektiv* 1999 (1), 25-38.
Sassen, S. (1996), *Losing Control? Sovereignty in an Age of Globalization.* Columbia.
Sassen, S. (1998), *Globalization and its Discontents: Essays on the New Mobility of People and Money*, The New Press.
Svenska Dagbladet, 10 October, 1999.

Temo 2001. Aktiefrämjändet. *Aktieägandet i Sverige.* December 2000. www.temo.se.

6 Magic and the Market: A Case Study of Warren Buffett and Shareholders of *Berkshire Hathaway*

KURT HARTWIG

In the United States, investing in the stock market has become a commonly available financial option, accessible through brokerage firms and even the Internet. With so many possibilities at hand, a wide variety of understandings have emerged regarding the market and its relation to the economy. A veritable industry of its own exists to guide would-be investors to potential wealth. One result of this development is that people speak in terms of wins and losses, indicating an attitude towards investing in the stock market as a great game.

In this chapter, I will discuss the behaviour and beliefs of stock market investors, using shareholders of one company, *Berkshire Hathaway*, as a case study. The information was gathered at the *Berkshire Hathaway* annual meeting in 1999, where I worked on the documentary 'Oracle of Omaha', and so was able to observe and carry out interviews.

This chapter represents only preliminary steps into this topic, which I plan to continue further. I will begin by describing my approach, detailing the rules as perceived by the investors, and continuing on to explore how their thinking is subtly influenced by unspoken reliance upon magic.

Background

By the late 1990s, close to 20,000 investors were attending the *Berkshire* annual meeting, in part to network and meet with other investors, but most importantly to see or speak with the chair and CEO, Warren Buffett. With a net worth of nearly $30 billion, Buffett has more money than most people can conceive. Importantly, he has made his fortune through investing, making him one of the most successful investors in US history. Furthermore, his success has brought his investors great wealth of their own. The sale of one share in 1998 at $81,000 was almost enough to put a single child through four years of private university education.

Investors react in a variety of ways to Buffett's success, yet the frame of investment-as-game stands out above the rest (Goffman 1974). Roger Caillois (1961) divided games into four primary classes, though only two are of interest here: *agon*, or competition, and *alea*, or chance. Competition suggests other players, but it can as easily refer to an investor going against his or her own history, or against any one of a number of market indices. Chance comes into play in the tumultuousness of markets generally. Beating unpredictable factors becomes the challenge. That some people achieve this feat with consistency implies esoteric knowledge.

In this sense, Buffett becomes a master player, given his astounding success. In only a handful of his forty-some years of investing have his returns fallen below most market averages. In fact, he generally beats averages by a large and wide margin. Naturally, people clamour to understand his method as though it were public property: one shareholder remarked about the annual meeting:

> I view it almost as an MBA course. There's a lot to learn here. These guys have a tremendous track record, and I want to know how they've done it... to learn the secret.

Other fans treat Buffett as less of a player than a force of the market himself, relying upon his consistency to counterpoint their own investment strategies:

> I've always been half *Berkshire* in my portfolio, and half I manage myself... I've got almost all techs in my half right now, they're

doing great. But the fact that I've got *Berkshire* in my other half gives me the confidence to gamble on the high fliers in that end... In a downturn, I think *Berkshire*'s going to shine as a great defensive position.

There are sceptics, those who claim that Buffett is a dinosaur, a relic of the past with an antiquated system. In its own way, this behaviour is a kind of grandstanding, as rival investors proclaim the superiority of their own system because of a superior process – necessarily superior because of the technology (computers) or location (New York City).

Systems are only as good as their results, and in this regard Buffett has managed to beat the odds – and other people's records – time and again. Most investors gauge rates of return against specific indices, reported as the Dow Jones in the US, London's FTSE, Tokyo's Nikkei 225, or Hong Kong's Hang Seng. These markers are averages only, and vary with each other on their percentage growth, often measured as a return against the investment. Beating any given average is the simplest way of assessing one's success, and the greater the difference between an investor's return and the market index, the more successful he or she is, especially when marked by consistency over time. Elements of chance creep in with all of the variables that affect any large economy – interest rates, governmental monetary policy, inflation, unemployment, elections, international conflicts, and so on. Predicting the vagaries of an economy is notoriously problematic, and historically downturns come as often with warning as they do with unforeseen and crippling force. And yet, people like Buffett suggest that the unforeseen can be anticipated.

The Rules of the Game

While competition and chance are the two poles that directly concern the game of investing, other issues must also be considered: how do players keep score, who plays, how, and to what end. In finite games, that is, games with marked beginnings and endings, there are generally clear winners and losers. Investment is typically an open-ended game, where one's record may be determined by several different means: net worth, sudden gains of wealth, strengths, and weaknesses. By any of these standards, Buffett does extraordinarily well. For example, in terms of wealth, he has frequently ranked in the top five on the Forbes 400 list of richest US citizens. From under $5,000 per share in 1991, his stock rose throughout the 1990s to nearly $70,000. His seeming weakness, an unwillingness to invest in high-tech stocks, seems less of a problem in the wake of their collapse in US markets.

The next issue is the players, broadly speaking. Anyone with sufficient money may invest. By considering players as competitors, we can problematise the notion of score keeping. An investor may rate him or herself on any of the accounts mentioned – worth, scores, strengths, or weaknesses – against his or her own record, or against others', whether other individuals, or other market indices. In the simpler systems of score keeping, wealth is the obvious primary factor: the richest person is the current leader. Precisely because the game is open-ended, however, that individual is always susceptible to a later defeat, and their system subject to adoption or manipulation.

How investors surpass one another raises the question of how the game is played. The first thing to note is that, in addition to fluctuating economies and government regulation, each investor plays by his or her own system. Investment-as-a-game is implicit, not codified, freeing people to adopt or reject both competitive attitudes and particular strategies as they see fit. The government's rules (laws) only tell you what you cannot do; they do not tell how you can or should invest. What is important here is that not all investors who match themselves to Warren Buffett need play by his rules: if they play by their own and still beat him, then not only have they succeeded in gross terms, but their system itself will be shown superior.

Before discussing systems of investing in more depth, I must address the last point of gaming: why do people play. As with any game, there is no one answer. Buffett claims no competition with anyone but himself:

I would like to see how far the company can be taken... It is a journey and not a destination... I would never sell under any conditions; it wouldn't make any difference if someone offered me five times what the company was worth. I don't measure it by the money, although I do measure it by the returns that it provides, because that's my job.

For others, it is a matter of making money: investor and analyst Peter Lynch makes the observation that,

People want an easy answer. They want, give me a stock that will triple, and thank you very much. I'd like to have it not go down, and if it could happen in the next week, that would be good as well.

One investor at the meeting made the frank admission, 'we're in this for money. He gets to spend his the way he wants to, I get to spend mine the way I want to'. These two perspectives may be simplified to being or becoming a good investor, and becoming wealthy. Though they would seem to entail one another, they do not. One can make money blindly, following the dictates or actions of others, for example. The more active investors often take Buffett's system and attempt to modify it, improve it for their own circumstances. In both cases, however, the frame of 'game' marks a consistent approach to investing.

Magic and the Market

For both kinds of people, there is a whiff of magic about their participation in the *Berkshire* annual meeting, suggesting Bronislaw Malinowski's remark that 'The function of magic is to ritualise man's optimism, to enhance his faith in the victory of hope over fear' (1954[1948]: 90). It is the institutionalisation of hope. Buffett's success seems preternatural to many, simply by having applied different standards. For the investors who follow his system rigorously, Buffett is emblematic as the Master. It is worth observing here that *Berkshire* pays no dividends, and therefore owning the stock unto itself provides no wealth; instead, it marks other factors. To be able to own one share, someone must have the necessary capital to cover the exorbitant price, indexing their general wealth. Possession of the stock means that a person can attend the annual meeting of the company. It also means that a person has enough acumen to invest in a demonstrably smart stock. It is, in other words, symbolic capital. Naturally, it may be redeemed (that is, sold) for financial capital, but only at the risk of losing access to Buffett's later returns (that is, selling at an even higher price) and, importantly, losing access to Buffett himself.

People's behaviour at the meeting is where an implicit belief in magic is often on display. Buffett takes this one weekend per year to be as accessible as possible to his shareholders, and they take full advantage of it, as though mere proximity were enough aid their aspirations. A reporter covering the event noted:

> When you get to the annual meeting on Monday, your goal is really (a) to get through the door as quickly as you can so that you can get a good seat, and (b) then to line up at one of the 15 microphones so that you can to ask a question of Warren.

The questions that Buffett faces vary from his opinions on foreign policy, to the US economic outlook, to his feelings on child-rearing, and what books he happens to be reading at the time; and although he famously does not give stock tips, at least one person will often ask him specific advice. It could be argued that people assume that if he is remarkable at one thing (namely, investing), he must be at least good at several (for example, being a parent), or that knowledge of the US market entails knowledge of the Chinese one. Instances arise in these circumstances that illustrate Sir James Frazer's definitions of magic (1930): sympathy, like calls to like; and contagion, affect by physical association. One investor referred to Buffett's 'golden touch', and his desire to learn it (contagion), while another was even more specific in an example of sympathy. Speaking of dinner the previous night at Buffett's favourite restaurant, he said,

> I had double hash browns, T-bone steak, and beans, just like Buffett. I want to do as well in my investments as he does on a percentage basis, so I figure if I eat what he eats, I'm halfway there.

People flock to the meeting, referring to it as a pilgrimage, or as a religious experience. They come to speak with Buffett, to shake his hand, to touch him, as though mere contact will make them somehow more special, more remarkable, or a better investor.

And to some degree, mere contact with Buffett does actually help investors, because contact – a conversation, or a photograph, or an autograph – contributes in its own way to symbolic capital as an anecdote. What mere contact does not do is make a person a better investor. The problem with emulating Buffett's system is twofold for most: it seemingly works best with investments of large sums of money (say, around $1 million), and it works relatively slowly. Recalling Peter Lynch's statement, that most people want a rapid return, time is a real concern. Dismissal of time as a factor suggests instantaneous returns and riches. What seems to happen is that people implicitly compare their own current wealth with Buffett's. It is not that anyone advocates removing time from their considerations, but that they foreground wealth as the primary factor. By emphasising that one feature to the near exclusion of all others, they simplify the system. Time is not in fact 'removed'; it is ignored. 'Instant' wealth implicitly reinforces magical notions.

The last major point to discuss with regard to chance and magic is beating the odds. Though economies and markets are notoriously difficult to predict, Buffett seems to have done just that. One investor in New York City wryly compared him to the chair of the US Central Bank:

> Seems like he's always right... Whenever Greenspan speaks, the market goes the other way. Whenever Buffett speaks, the market goes in his favour.

Buffett's secret for beating the market is that he doesn't play the market. He invests in companies, and focuses on each individually. By identifying businesses that he understands, led by chief executive officers of whom he approves, he minimises his investment risks, claiming, 'I never worry. If we buy something, we buy it because we like the business'.

For everyone around him, touching Buffett confirms unarticulated mystical convictions. While they may not become wealthier, or the investors that they hope to be, the principle of contagion nevertheless allows someone to increase their symbolic capital, by being able to say: 'I spoke with Buffett', or: 'he autographed a dollar bill for me'. Buffett's fame is transferable via personal contact – a conversation, an autograph – and without any loss of fame to him. His generosity actually increases his own capital. One woman, not a shareholder at the time, wrote to Buffett asking for entry to the meeting as a birthday gift. She carried with her a photocopy of the letter he wrote back to her and became a minor celebrity as the recipient of largesse. She told her story to all comers, including the several television and film crews. The principle of sympathy, meanwhile, is confirmed by simple, logical evaluation. If Buffett follows a certain course of action, then anyone can do the same. His success can be the success of any investor.

Buffett himself plays conservatively, by specific rules that minimise risk and maximise return over time. He is not known for self-aggrandisement, as were many of the tech stock companies in the mid 1990s. His simplicity of demeanour provokes a contrary reaction, however, encouraging in many people the belief that such a persona is a facade, that there is a wizard behind the mask, keeping his secrets from the general populace. His is, in fact, sometimes called the Oracle (after Delphi) or the Wizard (after L. Frank Baum) of Omaha. Given that Buffett's system is copy-able – one shareholder, for example, is well on his way to turning $1 million into $1 billion over the course of a decade – hidden or esoteric knowledge does not seem to be the real factor at play.

If most people in the US would not advocate a belief in magic per se, they may still find truth and reliability in its principles, which are not unique to magic alone – sympathy and contagion; and there is reason for them to do so, because they are confirmed in other ways. By looking at the game of investing from a market perspective instead of an individual business perspective, investors see Buffett as beating unbeatable odds; from his perspective, he is only reducing them.

The difference in perception is crucial. Homeopathic magic, the principle of contagion, is confirmed by the increase in their own fame when they speak to Buffett. Other people are interested in their story, at least in that one specifically. These people may not be famous to the degree that Buffett is, but they become locally, immediately recognised. Sympathetic magic, that like calls to like, may be confirmed by deduction or by example, such as the investor determined to do with tech stocks what Buffett has done with so-called brick-and-mortar firms. His adapted system is similar to Buffett's, and it yields proportionate returns.

Conclusion

Magic may seem superficially unreasonable until it becomes clear that the defining principles of magic work in everyday life, particularly when taken in concert with the theory of symbolic capital. While an individual might not believe in magic, its principles as defined in anthropology and folklore are demonstrated to be viable. There is also a selective application of both principles: investors tend to follow his life, not his strategy. Buffett's historian, Roger Lowenstein remarked:

> I don't think he's changed the way most people invest. Most people are going to be investing for the short term, or they're following what's hot right now.

And while this too may seem illogical, consider natural laws, and how they work only under specific circumstances. Quantum physics, for example, can make a mockery of classical physics. I raise this point not to compare magic to science, but to illustrate how selective application may be justified in context. The unknown, in this case the stock market, is not unknowable, but without a common base of knowledge about how it operates, investors make their own deductions, using knowledge both received and experienced. These forms of knowledge counterpoint and support one another, lending weight to the frame of a competitive game of chance. If winning is important, then all recourses should be employed, including the principles of magic, which are but one way of manipulating chance and fortune.

References

Caillois, R. (1961), *Man, Play, and Games*, trans. M. Barash, Free Press of Glencoe.

Frazer, J. (1930), *The Golden Bough: A Study in Magic and Religion*, abr. ed., Macmillan.

Geertz, C. (1973), *The Interpretation of Cultures*, Basic.

Gildehaus, L. (2000), *Oracle of Omaha*, Riveting Pictures.

Goffman, E. (1974), *Frame Analysis: An Essay on the Organization of Experience*, Harvard.

Malinowski, B. (1954[1948]), *Magic, Science, and Religion*, Doubleday.

7 Tradition in the Market Place: An Ethnographic Study of a Polish Amber Tradeshow

Amy Goldenberg

Amber art is one way in which Poles creatively express their identity. Archaeological evidence shows that workshops specialising in amber art in Gdańsk date back to at least the tenth century (Lepówna 1992; Tabaczyńska 1999). Its appearance today in the Gdańsk marketplace, museums, and churches is nothing less than pervasive. My fieldwork in Poland from September 2000 through June 2001 explored the creation and use of amber art in each type of context. The research also investigated how the modern Polish amber industry continues the tradition of amber crafting in a globalising economy while working towards proving to the world that Gdańsk is the international capital of amber art. In this essay, I focus on the central event in the Polish amber industry, an annual international tradeshow called *Amberif*. This trade fair highlights the specific qualities of amber art within a contemporary economic setting and celebrates Polish amber, while providing opportunities to network, exchange products, and learn about amber as a raw material.

Introduction to Amber

Amber is fossilised tree resin and can be found all over the world. The largest and most famous deposit is in and near the

Baltic Sea. Baltic amber, also known as 'succinite', differs chemically from that found elsewhere. This type of amber began forming approximately forty million years ago, in northern forests. It started as tree sap, stored in trunks, and then was released when the tree needed to heal external damage. As this resin oozed down the tree, it would sometimes capture portions of or entire insects and plants. During the ice age, glaciers pushed the fallen branches and trees with the resin towards what became the Baltic. Air, water, earth, and fire affected how individual pieces of the resin became amber (Grimaldi 1996; Poinar and Poinar 1999). Because of the variety of effects from the elements, natural amber can be many different colours – light brown, dark brown, red, yellow, white, blue. It can also be opaque or transparent. Amber can wash up on shore, and can also be found under sediment in the sea or on land. Some pieces are pebble-sized, others are larger than an adult's hand, and there are many pieces that fall somewhere in between.

It is precisely this variety in amber that appeals to many artists. As all of my contacts told me, no two pieces of amber are alike. With experience, one can make an educated guess about how the interior of a chunk of amber looks, but there is no method to know exactly how it will appear before slicing it open. Often artists maintain amber's natural shape in their work, creating unique, contemporary art. While amber has been used artistically for centuries in Poland and other countries, today's amber market also calls for smaller, more affordable pieces of amber art. Amber for such pieces is manipulated to give uniformity to a large amount of amber, which reduces the price while taking away much of what is so appealing about amber in the first place. For example, baking amber changes the colour of the outer layer without altering its chemical composition. With this method, amber can be consistently one of several shades of red, brown, or green. Such colour alteration usually occurs mainly among the large companies that have a line of amber 'for production'. Production lines usually target tourists and those looking to spend a conservative amount of money.

Context of Gdańsk

While amber products can be easily purchased throughout the country, the centre of Poland's amber industry is Gdańsk. This port city's complex history includes having been Prussian and Polish, as well as independent and occupied (Cieślak and Biernat 1995). Gdańsk is the birthplace of Solidarity. While today's efforts to become part of the European Union are clear in Gdańsk, people are maintaining and further developing various aspects and expressions of Polish identity. With a history and tradition of amber craftsmanship in this area, combined with political and social changes since 1989, the amber industry has grown into an extensive network of people who make a living working with this raw material (Gierłowski 1999). Furthermore, some members of this amber community have the specific goal of demonstrating to the world that Gdańsk is the international capital for amber, something accepted as fact by many in northern Poland.

Stores that primarily sell amber items are concentrated in the centre of the city, also the location of many museums and landmarks. As such, this area attracts tourists, who often purchase amber souvenirs as part of the search for and acquisition of the authentic (MacCannell 1999). The largest street in this area, Długi Targ, houses restaurants, cafes, bookstores, as well as amber jewellery stores. Nearby, the small Mariacka street runs parallel to Długi Targ and offers almost exclusively amber stores. The concentration of them on Mariacka is interspersed with several cafes and a few people selling non-amber items, with the Archaeology Museum and the immense St Mary's church marking either end of this short street. A third street, Długie Pobrzeże, connects Mariacka and Długi Targ. This one runs along the water and, again, is almost bursting with stores specialising in amber products. Amber jewellery stores exist elsewhere in the centre, but these three streets have the most. In other parts of the city, stores offer amber items either exclusively or among other products, but it is not nearly as concentrated as in this area. Outside the centre is where many amber artists work as well as the location of a multitude of amber art businesses that work directly with stores and professional buyers in lieu of a storefront.

An Outline of the Amber Market

As mentioned earlier, amber is fossilised resin found in the sea or underground. If all goes well in the amber market, it ends up in the hands of a consumer. The following is a brief description of how it gets there.

First, people gather the amber. This can be done on foot near or in the sea. Alternatively, it is mined. Next, the collected amber is sold either to wholesalers or directly to individual artists and companies. The artists and producers prepare the amber for use, or they create jewellery or other art with it. Some producers do not create complete pieces of amber art themselves, but shape and polish the amber to be ready to use. Such pieces are sold to other people, often at jewellery stores, who in turn incorporate the amber into a creative setting. After the piece of amber art has been created, it goes to consumers, usually via a store or gallery. Some stores have their own workshops, and have owners or employees who make the store's pieces. Other stores purchase finished amber products from producers or artists. Galleries work mainly with artists, focusing on particularly unique pieces of art. The consumers can be tourists or non-tourists and tastes vary widely. Successful artists and producers usually have regular clients who buy and sell their work. Meeting new potential business partners can, as with so many other dealings, happen through word-of-mouth, advertising, publicity, and so on. Within the amber industry, however, a key venue to expand one's business is *Amberif.*

Amberif

Amberif is a professionally organised annual trade show with a focus on amber products. It attracts many sellers and buyers with different goals and desires. Part of the *Międzynarodowe Targi Gdańskie* (International Gdańsk Fair Company), the first *Amberif* occurred in 1994. With the expanding amber market and the area's reputation as a centre for this art, an amber-themed trade-show in Gdańsk began in part to help develop amber as a cultural trademark, a cultural brand (Rachón 2000). Since the first *Amberif*, it has grown significantly in size, with exhibitors and buyers from Poland and around the world returning to Gdańsk for this March event. It is now the central event for the amber market, providing four days of exchange between people who are serious about amber.

Amberif is primarily for professionals, not for tourists. Participants mainly include exhibitors, sellers, buyers, and scholars. While the majority of participants are Polish, many come from abroad. Non-Polish exhibitors at the 2001 *Amberif* included companies from Russia, Lithuania, Ukraine, and buyers came from countries throughout Western, Central, and Eastern Europe as well as North American, the Middle East, and Asia. Amber art is indeed a centuries-old tradition in Poland, but this is a trade show, thus the real focus is on exchange. This involves making significant sales to people representing other businesses, such as other jewellery stores, art stores, and galleries. Within this context, there seems to be a rough division between sellers who offer their own amber art and those offering production pieces made by the company employees.

The eighth annual *Amberif* took place during March 8-11, 2001 in Gdańsk's Oliwa neighbourhood. Although *Amberif* itself spanned four days, not all the participants stayed the entire time. Buyers did not need to stay the whole time, especially if they had sites to see or family and friends to visit. Some exhibitors set up their booths a little late, while others packed them up a little early. The first day was the most hectic, with a good number of exhibitors finishing up their displays after the doors had opened. At the same time, quite a few buyers were trying to complete transactions as quickly as possible, not wanting to waste any time in accomplishing their goals. Also, people were orienting themselves to both the building with the amber exhibit and the second building with watches and jewellery in general. The stands in this other hall were for buyers searching for items besides amber. This hall was smaller, but also quite hectic on opening day. The third day, Saturday, was particularly busy because more of the general public came, paying an entrance fee for the day.

Ground Floor versus First Floor

The main hall, focused on amber, had two levels. The layout of the two levels physically separated the larger companies on the ground floor from the individual artists on the upper level. This organisational distinction emphasised two parts of the amber market: tradition and production. This separation was not total because quite a few firms have production lines while also offering unique art based in the amber crafting tradition.

The ground floor focused on large companies, with the most expansive exhibits in the middle with medium and even a few small ones along the sides. The large booths looked more like small stores erected in the middle of the trade show. Some were set up in an open, public fashion, while others were arranged so that deals would be negotiated in private.

Two of the large exhibits, *Venus* and *Art7*, exemplify these different arrangements. *Venus* had a large area with tables and chairs in the middle, while the back wall was covered with amber beads above the shelves filled with more amber. In this way, everything was on display: the products, the employees, the buyers, and the deal making. *Art7*, on the other hand, had a large booth, but, in comparison to many other stands, kept the display of amber pieces to a minimum. If a buyer was interested based on the representative samples, he or she could discuss it a more private setting, either in the back room or just behind one of the pillars that could obstruct the view of and from the aisles. While Jacek Leśniak and Wojciech Kalandyk, the respective owners of *Venus* and *Art7*, are artists as well as business people, they run companies with production lines to keep all aspects of the business funded.

Another firm on the ground floor with a production line is the *Drapikowski Studio*. This booth was smaller than those of *Venus* and *Art7*, but representative of a medium size booth at the trade show. The *Drapikowski Studio* exemplifies how some companies have a line of products for mass distribution as well as unique amber art. The production pieces are various types of glassware decorated with amber set in silver. The artistic pieces, by Mariusz Drapikowski, include sculptures with varying amounts of amber as well as amber book covers for liturgical texts.

While these firms have pieces for production, the owners of each have interests beyond those lines, which is clear from both their work and participation in the community of amber artists. However, some companies with displays on the ground floor at *Amberif* seem to focus solely on production and sale of fairly uniform amber items. Several such companies have stores geared towards tourists, and their booths at *Amberif* appeared to be an extension of the store.

The amber hall's upper level ran along the sides of the building, like an indoor balcony. This provided a good view of most of the ground floor. In contrast to the ground floor, the upper level housed many smaller exhibitions, including the *Designer's Gallery*, which featured works by individual artists. By drawing from and expanding on the tradition of amber craftsmanship, the artists add their own ideas to create contemporary amber art.

Danuta and Mariusz Gliwinski have a distinct style with their jewellery. Many of their pieces involve natural shaped amber set in a piece of square silver. Most artists create pieces that emphasise a certain quality of amber, such as its colour or natural shape, with the design and execution of the settings being equally important as the amber itself. For instance, much of Pauline Binek's jewellery can be worn in several different ways due to flexible design elements. Also, Janusz Wosik's work frequently combines several different materials, sometimes with amber as the focus, sometimes with it as just part of the piece.

The upper level also had a display of the pieces that won prizes in the *Amberif* design competition, a collection of a single artist's paintings, and a folk art exhibition of wooden sculptures. Including these items here further emphasised the upper floor as the place for unique art.

One side of this level was devoted to booths focusing on other aspects of amber. For instance, the Amber Laboratory offered to verify the authenticity of amber through simple and complex methods. Next to the Amber Laboratory, the Amber Association provided information about this natural material as well as the association's activities. At the end of the row, the Museum of Inclusions, part of the University of Gdańsk, had a display of amber with insects trapped inside.

In addition, there was a demonstration of traditional amber working techniques: sanding down a piece of spinning amber with a piece of flint. Other informational stands included the Amber Museum and amber altar project. This area provided both exhibitors and buyers with the chance to learn more about amber and see its importance beyond the market atmosphere of the trade show.

Amber at *Amberif*

There was great variety in the amber items being displayed and sold. Artists work hard to show their unique designs and concepts. Today's amber art certainly should be viewed as a continuation and expansion of the tradition within the culture. This tradition now also includes the ability to draw on ideas and be influenced by other cultures. For instance, one artist at *Amberif* is Polish, but Italy has been her home for ten years. She does not identify her work as Polish or Italian, just hers. At *Amberif,* all the exhibitors try to show how their amber pieces are distinct.

Similarities mainly occur among the amber pieces 'for production'. These items are more affordable and less unique due to their standard sizes, shapes, and settings.   Such production pieces could be found pretty easily at the booths of companies that also have storefronts in the city. While these pieces dominate the tourist shops in central Gdańsk and are ideal for limited budgets, they were easily overshadowed by the designers' work.

The four days of *Amberif* were filled with special events as well as the actual business of buying and selling amber. The surrounding events included an opening and closing press conference, a meeting for the Polish Jewellers' Association, a seminar about amber imitations, an auction for pieces of amber with inclusions, and a fashion show. In addition, awards were presented to the winners of the amber art competition, folk art competition, and to the Amber Artists of the year and the century. Except for the fashion show (which included the presentation of the amber art awards), the non-business events provided a nice break during the exhibition hours. The fashion show took place on Saturday night, giving people an opportunity to socialise outside the fair centre while also showcasing unique amber jewellery created by selected exhibitors. All these events, in conjunction with the floor activity, worked to give *Amberif* a festival atmosphere.

Conclusion

In talking with people before, during, and after the trade show, it became clear that *Amberif* is the highlight of the amber industry's year between businesses. While this trade show gives artists and buyers the chance to meet and focus on amber products, *Amberif* also helps further Gdańsk's status as a leader of the amber industry. It showcases innovative amber art as well as standard lines. *Amberif* also draws on other parts of the amber community to make this more of a cultural event than one of pure business. This trade-show also helps promote amber as a cultural brand, as explored by Ewa Rachón (2000) in her recent thesis.

The success of the past *Amberif*s prompted the organisers to create a second annual amber trade show, called *AmberMart*. The first *AmberMart* took place in September 2000. It was small, but so was *Amberif* seven years ago. According to Ewa Rachón, the main organiser of both, it was as successful as the first *Amberif*. Both will continue to be the best time for buyers to dive into the market for all kinds of amber art and, together with the community of amber artists in Gdańsk, strengthen the city's reputation as the world capital of the amber industry.

Acknowledgements

I am grateful to the Polish Studies Centre at Indiana University for a travel grant that supported my participation in the Budapest SIEF conference, where I first presented this essay. In addition, the field research was made possible in part by the financial assistance of the Indiana University

Russian and East European Institute through their Andrew W. Mellon Foundation Endowment. I heartily thank both organisations for supporting my research and making this publication possible.

References

Cieślak, E. and Biernat, C. (1995), *History of Gdańsk*, trans. B. Blaim and G. Hyde, Fundacja Biblioteki Gdańskiej.

Gierłowski, W. (1999), *Bursztyn i gdańscy bursztynnicy*, Marpress.

Grimaldi, D. (1996), *Amber: Window to the Past*, American Museum of Natural History and Harry N. Abrams.

Kosmowska-Ceranowicz, B. and Paner, H. (eds) (1999), *Investigations into Amber: Proceedings of the International Interdisciplinary Symposium: Baltic Amber and Other Fossil Resins*, Archaeological Museum in Gdańsk, Museum of the Earth, and Polish Academy of Sciences.

Lepówna, B. (1992), 'Pracownie bursztynnicze w południowo-wschodnim rejonie gdańskiego grodu na przełomie X-XI wieku', in *Acta Universitatis Lodziensis: Folia Archaeologica* 16, 209-20.

MacCannell, D. (1999[1976]), *The Tourist: A New Theory of the Leisure Class*, California.

Poinar, G. and Poinar, R. (1999), *The Amber Forest: A Reconstruction of a Vanished World*, Princeton.

Rachón, E. (2000), *Kreowanie wizerunku bursztynu bałtyckiego jako marki narodowej*, unpubl. Master's thesis, Wyższa Szkoła Administracji i Biznesu w Gdyni.

Tabaczyńska, E. (1999), 'A Thousand Years of Amber-craft in Gdańsk', in Kosmowska-Ceranowicz and Paner, 177-81.

8 Traditional Textiles and Economic Development: Lithuanian Groups in Latvia's Border Regions

Vida Savoniakaitė

This essay is concerned with how the economy controls the culture of ethnic minorities. Using fieldwork, the chapter examines Lithuanian migrant groups in the border regions of Latvia. These people are mostly twentieth century economic and political refugees. It is interesting to study how these Lithuanians determine themselves in Latvia by examining the creation of textiles as a household tradition at the same time as the development of the Latvian souvenir business inspires the assimilation of the culture of ethnic minorities. In the process of globalisation and the market economy, ethnic minorities often use traditional crafts to produce income from tourism as well as from export. Working for Latvian companies, Lithuanian women adapt to Latvian ways of textiles creation while retaining their Lithuanian roots. The market economy and the traditions of the homeland thus protect the survival of a native culture evident in domestic textile production. Lithuanian people in Latvia keep some of their heritage in everyday practices by making souvenirs.

Traditional Textiles for Lithuanians

At the end of the twentieth century there is a growing interest in culture. In cultural studies, there is a turn away from materialism; there is talk about modernity and postmodernity (Ray and Sayer 1999). In the latter, according to Baudrillard, the 'order of simulacra' (1998: 50) thrives. Traditions of ethnic culture that have developed in the way of simulacra bind differently with new environments and information, yield to the influence of fashion and break free of it again. Lithuanian culture, as Lithuania seeks to integrate into the European Union, remains valuable with its signs of traditional culture that do not lose their originality in the way of infinite simulacra of cultural phenomena, or on cultural crossroads. One such ethnic sign of Lithuanian culture can be seen in traditional textiles.

Lithuanian textiles are an original 'sign' and identify the nation. As Baudrillard states, 'a sign has itself only an allusive value'. All the great humanist criteria of value, the moral, aesthetic and practical judgement of civilisation are influenced by certain 'signs'. Known in culture, art, and politics for a long time, they also affect the economy (Baudrillard 1998: 7-9). Even the strongest enthusiasts of cultural studies, of the so-called 'cultural turn', cannot deny the continued importance of economic questions (Ray and Sayer 1999). The traditional culture of any society is closely but flexibly connected with its developing economy. The place of traditional textiles in a culture responds sensitively to the changing needs of a society that is modernising, and to the development of its economy. Every society uses textiles for everyday and special occasions (Harris 1995: 11). Traditional textiles as a cultural 'sign' are valuable from the aesthetic, historical, social and economical point of view. They are inseparable from the economic development of a country. The production of traditional textiles satisfied the economic needs of a family, a small village community, or a group of people. It lives on in a family as long as it has a utilitarian function for the members of that family and their relatives. Having lost its necessary functional meaning, it remains for a long time as a relic. Having passed the boundaries of a family or a small community, traditional textiles become a souvenir.

Modernisation is a process of 'time-space distanciation', in which, according to Scott Lash and John Urry, 'time and space "empty out", become more abstract; and in which things and people become "disembedded" from concrete space and time' (1999: 13). The production of well-known textile brands is penetrating quickly into the Baltic States, more so in the cities than in the countryside. In remote districts traditional cultural values are still strong. The migration process, according to Lash and Urry, is clearly seen in the fashion industry. The clothing industry shows that immigrant models hold exceptionality (Lash and Urry 1999: 158-79). In this essay, I will augment and illustrate their statement with examples of traditional culture, which demonstrates that analogous actions are going on in the creation of traditional textiles. At the threshold of the twenty-first century, this migration process can be observed in the interiors of houses in the Latvian border region. The interiors of houses occupied by Lithuanians can be identified by specific patterns of traditional fabrics, and especially by their colours. Colour combinations, adapted or quasi-inherited elements of taste, remain for a long time, in the words of Marshall Sahlins, 'semiotic codes' (1977: 167). As the culture assimilates, favourite Lithuanian colours (see Savoniakaitė 1998: 180-4) distinguish articles of the second, the third generation. How, then, does the manufacture of traditional textiles, with its national Lithuanian values, exist in the life of a multi-cultural society? How does economic development affect the culture of ethnic minorities? The case study of Lithuanian groups in Latvia's border regions aims to examine how homeland traditions of ethnic minorities survive in the market economy.

The local cultural features that still remain in the village culture are important to Lithuanian ethnologists. The works of Paulius Galaunė (1931: 260-72), Antanas Tamošaitis (1937: 114-7), Angelė Vyšniauskaitė (1977), Regina Merkienė (1998), Giedrė Tallat-Kelpšaitė-Niunkienė (1964: 286-331), Juozas Balčikonis (1961) and many other Lithuanian authors identify peculiarities of Lithuanian traditional textile art and its use in their historical context. Geometric patterns, original subtle and resonant colour combinations, gifts of traditional textiles as part of family customs, all characterise traditional Lithuanian art. Until now very little research has been done on Lithuanian emigrant culture. History shows how already in the second half of the nineteenth century humanistic academic associations, established in many European countries, were concerned with research on their own country or nation, and also on neighbouring nations (Milius 1993: 143). The skills of the Latvian weavers were most extensively researched by Aina Alsupe (1960: 173-86; 1982). Latvian border region textiles are defined in the research by Alvydas Butkus (1995: 98-113), and in the Historical Ethnographical Atlas of the Baltic States (1986: 15-162). This earlier research has no answers to questions that I am concerned with here, about Lithuanian textile art in the context of economic change, which means that in my research on local history the reliability of my own sources is very important.

In this chapter, I refer to fieldwork conducted during the period 1996-1999 in the districts of Bauska, Daugpilis, Jekabpilis, Kraslava and Liepoja. Observation helps to unveil the relationship between society and environment. It enables us to move away from well-known defined schemes and to look for new ones. Social researchers have to be more like 'critics, than architects of grand theory' (Wolf 1999: 132). When theorising about the influence of the environment, it is thought that even a defined environment does not influence all individuals in the same way (Larsen 1998: 19). Hence it is especially important to perform thorough social observations. In contemporary social sciences, such a path is appreciated because it helps understand people's perceptions and motives (Bull and Bergua 1998: 77). In Lithuanian ethnology, field research remains a traditional method, the roots of which reach back to the oldest written sources.

The research team tried to show by local research how the development of the economy and the environment affected the ethnic culture and traditions of Lithuanian emigrants. To this end, we analysed if cultural and national orientations always remained important to people. We methodically accented the concepts of 'nation' and 'tradition'. Through the interviews, we wanted to find out how the interviewees kept and evaluated Lithuanian and Latvian customs and textile traditions, what customs they observed, and which ones were more important and dear to them. We tried not to use literary language or scientific concepts, and showed picture material. Researchers use directional 'arrows' in questionnaires (Miles and Huberman 1994: 23) to help define social phenomena. We used repetitions with regard to nation, tradition, own and foreign culture on purpose in the questionnaire. When people are asked again about the same occurrence in other words, they give new data. We evaluated social cultural orientations, works, deeds, textile creations, and traditions after having questioned people of different age, interests, education, religion, and nationalities. Three people carried out the interviews in this research, which enabled us to gather multi-facetted objective data.

Lithuanian Tradition in Latvia's Border Region Market

In a market economy after the 'cultural turn', the importance of 'recognition' and identity questions remains, in the words of John O'Neill, a 'variation on an old theme' (1999: 80). It is known in Latvia's border region society that Lithuanian women stand out with their liking for handicrafts and their ability to create traditional textiles, in this way expressing their identity. The traditional textile market stimulates the survival of Lithuanian ethnic art together with culture in two ways:

- traditional textiles in a market economy remain as a 'sign' of ethnic culture, and

- local problems and a small market for traditional crafts accelerate the assimilation of ethnic culture.

Let us look into the specific reasons that let the traditional textiles of Lithuanian emigrants and craftspeople survive and compete with the products of Latvian small industry in the Latvian border region market.

In the twentieth century Lithuanian people migrated into Latvia mostly for economic and political reasons. The strong economic market helped people find a tastier bit of bread, and their traditional culture could survive. In the Soviet period, political exiles, with no right to return to Lithuania, settled in Latvia's border region. People's emigration was influenced by the state's politics. Farmers and workers looked for better working conditions. In the early twentieth century, the Lithuanian economy felt the consequences of the Czarist economic policy (Šalčius 1998: 194-7). The land reform, started in 1919, which, according to Domas Cesevičius, was mostly not economic but a means of social policy (1995: 46-7), did not stop the emigrant stream. Land famine in Lithuania was great. In 1930 there was more unemployed labour in Lithuania than in Latvia, productivity in agriculture was smaller, and there were not enough hired labourers in Latvia (Vaskela 1998: 7-8). Therefore, thousands of workers from abroad, including from Lithuania, worked in the fields of Vidžemė, Kuržemė and Žiemgala (Vaskela 1992: 105-6). Another reason that attracted people was the right, provided by the 1940-41 Latvian land reform (Vaskela 1990: 95-8), for Lithuanian farmers who wanted to live in Latvia to get land. This possibility later attracted also exiles who came back from the Soviet Union.

Some homeland *oiconomikē* principles remained in use in emigrant agrarian families. Lithuanian women who moved to live in Latvia in the twentieth century wove textiles for family needs, and also for others who asked. They brought weaving instruments. Many Lithuanian families lived in Subatė where women wove in the winter during their free time. It made good economic sense for farmers who raised sheep, or grew flax and hemp, to weave their own textiles, because thread was expensive to buy. Weaving traditions had existed for a very long time in Lithuanian families. Interviewees born in the middle of the twentieth century talked and knew about homemade fabrics only from childhood memories from Lithuania: 'I don't remember all from those old times. We were kids, when we left'. Between the wars many people wove for themselves. During World War II, people wove fabrics for clothes because they could not afford to buy them.

According to Bauman (1999: 73), the development of any culture consists of inventing new things and forgetting old ones. As production specialises, technologies change, trade flourishes, and economic development becomes more intense, home industry becomes too expensive and of no importance to people. Such a decline in the market, together with more intense foreign trade, was the reason for the disappearance of traditional textiles in conjunction with the assimilation of emigrant culture. In 1950, compared to 1940, more fabrics and thread articles were sold to residents in the state co-operative stores. Lithuania was known in Europe as a big producer of flax. In the British market in 1939, Lithuanian flax was cheaper than that produced in Latvia or other Baltic countries. Besides, Lithuania had the lowest protective duties (Šalčius 1998: 294, 359-60). It is known that with the development of trade, independent craft businesses vanished (Žvinklys and Vabalas 1998: 63). In the second half of the twentieth century, handicrafts became a way of spending free time. Lithuanians and Latvians ordered carpets to be woven in Juodupė. Latvians bought textiles in Lithuania. Cheaper Lithuanian fabrics find buyers faster in the market today, too, which appears to confirm that a decentralised market is superior to a centralised system with a planned economy (Isachsen and Hamilton 1994: 29). Small Latvian enterprises that were part of the planned economy are now competing with the cheaper products of craftsmen that can be bought in Lithuania.

In the process of globalisation of the market economy, ethnic minorities often use their traditional handicrafts as an income producing business for visiting tourists as well as for export. While working for Latvian companies, the Lithuanian women adapt to the Latvian methods of creating these textiles, while still showing their Lithuanian roots.

Latvian pattern fashions were dictated by women from surrounding districts who had studied a little of weaving and who wove in fabric workshops of Ilukstė. Women of different nationalities, including one Lithuanian, were weaving Latvian patterns in this enterprise. People would give threads to the masters of these workshops, and they would weave bed covers for them. There were exchange points in the district where people could obtain the finished articles. Thus in every house, regardless of who lived there – Lithuanians, Latvians or Russians – one could see fabrics with Latvian traditional patterns. People bought fabrics in the market of Daugpilis. From weaver home-workers in Liepoja, one could order towels made by hand. There was a weaving factory in Priekulė. The Latvian small industry production was being sold in stores of bigger cities and in markets.

Not without reason it is said that there were not many people who lived off weaving. At the end of the twentieth century, the same fate befell small business. Although the Latvian Government promised to create 10,000 new jobs each year (Kontrimas 2000: 8), the weaving shop in Ilukstė has difficulties maintaining its workers. Weavers get fewer orders. Demand for fabrics decreased. This is related to the decline of people's living standard. Expensive threads increase the cost of producing fabrics.

The economy developing in Latvia's border regions does not use the potential of traditional art as a basis for creating new jobs, a small textiles or souvenir industry. Beautiful articles could find their place in the market for European souvenirs. Original creative components, showing the roots of traditional culture and increasing the value of this production, could be combined with contemporary creations. These original textile patterns could be a source for the creators of modern textile production. Latvia's Lithuanians do not push into the Latvian souvenir industry at all; they do not decorate it with patterns of ethnic minority textiles.

Working together in the weaver and knitter circle *Dailradė* in Priekulė, in Barta, weavers exchange their experience and are proud of their work. Technologists and artists created patterns for them. Latvian and Lithuanian women knit in a similar way. Women state timidly that probably there is no difference between the handicrafts but also they contradict themselves by singling out very skilled, so-called 'golden-handed', Lithuanian women. It is said that embroidery is less common in Latvia, and that in Lithuania there was greater appreciation of embroidered items. An assimilation process is continuing. Lithuanian children become Latvianised, marry Latvians.

market for traditional crafts, standard of living	survival ↔	TEXTILE TRADITION	assimilation ↔	*production specialisation, new technologies, information*

Figure 8.1   Textile tradition

The reason for cultural assimilation was people's adaptation to their environment. The existence of textile traditions (Figure 8.1) and the culture of ethnic minorities depended on the market and the environment – the market for traditional crafts, the standard of living, specialisation of production, new technologies, and information. As Latvian small industry and new technologies developed, the number of Latvia's Lithuanian commercial weavers decreased. It did not pay to weave, threads were expensive. Weaving became inaccessible for people as there were only few weaving looms left. People burned them as they were no longer needed, or left them in their parents' homes. There was nothing worth learning. This is the natural disappearance of traditional weaving. Besides, the traditional textile market was small. The popularity of other crafts was conditioned by the spirit of the time. People chose cheaper materials, a craft that demanded less means. Yet the nation's feature – the women's liking for making handicrafts – did not disappear.

Textiles remained the 'sign' of Lithuanian traditions. They were still in demand in the border regions of Latvia. This prompted Lithuanian women to weave. It is pointed out that Lithuanian women made more souvenirs and that even television had influenced this. In this way, textile demand in Lithuania encouraged the existence of Lithuanian ethnic traditions in Latvia.

Emigrants and Traditions

Kasja Friedman offered two dramatic perspectives in cultural change: people have problems when they find themselves in a new social world, and they tend to freeze their 'mind models'. In time the cultural creation process breaks the 'frozen models' (Ekhom-Friedman 1991: 225) of a traditional order. Such cultural change in Lithuanian traditional art may happen a little differently than in political and social life, but it happens all the same. Women are not afraid to demonstrate their 'Lithuanian patterns'. Craftswomen adapt themselves to the buyers' taste, because it is usual in this society to admire and decorate with 'Latvian patterns'. Working with Latvians, women start liking the new patterns. Do 'Lithuanian patterns' sink into oblivion?

The first generation of Lithuanians cannot forget the 'symbolic frames of self-consciousness', formed in the homeland, that 'make up the essential part of human cultural history', according to Kavolis (1998: 151). Emigrants connect 'beautiful patterns' with their homeland. For describing patterns, people take notions from the past; they choose 'historical concepts' (Balkenbarg 2000: 24-34) like individual painters. One can feel nostalgia for the homeland in the expressions of women. To the question of what patterns are beautiful, there is the answer that 'Lithuania's patterns are very beautiful'. People describe national patterns according to the colours of the Lithuanian flag that strongly bind together communities of ethnic origin (Merkienė 1999: 11). The flag remains a symbol of nationality, especially to Lithuanians of the first generation.

Textile traditions, created, passed on and developed from generation to generation, were brought from the homeland. Original taste elements defined the long history of textiles as an exceptional 'sign', compared with the changing industrially produced fashions. The disappearing in the twentieth century of the agrarian family hardly affected the tradition of teaching girls weaving and handicrafts from childhood. This may be illustrated with an 'interval line' (Kalnius 1999: 8). According to statistical data from the border regions of Eastern Latvia and Lithuania, women born in the early twentieth century and in the second half of the century both used to weave at the age from 14 to 18; they learned to knit earlier, between 7-13 years of age, and to embroider at about 12. The young generation took over the experience of their mothers and grandmothers.

In time the attitude of generations towards handicrafts was changed by social needs. Firstly, it may be noticed that farmers' women made handicrafts more for their own use, and employees made them for pay and for pleasure. Farmers continued as if by intuition the childhood habit to weave, knit, or embroider during free time. Employees, descending from farmers, the so-called second generation, made handicrafts to earn money for a living. Obviously, these are only the views of the interviewees questioned, and exceptions happen everywhere. It is clear that in the end of the twentieth century women made handicrafts for their own pleasure.

There are similar regularities in the history of professional and non-professional art. The art of today, according to Algirdas Gaižutis, 'emerges from the social and cultural aspirations and crisis symptoms of the past century, from the broken ties with the classic and convulsive search for a new "language" and a new "way of seeing" the world' (1998: 204). How did women of the twentieth century learn to weave and make handicrafts? Of the 36 interviewees, most learned to weave from their mothers (12) or by themselves (8). Some (2) adopted their mothers' experience and learned by themselves. Women also learned to make handicrafts from other women, from close relatives or neighbours (2 interviewees), and girls learned to embroider at school (2 interviewees). Women of different nationalities learned to make handicrafts at about the same age. This depended on family traditions (cf. Bauer 1972: 61) and schooling.

Humanity gives essential meanings, according to Benedict Anderson, 'to the fatality of everyday existence ... and gives sacrifices in different ways for their redeeming' (1991: 36). Does the wish to make things for their life, to create, to be proud and to boast of the things made by their own hands remain in the consciousness of people? There were not many such creators found in this study. According to the data from East Latvia, there were only two 'creative' women among those questioned. Mostly, women would take their creative ideas from others (7 answers), from others and from books (5 answers), or only from books (5 answers). The creativity of people increased the beauty of the textiles while accelerating further the assimilation of ethnic culture. Curious women, after having seen beautiful articles in the press, visiting friends or in the market, tried to make something similar themselves. Women would grow bored with patterns brought from Lithuania, and changed these for new ones.

The young generation grows used to its environment, including to Latvian school. Lithuanian ethnic culture of the second generation assimilates. The loss of ethnocentrism (Gaižutis 1999: 9) leads to assimilation. Consumer goods that fill the markets of the world (Harrison 1999: 246) are more acceptable for the younger generation. However, there are individuals in the context of Latvian culture who stand out with their knowledge and Lithuanian creative works.

There are 'strong' and 'weak' ties in the globalisation process (Werbner 1999: 27), where the so-called 'strong' ties consolidate social ties, because 'weak' ties connect different social relations. When we examine the traditional art of Latvia's Lithuanians, we have noticed how emigrants keep strong ties with Lithuanian culture and entwine with Latvian culture at the same time. We can feel the love for their homeland and their roots in the definitions of 'Lithuanian patterns'. Cultural symbols and language are generated by the 'power of ethnic perception' (Kapferer 1988: 110). The 'beauty' of patterns, related to the homeland, is inseparable from an apprehension of 'Lithuanian patterns'. The first generation of emigrants living in Latvia say that 'Lithuanian patterns are very beautiful', Lithuanian textiles are more acute, clearer, more beautiful, more vivid, having more colours. Lithuanian colours are even poeticised with such notions as 'good', 'cheerful', 'kind', 'romantic', 'coordinated'.

The market for traditional textiles helps preserve elements of customs of native ethnic culture from memories, and the concept of 'beauty' and the perception of 'Lithuanian patterns' among emigrants of the first generation show a rather strong connection with the homeland especially for this generation.

Conclusions

The market economy in Latvia's border region appreciates the culture of ethnic minorities: the demand for Lithuanian traditional textiles encourages the existence of their ethnic traditions in emigration. Traditional textiles remain as a 'sign' of ethnic identity.

As economy and production specialisation develops, as farmers' life changes, weaving for themselves as a fulfilment of needs of daily living is disappearing. Firstly, it is becoming too expensive because farmers do not grow the raw materials themselves anymore. It is becoming cheaper to buy textiles. Secondly, expensive raw materials determine the fact that traditional textile remains as a thing of pride and luxury. Thirdly, the second generation does not take over the weaving experience any more; it only adopts inherited taste elements and a desire for handicrafts.

The assimilation of 'sign' in the way of simulacra is encouraged by an underdeveloped or absent market, by changes in production, Latvia's small industry, and new information. Women working together in Latvia's border regions start liking each other's creative works. In the way of infinite repetitions, specific features of traditional art are assimilated. Creators adapt to their environment. Curiosity for new information encourages people's innovations in their own creative work. The art of the first generation is more an element of modern culture, and the articles of the second generation are closer to the postmodern culture where the taste of previous generations lies as if coded, brought from Lithuania.

Beautiful aesthetic textiles hide within themselves clearly visible ties with family roots, and textile articles identify such family roots. Specific patterns and colours help to find out the history of textile creators, the paths of a Lithuanian emigrant family, how they came to Latvia's border regions. Colours show people's taste and emigrants' ethnic origin.

The periphery of Latvia's border region is a suitable ground for that 'sign' to survive. Local culture differences may still be found in textile articles. In the cultural assimilation process traditional textile art remains livelier than language. Those who cannot speak the language still know and keep traditional Lithuanian customs.

Translated by Greta Rinkevičiūtė and Sigita Clark

References

Abram, S. and Walden, J. (ed.) *Anthropological Perspectives on Local Development*, Routledge.

Alsupe, A. (1960), 'Audumu veidi Vidzemē (19. gs. otrā un 20. gs. pirma pusē)', in *Archeologija un etnogrāfija* 2, 157-86.

Alsupe, A. (1982), *Audēji Vidzemē 19. gs. otrajā pusē un 20. gs. sākumā*, Zinātne.

Anderson, B. (1991), *Imagined Communities: Reflections on the Origin and Spread of Nationalism*, Verso.

Balčikonis, J. (1961), *Audinių raštai*, Valstybinė politinės ir mokslinės literatūros leidykla.

Balkenbarg, R. (2000), 'Nature Teaching: Art Painted Landscapes in the Low Countries', in *The Low Countries Arts and Society in Flanders and the Netherlands: A Yearbook 1999-2000*, Stichting Ons Erfdeel, 24-34.

Baudrillard, J. (1998), *Symbolic Exchange and Death*, trans. by H. Grant, Sage.

Bauer, G. (1972), *Gesellschaft und Weltbild im Baltischen Traditionsmilieu*, Inaugural Dissertation, Ruprecht-Karl-Universität, Heidelberg.

Bauman, Z. (1999), *Culture as Praxis*, Sage.

Bull, G. and Bergua, J. (1998), 'From economism to culturalism: the social and cultural construction of risk in the River Esera (Spain)', in Abram and Walden, 75-95.

Butkus, A. (1995), *Latviai*, Aesti.

Cesevičius, D. (1995), *Lietuvos ekonominė politika: 1918-1940*, Academia (Vilnius).

Dolgin, J., Kemnitzer, D. and Schneider, D. (eds) (1977), *Symbolic Anthropology*, Columbia U.P.

Ekhom-Friedman, K. (1991), *Catastrophe and Creation: the Transformation of an African Culture*, Harwood.

Gaižutis, A. (1998), *Meno sociologija*, Enciklopedija.

Gaižutis, A. (1999), 'Kultūrinis reliatyvizmas ir etnocentrizmas', in Merkienė, 7-10.

Galaunė, P. (1931). *Liaudies menas*, L. U. Humanitarinių mokslų fakulteto leidinys.

Harris, J. (ed.) (1995), *5000 Years of Textiles*, British Museum Press, 8 -16.

Harrison, S. (1999), 'Identity as a scarce resource', in *Social Anthropology* 7 (3), 239-52.

Isachsen, A. and Hamilton, C. (1994), *Ekonomikos pagrindai. Perėjimas nuo plano prie rinkos*, Alma littera.

Kalnius, P. (1999), *Statistikos taikymas etnologijoje*, Vytauto Didžiojo Universitetas.

Kapferer, B. (1988), *Legends of People, Myths of State*, Smithsonian Institution.

Kavolis, V. (1998), *Civilizacijų analizė*, Baltos lankos.

Kontrimas, R. (2000), 'Žada mažiau mokesčių', in *Verslo žinios*, 90(765), 8.

Larsen, A. (1998), 'Discourses on development in Malaysia', in Abram and Walden, 18-35.

Lash, S. and Urry, J. (1999), *Economies of Signs and Space*, Sage.

Maslova, G., Slava, M., Viires, A., Morkūnas, V., and Cimermanis S. (eds) (1986), *Istoriko-etnografičeskij atlas Pribaltiki*, Zinatne (Odežda, Riga).

Merkienė, R. (1999), 'Etninė kultūra pilietinėje visuomenėje', in Merkienė, 10-2.

Merkienė, R. (ed.) (1999), *Etninės kultūros paveldas ir dabarties kultūra*, LII (Vilnius).

Merkienė, R. and Pautieniūtė-Banionienė, M. (1998), *Lietuvininkų pirštinės*, Lietuvos etnologija 3, Žara.

Miles, M., Huberman, A. (1994), *Qualitative Data Analysis. An Expanded Sourcebook*, Sage.

Milius, V. (1993), *Mokslo draugijos ir lietuvių etnografija (XIX a. antroji pusė-XX a. pirmoji pusė)*, Mokslo ir enciklopedijų leidykla.

Niunkienė, G. (1964), 'Audiniai ir jų gamyba', in Vyšniauskaitė, A. (ed.) *Lietuvių etnografijos bruožai*, Valstybinė politinės ir mokslinės literatūros leidykla, 286-7.

O'Neill, J. (1999), 'Economy, Equality and Recognition', in Ray and Sayer, 76-91.

Ray, L. and Sayer, A. (eds) (1999), *Culture and Economy After the Cultural Turn*, Sage.

Sahlins, M. (1977), 'Colors and Cultures', in Dolgin et al., 165-82.

Šalčius, P. (1998), *Raštai. Lietuvos prekybos istorija*, Margi raštai.

Savoniakaitė, V. (1998), *Audiniai kaimo kultūroje: lietuvių geometriniai raštai XIX-XX amžiuje*. Lietuvos etnologija, 4, Alma littera.

Tamošaitis, A. (1937), 'Lietuvių audiniai', in *Naujoji Romuva* 4-5, 114-7.

Vaskela, G. (1990), *Žemę išdalinsim iki rudens*, Mintis.

Vaskela, G. (1992), *Lietuvos kaimo gyventojai 1920-1940 (Socialinis ir ekonominis aspektas)*, Academia.

Vaskela, G. (1998), *Žemės reforma Lietuvoje 1919-1940*, LII.

Vyšniauskaitė, A. (ed.) (1964), *Lietuvių etnografijos bruožai*, Valstybinė politinės ir mokslinės literatūros leidykla.

Vyšniauskaitė, A. (1977), 'Lietuvos valstiečių lininkystė', in Vyšniauskaitė and Laniauskaitė, 7-138.

Vyšniauskaitė, A. and Laniauskaitė, J. (1977), *Valstiečių lininkystė ir transportas*, Iš Lietuvių kultūros istorijos 9, Mokslas.

Werbner, P. (1999), 'Global pathways. Working class cosmopolitans and the creation of transnational ethnic words', in *Social Anthropology* 7 (1), 17-36.

Wolf, L. (1999), 'Anthropology among the powers', in *Social Anthropology*, 7 (2), 121-34.

Žvinklys, J. and Vabalas, E. (1998), *Įmonės ekonomikos pradmenys, I dalis*, Vilniaus universitetas.

9 Transboundary Co-Operation as a Vehicle for Cultural Interchange: A Case Study of Poland

Ann Kennard

Transboundary co-operation has become part and parcel of the European integration process with its endeavour to dovetail policies and practices of different national systems. The brave new world of co-operation between Poland and Germany along their border, for example, has surprised many by the cordiality of its relations and the success of its project-led development, supported by the European Union (EU). The interchange has generated further bilateral arrangements around more or less the entirety of the Polish borders, not to mention links further afield in the Baltic and elsewhere. With the help of a series of interviews held in the eastern, western and southern Polish border regions with actors closely involved in the transboundary co-operation process, this essay examines differences in the approach to the co-operative agendas of different national groupings, and tries to assess whether this interchange may create a new identity with its own cultural dynamic, or whether it is a rather ephemeral phenomenon, generated by financial incentives.

Borders as Agents of Social Change

The study of political boundaries between states is by no means new and occupied political geographers more or less throughout the twentieth century, with the period between the two World Wars being most important for the establishment of boundary terminology (Paasi 1999: 13). It is, however, true to say that interest in border studies has increased dramatically since the fall of the Berlin Wall in 1989 and subsequent demise of the Communist governments in Central and Eastern Europe. Previously two adjacent blocks, hermetically sealed off from one another, did not lend themselves to any kind of comparison, and although borders became more permeable in the institutionalised west of Europe, in the east, as Langer points out 'cross-border relations were reduced to the lowest level since perhaps the Ottoman invasion in the 16th and 17th centuries' and during the Communist period 'almost every cross-border interaction had a political connotation' (Langer 1999: 27). These borders were, in a sense, accepted and for practical purposes, forgotten about, since those who found themselves living beside them, who remembered their previous culture when the border was somewhere else, were not in a position to return to this situation, and could only try to pass on their cultural and ethnic heritage to the next generation. Paasi's comment on the Finnish border situation is germane here too:

> The generations who have not experienced the war live in a socio-spatial context which is characterised and limited by certain geopolitical facts. For them the boundary has always been where it is now, they simply have no experience of other situations (Paasi 1994: 109).

Rather paradoxically, then, since the disappearance of the Cold War divide there has been increasing interest in the lines that separate the countries which constitute today's 'pan-Europe'. The countries of the former Soviet bloc, amongst them Poland and all her present-day neighbours to the south and east (eastern Germany having been absorbed into her western counterpart), have become more aware of their borders just at the point where the rest of the developed world is observing a withering away of the significance of international borders in the face of globalising economies and the predicted demise of the nation state as the pre-eminent political entity. It is understandable in newly independent states, perhaps in Poland in particular, that they should wish to guard their borders, to see them as the edge of the state's identity, and to emphasise their national material culture. In these most sensitive of border regions, the collective memory will always have a role to play, and will reach back to the respective political, cultural and social environments that different generations remember (Kennard 1996: 117).

Poland's New Borders

Perhaps more than any country in Europe, Poland has seen its borders wax, wane and even disappear altogether down the centuries, as invading empires, wars and other international conflicts took their toll. Relationships with Germany, Russia, and to a lesser extent Austria, have been a determining factor in the shaping of each new manifestation which Poland has taken. Martin Broszat points to the different cultural background to Poland's relationships with Prussia and Russia respectively: whilst Poland and Russia have related Slavic languages, common eastern European experiences and fates, centuries-long conflicts with Mongols and Turks, and both accepted a certain cultural influence from the other, Prussian ambitions in Poland emerged quite simply as powerful and 'naked' territorial interest. The latter also had a totally different approach to state-building, which took on the form of 'foreign rule', initially during the Polish partitions and this ensured the development of conflicting national stereotypes (Broszat 1972: 41-2).

During the Communist period also, there was a certain sense in Poland that Russia (as the leader of the Soviet Union) albeit in a hegemonic position, was guaranteeing her borders in the context of the Cold War with the German threat to the west, this time as America's ally. That said, the Katyn massacre and the fact that Stalin carved off a large slice of Poland's recently regained eastern provinces after the Second World War indicate that the Soviet Union's attitude to Poland was basically one of a master to a vassal – very comparable to that of Hitler's Germany.

It would be difficult to overestimate the significance to her of Poland's borders, and the recent period has indeed been no exception. Since 1989 Poland has had to make massive adjustments where her borders are concerned, changed as they are from a relatively simple situation of being surrounded by allies (although the relationship with the GDR was never a relaxed one, especially after the advent of Solidarity) to one of being adjacent to seven different and largely independent countries, each with its own geopolitical attitude to Poland. One of these, Kaliningrad Oblast, is in fact anything but independent, since it has been a Russian exclave since the Baltic States reclaimed their own independence; also, an 'extra' country was added to the number surrounding Poland's borders when the 'velvet divorce' between the Czech and Slovak Republics took place in 1993.

These attitudes are coloured by a variety of historical, cultural and political phenomena, each with its own dynamic, due to overlapping experiences of neighbourhood. If border zones can be said to be 'characterised by intensified political as well as cultural negotiation and contestation', and if it is here that 'states and national ideologies meet, often with local attempts to [sic] cultural and/or political self-identification against national currents' (Thomassen 1996: 1), then there should be some room for positive developments in this region of post-thaw Europe. After all, borders are in one sense simply lines on a map, created usually as a result of some wider conflict, historical or demographic development which has little directly to do with the peoples living on either side – they are not *sui generis* bound to set up confrontational discourses. On the other hand, the division between states that borders constitute does not take into account the many ethnic and national groups which find themselves on what they consider to be the wrong side of the latest borderline. As Kockel points out, not only do people move across borders, but borders also move 'across' people (Kockel 1999: 265). And so it is *par excellence* with Poland.

It is worth asking the question as to whether the way in which transboundary co-operation currently works in this part of Europe makes a positive contribution to refashioning the cultural relationships there, since almost the entirety of Poland's borders are new: they were altered as a result of the Great Powers' agreements after the Second World War. Even the northern region bordering the Baltic Sea shifted westward, to incorporate previously German coastal areas and ports (such as Szczecin) both to the west and east. The result was a very confused one in cultural and ethnic terms, and there are perhaps two major points to be made here concerning government policies on forced migration and assimilation, which had a profound psychological effect on the peoples of the regions around Poland's periphery.

Firstly, not only were ethnic and national groups left on the 'wrong' side of various new borders, but in addition, others were forcibly expelled, such as the Germans from what became western Poland. Their places literally taken by others who were transferred from other territories, such as the Poles who went westward from what became part of the Ukraine or Belarus due to Stalin's takeover of the eastern strip of Poland, which had only been regained in 1918. These expellees were promised 'beautiful new houses' and a wonderful life, but they were subjected first to an arduous trek, often carrying such things as altars from their churches in horse-drawn carts and accompanied by Red Army soldiers with fixed bayonets as far as the new Soviet border. When they eventually arrived in the Oder-Neisse region, they found towns and cities destroyed, and most of the houses plundered, either by the Soviet army or by raiding parties from elsewhere in central Poland (Urban 1993: 64-5). This was obviously a huge cultural upheaval, both for those being transferred and for the receiving communities. Indeed, there are Polish minorities in all of the neighbouring countries, and although post-War Poland is the most homogeneously Polish manifestation of the state for centuries, there are still several hundred thousand Germans living there, as well as small minorities of Ukrainians and Belorussians, not to mention the remaining small Jewish group.

Secondly, all these movements took place in a situation where the underlying cultures were forced into subordination to the Soviet system – a situation that endured largely unchanged until the upheavals of 1989 and the early 1990s. Thus relationships since then across all Poland's borders to the east, west and south have been in several senses new ones which were waiting to be developed on a bilateral level, and they are bound to differ from each other due to the varied historical events and memories.

So, to what extent have the co-operation initiatives since 1989 changed the relationships across Poland's borders? Have these been changes in territorial perceptions? And is there any evidence that cultural interchange is becoming a vehicle for modernised relationships in the centre of Europe?

The Development of Cross-Border Activities

Activities across Poland's borders and in the border regions can perhaps be broadly categorised as either official or unofficial: unofficial activities emerged as soon as the borders were opened, when the restrictions of the planned economy were shown to have been something like a suit which did not fit, and the freedom of the market was immediately embraced, albeit on the level of small-scale trade and other interchange. Official activities came somewhat later in the form of co-operation in an EU context, initially therefore on the border with Germany, since this new dividing line was a region that quickly became influenced by the political decision-making of the EU (Bertram 1998: 215).

As far as unofficial activities were concerned, the new situation very quickly spawned one new phenomenon, which has become known as the 'bazaar economy'. Initially most evident on Poland's western border with Germany, this was undoubtedly the most visible and fastest-growing of the cross-border activities and it can be said to have been the single most powerful factor bringing together the border peoples of Central and Eastern Europe. The 'bazaars' or markets on the Polish side of the border with Germany have become legendary, selling a very wide variety of goods at low prices to Germans seeking bargains. Queues at the border crossings have also become a significant if rather negative feature, for instance at Frankfurt (Oder)/Słubice, where cheap Polish petrol is the greatest draw. Another cause of these queues is the fact that this is currently the external border of the EU and lorries can be held up for days at a time whilst documentation and goods are checked.

On the eastern border of Poland the situation is, in a sense, reversed. Firstly there is very little habitation, let alone urban development, along the border itself, so that there are not the centres of activity that exist along the border with Germany, such as Frankfurt/Słubice, Guben/Gubin, Görlitz/Zgorzelec, as well as metropolises nearby, such as Szczecin, Wrocław and even Berlin. Poland's eastern border runs largely through agricultural areas, where there is much poverty, particularly in the neighbouring countries. The other major difference is that although similar bazaars or markets have sprung up here, they have almost exclusively done so inside Poland. In other words, those with goods to sell do so by crossing the border into Poland, rather than the potential purchasers going eastward. This is now likely to become a problem as Poland adjusts to the Schengen requirements ready for entry into the EU, since this will become the new external EU border.

But there is more to co-operation than this very basic economic exchange. Experience on the border with Germany has shown that even the most sensitive relationship can be developed in a pragmatic manner if both sides see that there is much to be gained from co-operating in a practical way, given an appropriate context. Just such a context has been offered by the proximity and attractiveness of the EU, with its markets, its funding arrangements and its role in bringing the new 'Europeanness'.

Official Border Co-Operation Frameworks

The official structures of transboundary co-operation between Poland and her various neighbours are situated on several levels and can be summarised as follows:

- At the European level, cross-border co-operation is now promoted by the EU both inside and outside the Community borders: since 1990 border regional development inside EU member countries, such as Germany, has been funded via the Community Initiative *INTERREG*, and countries of Central and Eastern Europe bordering the EU have also benefited from a similar arrangement via a special allocation of the aid package, PHARE, known as *PHARE-CBC,* or *TACIS* in the case of the post-Soviet republics. Since the decision was taken at the Amsterdam summit in 1997 to initiate membership negotiations with the most advanced of the Central and Eastern European countries, this funding has been seen as part of the pre-accession strategy. Moreover since 1998 this approach was extended to include further funding of cross-border co-operation between accession countries, that is, without a border with a current EU member. This later package, *CREDO* has given rise to development planning and co-operation in eastern border regions which would not otherwise have been possible.

- At the national level, *Intergovernmental Commissions* have responsibility for transborder co-operation between Poland and all her neighbouring countries, with the exception of the Russian exclave, Kaliningrad, which ceased such co-operation in 1996, at least for the time being. These Commissions have a variety of Sub-Commissions also, responsible for the border zone, and local and regional economies.

- At the regional level, on the western border the *Länder* have a role to play in Germany, as they are responsible for the regional development plan *(Landesentwicklungsplan),* preparing the Operational Programme for EU funding, and they are also involved in putting up (or procuring) the matching finance, which is a condition of this funding. The Polish regional units, *wojewódstwa* (voivodships), although they gained in size and responsibility in a major administrative reorganisation in 1999, still have no real function in EU funding applications, since where *PHARE* and *TACIS* are concerned, this is required to be centrally administered. This obviously applies to the other neighbouring countries around the south and east, but these countries are, on the whole, still politically very centralised and do not allow any real decentralised decision-making anyway. The Czech Republic introduced fourteen new 'self-governing' regions in 2000, but it will be some time before they are functioning properly and all subjects and organisations become accustomed to the new institutional framework (Blažek and Boeckhout 2000: 312).

- At the local level, fourteen *Euroregions* have now been set up around almost the entirety of the Polish borders (Fig. 9.1). The only area currently not covered by these relatively informal organisations is the western coastal area between Gdańsk and Szczecin, presumably because it is not considered near enough to any of its neighbours. This may change at some future date, if only to provide a framework for project-led development. Euroregions are made up of local associations of municipalities and in the German case, also organisations such as the trade unions and the Church. This means that they are at a certain disadvantage, since they neither belong to either national administration structure, nor do they have an independent legal identity; they make project proposals on the basis of special agreements which do however carry weight in both countries.

These structures interlink and demonstrate that Poland is very much part of the growing and developing larger Europe. It has to be said, unfortunately, that the enthusiasm for co-operation on the part of Poland, and indeed in Central and Eastern Europe in general, is not always matched by the efficiency of the funding mechanisms, due to regulatory dissonances between, for instance, *INTERREG* and *PHARE/ TACIS*, but there has been some effort on the part of the European Commission to improve on these technicalities in the new funding period.

Cultural and Social Interaction around Poland's Borders

The fact that petty traders started to cross Poland's various borders immediately after the fall of the various Communist governments demonstrates that there was potential for interaction from the start. The trend tended to be westwards, so that Polish traders went initially to Germany, and people from the former Soviet Union came to Poland.

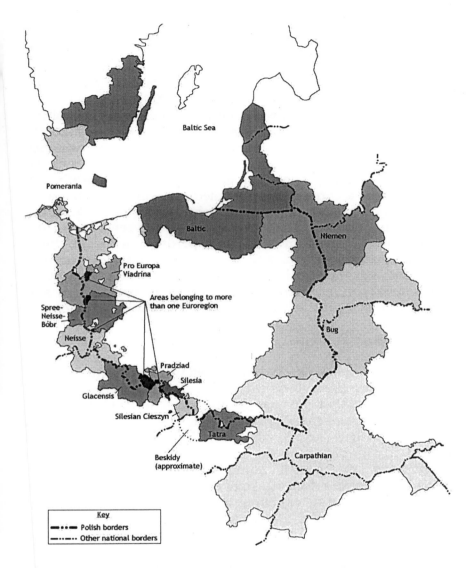

Figure 9.1   Euroregions around Poland's borders

Source: *Euroregiony w nowym podziale terytorialnym Polski,*
               Central Statistical Office, Warsaw/Wroclaw 1999 (English
               text added)

In both cases there was also a tendency to seek work on the black market in the target country, generally with some success, even if only for a short period. Investigations in the Ukraine and Poland show that, in 1995, some 500,000 Ukrainians may have been in such short-term illegal work in Poland, whilst also trading (Iglicka 2000: 204).

The work of the intergovernmental Commissions and of the Euroregions shows that serious attempts are being made to regularise these cross-border relationships, and the evidence is that the Euroregions have become aware of the relevant issues in their own specific regions, and are attempting to place them in a context of project-led development. The quite intensive activity on Poland's western border with Germany has become a model for other borders in the region, and the exploration of possibilities for co-operation with the 'poor relations' in the east, as well as working on specific mutual problems with the Czech and Slovak Republics to the south, demonstrates a recognition that much has been learnt and indeed gained from transboundary relationships hitherto.

Poland's Western Border

As indicated above, much has already been written about post-1989 relations between Poland and Germany: the success story that no one expected. Cultural and social interaction across the German-Polish border has been, and continues to be, surprisingly lively. Not only do the various institutions outlined above work smoothly, in spite of a background of different administrative cultures (broadly: centralised versus federal structures), but it is the more specifically cultural exchange projects which have been particularly successful and dynamic. The most significant of these by far is the establishment of the German/Polish Viadrina University in Frankfurt/Oder, which has had enormous support from both sides of the river Oder and indeed its buildings span the river. There were political and funding difficulties along the way, but the result so far is a really dynamic international institution, where students are expected to be fluent and attend lectures in at least two languages. The graduates are in great demand, particularly in Poland's burgeoning economy (interview with Bettina

Morhard, International Relations Adviser, Europa-Universität Viadrina and member of the *Pro Europa Viadrina* Euroregion Secretariat, 7 January 1999).

Colourful dual language magazines, such as *Trakt* in the Euroregion *Pro Europa Viadrina* with information about cultural and sporting events shared across the border, personalities involved in the exchanges, funding opportunities and general information about towns and villages in the region as a whole contribute to a feeling of being part of a wider European culture. This is an example of the type of smaller project which is supported by the *PHARE-CBC* fund, and which helps to soften the hard edges between two historically antagonistic nations about to become bedfellows in the European Union. The annual *Oderfest* also makes an enormous contribution here, with tens of thousands of visitors from widespread regions in both countries and further abroad, coming to participate in this cultural festival spanning the bridge over the Oder between Frankfurt and Słubice (interview with Klaus Baldauf, International Relations Officer, City of Frankfurt/Oder and Chair of *Pro Europa Viadrina* Secretariat, 7 January 1999). There are many other examples of sports and music festivals, tourist and cycling trails, language classes in schools on each side and indeed, schools exchanges, all of which aim to break down prejudices gradually, both horizontally between the two sides and vertically through the generations.

These official EU-backed activities have given rise to other non-funded trans-border initiatives, such as the magazine *Regional Business*, printed in the city of Szczecin in the Euroregion *Pomerania*, and promoting business links across the border. It is printed in German, Polish and English, has interviews with public figures aimed at promoting business in the area, in particular with Germany. Such initiatives are to be applauded, not least because conflicts do still occur: fear of competition has led to repeatedly reported attacks on foreigners, including Polish tourists and business travellers (Krätke 1999: 639). Nevertheless, there are now at least structures in place that can mitigate against the emergence of old prejudices.

Poland's Southern Border

Turning to the southern border of Poland, here there is a very different situation, in the sense that the two sides are much more compatible in size, political and economic development, or cultural heritage than either Poland or the Czech Republic are with Germany, their powerful neighbour, a long-time member of both EU and NATO. It is also very different physically, in that the entire border between Poland and the Czech and Slovak Republics follows the northern edge of a mountainous range from the Sudeten through to the Carpathians. This has meant that relationships between the populations above and below this line have been characterised on the whole by small-scale trade, cultural and recreational exchanges and pursuits between communities which are limited in size and regional in nature. Much of the border between Poland and the then Czechoslovakia was closed during the Communist period, and relations between Poles and Czechs are generally recognised to be somewhat problematical – problems of 'mentality' – whereas Poles and Slovaks appear to understand each other better, to share perhaps more of the traditionally Slavonic traits (interview with Vàclav Laštůvka, Director of the Třinec Economic Development Agency and Secretary of the *Silesian Cieszyn/ Těšín* Euroregion, Czech Republic, 15 June 2000; the author, a non-Czech speaker, was able to conduct the interview with this Czech official in Polish – a practical demonstration of the general bilingualism in this transnational region).

Nevertheless, and perhaps because of their closer proximity to Germany and the rest of the EU, it is between Poland and the Czech Republic that co-operation has developed more consistently in recent times. Euroregions have been formed across the border, gradually covering its entire length, and the Polish-Czech Intergovernmental Commission's Development Strategy for the Borderlands forms part of the *PHARE-CREDO* programme for the funding period of 2000-2006. It contains a wide-ranging survey of cross-border issues, including proposals for solutions of unemployment, transport and communications, air pollution, but also such social issues as the removal of prejudice.

Perhaps the divided town of Cieszyn/Český Těšín and its surrounding region is the most interesting example of how co-operative projects can make a positive contribution to transboundary social and cultural interaction. There is a history here of conflict, with not only Poles and Czechs contesting their territorial rights, but also German claims to this eastern part of Sudetenland. Nevertheless, this region of Silesia was a largely integrated territory before 1920 as part of the Austro-Hungarian Empire, with the Polish and Czech sides sharing similar cultures, languages and other characteristic features. After the conflict and division in 1920, this situation changed and antagonisms appeared, although it is probably fair to say that from a purely local point of view, the border has been a rather artificial barrier (interview with Vàclav Laštůvka; as above). Co-operation on that level has in fact continued almost throughout, despite the vicissitudes of state diplomacy and since 1989, it has become possible to contemplate reintegrating this region in a way which is likely to benefit the population.

Much of the border region was closed to international traffic during the Communist period, and with the reopening since 1989 of existing crossing points and opening of new ones, there has been a flowering of both trade and tourism. As with Poland's other borders, local cross-border trade – initially in alcohol in particular! – was the first concrete evidence of exchange between the peoples on either side (interview with Maciej Borsa, Director, Government Centre for Strategic Studies, Katowice, Poland, 14 June 2000). The location of Cieszyn/Český Těšín, close to the Silesian Beskid Mountains rising to 1250m, makes transboundary tourism, both winter and summer, a very attractive prospect. This is a region renowned for its beautiful historical buildings, mountain villages with traditional wooden houses, crafts and folklore, as well as being a skiing and hiking centre, where the border has indeed little role to play. The establishment of a Euroregion here has a logic in terms of regional integration which might otherwise not have emerged, and which encourages both trade and social and cultural interaction via project-led development (interview with Maciej Borsa; as above). One of the most useful *PHARE-CREDO* projects has been the setting up of an information system, *Inforeg 2000*, both as a website and in glossy folkloristic publications, giving visitors up-to-date information about events on either side of the border and in both languages.

The Euroregion *Silesian Těšín/Cieszyn*, set up in 1998, has already achieved the publication of the first historical map since 1920, describing both parts of the transboundary region and thus demonstrating a will to accept past differences and progress to a new era of neighbourliness. Indeed, local Polish tourist information describes Cieszyn as 'the Polish part of a single municipal entity functioning in two countries' and shows its 'rich, living cultural tradition' with a list of events on the cultural calendar including an *On the Border* Theatre Festival and an *Autumn of Jazz* Festival.

A further interesting aspect of integration in this region is the fact that since 1993 it lies alongside the Slovak state border, which is topographically and in economic terms part of the same region. Co-operation between Poland and Slovakia is evidenced, for instance, by PHARE/CREDO support for a publication of the Regional Chamber of Industry and Trade in Bielsko-Biała in 1999, on 'Polish-Slovak transborder co-operation in the region of Bielsko-Biała/ Żylina'. This document constitutes a praiseworthy strategy or vision for the region as a whole, covering not only the region's economy and trading opportunities, but also environmental issues, tourism, and cultural heritage. Subsequent to the publication of this document, a new Euroregion, *Beskidy/ Beskydy*, was established in 2000, with the intention of continuing with this overall mission.

There are nevertheless continuing ethno-cultural issues in this whole tripartite region, especially since the 'velvet divorce' of 1993, dividing the Czechs from the Slovaks. For instance there are little-known complications, such as the fact that around the now unified Czech town of Fridek-Mystek there are still lingering allegiances to Silesia and Moravia to which the two parts of this town originally respectively belonged. This caused considerable difficulty, and indeed held up negotiations for a lengthy period, when trying to find an appropriate name for the transboundary Euroregion around Český Těšín/Cieszyn. The Polish proposal of '*Silesian* Těšín/ Cieszyn' was not well-received on the Czech side, out of deference to the Moravians – indeed there are considered to be three 'nations' in this transboundary region: Poles, Moravians and Silesians. The end result of the negotiations was to accept the Polish proposal, but a number of Czech municipalities to the east of (Fridek-)Mystek in fact chose not to join this 'Silesian' Euroregion. Ultimately they joined the Slovaks – without reference to the Poles – in their new venture with Poland in the *Beskidy/Beskydy* Euroregion (interview with Witold Dzierżawski, Director of the Silesian Regional Office, Bielsko-Biała, Poland, 15 June 2000).

Poland's Eastern Border

The complex national and cultural situation on Poland's southern border is more than replicated on her eastern border, where the national boundary has been redrawn many times, as a result of wars and other conflicts usually unleashed by outside forces. This has caused enormous upheavals of the indigenous populations throughout the region and ensured that the political borders rarely coincide with the linguistic and cultural ones. Three of Poland's eastern neighbours since 1989, all emerging from the monolithic Soviet Union – Ukraine, Belarus and Lithuania – contain substantial territories which were part of Poland until after the Second World War, and which therefore still have areas of Polish influence present. The fourth neighbour, the Russian district of Kaliningrad, formerly the East Prussian capital of Königsberg, has *ipso facto* its own identity problems, exacerbated by its exclave status with regard to 'mother Russia' and the future possibility of being surrounded by an enlarged European Union.

Perhaps because of these overlapping histories and possibly to forestall any animosity which might otherwise emerge, attempts at region-building across this border started very early after the events of 1989. Formal agreements have existed between the governments of either side from the early 1990s, such as treaties of friendship and co-operation with Lithuania and Ukraine leading to the formation of intergovernmental commissions for spatial planning, which were later combined with commissions for cross-border co-operation (Biuletyn Informacyjny 2000). A similar cross-border commission has existed with Belarus since 1994, but did not become active until 1996, the year when the preparatory work to establish such a commission with Kaliningrad effectively ceased, although it is hoped that this will soon restart (interview with Dr Katarzyna Ufnalewska, Transboundary Group project leader, Institute of Physical Planning and Municipal Economy, Warsaw, 9 March 2001). Petty cross-border trade between Poland and Kaliningrad does, however, continue to be lively.

Slightly surprisingly due to their great distance from EU centres of activity, Euroregions have also been set up along the entire length of Poland's eastern border, but they have a rather different character from the ones in the south and west. Firstly they are much greater in size than their counterparts elsewhere, mainly because the regions here are very sparsely populated: even on the Polish side, only approximately half the average national population density. This whole eastern region is also very poor, with an enormous 47.9% of the working population engaged in agriculture, 32.3% in various service industries, and only 19.8% in industry (interview with Dr Katarzyna Ufnalewska; as above). Comparable in its physical geography with Poland's western border, that is, very flat, this region has no definable geographical features other than the rivers Bug and Niemen, no large centres of population, and is altogether economically backward. Far from having a rich neighbour, as does the western border region, here it is the Polish side which is considered to play this role, not least because it has access to EU funding. Indeed a professor from Lublin Technical University was of the opinion that 'the only chance of economic development for the eastern regions of Poland, where investment is low, the technical infrastructure weak and the GDP per inhabitant low, is integration in a Euroregion' (Cielemęcki 1998: 44).

Actors involved in cross-border initiatives vary in their opinions as to whether the region needs more or less administration or institutionalisation. Due to the poverty of the region, it is clear that most of the ideas and initiatives here have been aimed at economic development, with particular concern for improving roads and border crossing facilities. There is certainly potential here as a crossroads of trans-European communications between the Baltic and the

Black Sea: the 'Via Intermare', which could ultimately include connections through to China and the Pacific (Rościszewski 1997: 45). In the cultural sphere, there is also potential for interchange, if only because of the overlapping histories of the peoples on either side. But the fact that there were only two border crossings – vehicular only, walking across was not permitted! – between Poland and the Ukraine during the Communist period, and the Ukrainian side of the border being approximately 5-8 times poorer than the Polish side, has meant that cultural exchange tends to be seen as a secondary priority (interview with Dr Waldemar Gorzym-Wilkowski, Institute for Spatial and Urban Management, Lublin, 9 March 2001).

Organisations like the Stefan Batory Foundation, based in Warsaw and funded by George Soros, organise seminars and workshops in their Central and East European Forum on many aspects of public life, and in recent years they have devoted their attention in particular to collaboration with Ukraine and Belarus. In 1998, 'much attention was devoted to issues related to the common Polish and Ukrainian heritage, and the aftermath of their history, in which hardship and tragedy were all too frequent' (Stefan Batory Foundation Annual Report 1998: 182). In attempting to help to improve relations between states in the region, the report concludes that 'in many cases culture proves to be the unifying element though which arguments can be settled amicably' and therefore 'the reconstruction of contacts between creative artists seems particularly important' (ibid.: 188). Other than the interaction of those working for this and other institutions, however, having discussions on the subject both inside Poland and in neighbouring countries, it is difficult to find concrete evidence of cultural exchange as such.

The *Bug* Euroregion shows the institutionalised face of border co-operation between Poland, Belarus and Ukraine, covering comparable areas in Poland and Belarus of around 30,500 sq. km and in Ukraine approximately 20,000 sq. km. However, approx. half the population of the whole region lives in Poland, and it is here that the overall economic and cultural infrastructure is most developed. There are considerable disproportions between Poland and Ukraine, for instance, in the socio-cultural sphere, since the numbers of schools and other education institutions, museums, theatres, tourist hotels and indoor swimming pools are much greater in Poland than in Ukraine, although the situation is reversed as regards public libraries, and mixed as regards health provision (Mindur 2001: 44).

The southwestern region of Belarus has very few centres of population, the Brest district with 1.5 million inhabitants being the only one of any significance, or 14.7% of the entire Belorussian population (Gorzym-Wilkowski and Miszczuk 1997: 53). Apart from the inevitable small-time border trade, there is little exchange between Poland and Belarus here. The only significant trading centre is further north around Białystok (in the *Niemen* Euroregion), where the biggest 'employer' in northeast Poland is said to be the bazaar at the Hetman Stadium in Białystok itself. Including salesmen and saleswomen, people working on transport and in hotels it is calculated that ten thousand local people obtain their income from eastern trade (Holm-Hansen 1999: 47).

Against this generally impoverished background, European funding is being used to highlight the possible benefits to be gained from working together. Under the Small Projects Fund, the *Bug* Euroregion as a whole was allocated some €120,000 in 1999/2000 within the *PHARE-CREDO* programme for fourteen projects in the areas of culture, sport, science and the economy. In December 2000, a successful European Student Forum conference was held in Lublin, part-funded by the Konrad Adenauer Foundation, on 'The Euroregions and cross-border co-operation', attended by political scientists, lawyers and economists (Letter from the Director of the *Bug* Euroregion Secretariat to the Director of the Regional Policy Department, Lublin voivodship, 18 January 2001).

Conclusion

What is clear from this short investigation is that there are somewhat different approaches to the respective co-operative agendas on Poland's various borders. There are a number of reasons for this, including the different historical narratives, but also the fact that each of the three transboundary regions is at a different stage of development, in terms of both its internal dynamics and also its relationship with its national government and the EU. All these factors mean that inevitably the actors involved see transboundary co-operation as bringing different benefits. It is probably true to say that all are aware of the need to aim for better relations, in some cases reconciliation, in order for both/all sides to achieve these benefits. The globalising world into which the countries of Central and Eastern Europe were unexpectedly propelled after 1989 makes this co-operation essential, at least in the sense of the need to improve communications, border crossings etc. This is something which they would be quite unable to achieve unaided, so that the EU regional agenda, with its invitation to decentralise where possible and cooperate across borders in setting up projects was perfectly timed. But are these developments simply to be seen as solutions to practical problems, or is something more fundamental happening in terms of the identity and acceptance of neighbouring cultures, which has been difficult, if not impossible, in this part of Europe for much of the last century?

One can, at this stage, be accused of using hindsight, but it is difficult to imagine in retrospect that without the intervention of EU policies relations along the border between Poland and Germany – the first to be thrown together, as it were – would have improved as quickly as they did. Intergovernmental Agreements and Commissions have provided a context for a broad-based interchange, for the establishment of issue-based groups, and for co-operation on a number of levels. Extreme environmental problems, such as existed between Germany, Poland and the then Czecho-slovakia were in urgent need of a solution, but the availability of the Euroregion model, which here became the *Neisse/ Nysa/Nisa*, undoubtedly accelerated the start of a solution, with help of the *INTERREG* and *PHARE* monies. The speed with which the other Euroregions covered the German-Polish (and German-Czech) borders took most of those with a professional interest in this part of the world by surprise. But the difficulty of juxtaposing the two funding mechanisms and their different conditions created a hiatus, which was partially solved by the advent of the Small Projects Fund, and it is here that it became more obvious, perhaps, that cultural issues could be addressed. On this of all borders, it would be fanciful, even misguided, to maintain that anything like a single border identity was even now in the making, so bitter has been the alienation between the two nations. But cultural exchanges and projects such as those described above do indicate that, in spite of occasional incidents, there is an acceptance of the status quo and a willingness to grow closer together.

On the southern border with the Czech and Slovak peoples, this process is probably easier, due to the greater comparability of historical experience, national size and influence and indeed, linguistic and cultural background. It may also be true to say that mountain peoples have that physical link which transcends human conflict and which may help to erase the negative aspects of national emotions. On the other hand, national and regional histories have a role to play and are a necessary part of identification, which was lost, at least on the surface, for fifty years. It is likely, then, that the boundary lines between Poles, Silesians, Moravians and Slovaks will continue to exist, but perhaps once there is acceptance of the postmodern relative borderlessness of the EU, then these may recede into the background and allow a common border culture to emerge.

In the east, the paradoxical situation of ethnic intermingling and the fact that it is unlikely that all the border partners will become part of the same international organisations may cause the situation to remain tense. The Euroregion *Niemen*, which includes the northwestern region of Belarus, the western part of Lithuania, the northeastern corner of Poland and a small section of Kaliningrad, is seen by some regional actors as focussing on economy and development only, as a way of securing support for infrastructural activities, such as the construction of better roads and border crossing facilities. It is considered that 'cultural cooperation already exists' (Holm-Hansen 1999: 56). There are a small number of NGOs and other centres which work to develop 'a common interethnic and intercultural borderland identity', such as the *Fundacja Pogranicze* (Borderland Foundation). This includes a number of small groups of young activists who have initiated cross-cultural activities which, apart from reviving ethnic cultures of the past, also try to develop a contemporary sense of living in the borderlands, in order to give the region a dynamic multi-culturalism (ibid.: 50-1). It is, however, reasonable to see a role here for the Euroregion also in integrating the region as a whole with a broad range of activities, including cultural and scholarly exchange, since this has been shown to be one of the most successful areas of activity in other border regions in Europe with more experience of such co-operation.

It would be difficult to claim at this relatively early stage in post-1989 central Europe that border regions here were already able to create a new integrated transboundary identity. But there is much scope nevertheless, and the presence of interethnic and linguistic overlaps, together with the catalyst of EU regional policy and the use of Community Initiatives and *PHARE-CREDO* as part of the pre-accession policy should certainly soften the edges of some previously difficult relationships.

References

Bachtler J., Downes R. and Gorzelak G. (eds) (2000), *Transition, Cohesion and Regional Policy in Central and Eastern Europe*, Ashgate.

Bertram, H. (1998), 'Double Transformation on the eastern border of the EU: the case of the Euroregion Pro Europa Viadrina', in *Geojournal* 44 (3), 215-224.

Biuletyn Informacyny (2000), nr.14, Urząd Mieszkalnictwa i Rozwoju Miast, Warsaw.

Blažek, J. and Boeckhout S. (2000), 'Regional Policy in the Czech Republic and EU Accession' in Bachtler et al., 301-17.

Broszat, M. (1972), *Zweihundert Jahre deutsche Polenpolitik*, 2nd ed., Suhrkamp.

Cielemęcki, M. (1998) 'Przyczółki Unii', in *Wprost*, 10 May.

Eberhardt, P., Gorzym-Wilkowski, W., and Miszczuk, A. (eds), *Przemiany Demograficzno-Osadnicze na Pograniczu Polsko-Białorusko-Ukraińskim*, Bug Euroregion Series 8, Norbertinum.

Eskelinen, H., Liikanen, I. and Oksa, J. (eds) (1999), *Curtains of Iron and Gold: Reconstructing Borders and Scales of Interaction*, Ashgate.

Gallusser, W. with Bürgin, M and Leimgruber, W. (ed.), *Political Boundaries and Coexistence*, Peter Lang.

Główny Urząd Statystyczny (1999), *Euroregiony w nowym podziale territorialnym Polski*, GUS, Warsaw – Wrocław.

Gorzym-Wilkowski, W. and Miszczuk, A. (1997), 'Procesy demograficzne I Struktura Osadnictwa na Pograniczu Polsko-Białorusko-Ukraińskim', in Eberhardt et al., 11-159.

Holm-Hansen, J. (1999), *Polish Policies in the European Borderlands: Ethnic institutionalisation and transborder cooperation with Belarus and Lithuania*, Norwegian Institute for Urban and Regional Research (NIBR PLUSS).

Iglicka, K. (2000), 'Trendy w migracji do Polski po roku 1989 w swietle rozszerzenia Unii Europejskiej', in *Polska droga do Schengen: Opinie ekspertów*, Institut Spraw Publicznych, 201-21.

Kennard, A. (1996), 'Issues of Identity in the Polish-German Border Region', in *Journal of Area Studies* 8, 106-19.

Kennard, A. (2000), 'Transnational Cooperation on the German-Polish border', in Parker and Armstrong, 128-52.

Kockel, U. (1999), *Borderline Cases: The Ethnic Frontiers of European Integration*, Liverpool.

Krätke S. (1999), 'The German-Polish Border Region in a New Europe', in *Regional Studies*, 33 (7), 631-41.

Langer, J. (1999), 'Towards a Conceptualization of Border: the Central European Experience', in Eskelinen et al., 25-42.

Mindur, M. (2001), 'Charakterystyka Euroregionu "Bug"' in *Wspólnoty Europejskie*, 6 (118), 42-45.

Miszczuk, A. (ed.) (1997), *Zagadnienia wielokryterialnej delimitacji Euroregionu na pograniczu polsko-białorusko-ukraińskim*, Norbertinum.

Paasi, A. (1994), 'The Changing Representations of the Finnish-Russian Boundary' in Gallusser et al., 103-11.

Paasi, A. (1999), 'The Political Geography of Boundaries at the end of the Millennium: Challenges of the De-territorializing World' in Eskelinen et al., 9-24.

Parker, N. and Armstrong, W. (eds) (2000), *Margins in European Integration*, Macmillan.

Rościszewski, M. (1997), 'Euroregion Bug a geopolityczne dylematy polskiej granicy wschodniej', in Miszczuk, 27-51.

Stefan Batory Foundation Annual Report 1998.

Thomassen, B. (1996), 'Border Studies in Europe: Symbolic and Political Boundaries, Anthropological Perspectives', *Europaea – Journal of Europeanists* 2 (1), vaxca1.unica.it/europaea/1996ii1.html.

Trefon, A. (ed.) (1999), *Polsko-Słowacka Współpraca Transgraniczna w Regionie Bielsko-Biała – Żylina*, Regional Chamber of Trade and Industry, Bielsko-Biała.

Urban, T. (1993), *Deutsche in Polen: Geschichte und Gegenwart einer Minderheit*, C.H.Beck.

10 Culture, Transactions, and Profitable Meanings: Tourism in Andalusia

Antonio Miguel Nogués

The relationship between culture, commodities and tourism has long since been a topic for debate. Many authors have used ethnography to demonstrate links between the tourism industry and the commodification of culture (e.g. Smith 1989; Boissevain 1996) in situations when traditional culture serves both to promote cultural tourism as an industry and, more recently, as a resource to ensure economic growth in the region. In this sense, the 'production' of culture faces a challenge. Whether or not we conceptualise culture as a set of human activities that allows adaptation to a given ecosystem, the fact is that throughout the westernised world, once 'nature' has been brought under almost total control, a rather reductionist notion of 'culture' has been propagated, and one that follows an instrumental, rationalist logic rather than an expressive one. In other words, 'culture' is conceived as useful for achieving tangible objectives rather than for making social space comprehensible. Due to this shift in perspective, a new commodity, packaged under the term of 'cultural heritage', is being deliberately created, and even re-presented as both a basis for the creation of regional, local or group identities, and an endogenous resource for developing a given territory. This duality highlights a key point: the more globalism is attained in every social dominion, the more culture becomes de-moralised, stripped of any moral content. This is merely a consequence of the dialectics of being and action, between a group's self-recognition and its capability to exercise power over 'nature' as well as the culture of others.

Colonisation, imperialism and, nowadays probably, the tourist industry are good examples of this. Nonetheless, this once dominant concept of development seems to have failed. As early as 1972, a UN Conference in Stockholm stated that development policies needed to be changed radically to avoid a global ecological crisis. In the report *Our Common Future* (1987), the Brundtland Commission advocated a strategy of sustainable development as a way of correcting the negative effects of out-of-control capitalist development.

This new awareness led to a serious concern about the need to merge nature and economy at the decision making level. Briefly, it could be argued that within a sustainable development strategy, 'nature' ought to be considered in any action taken, and by every agency involved. At the same time, this concern for 'nature' evolved into the more comprehensive concept of the 'environment'. Whereas the idea of 'nature' allowed a restricted view of the global ecological problem as merely a question of trees, birds, rivers and air-quality, the notion of 'environment' included mankind not only as another biological species, but also and primarily as a social entity. This shift in outlook has required a new development paradigm that understands 'environment' as 'the physical, living and non-living surrounding of society with which it stands in a reciprocal relationship' (Udo 1991: 10).

To understand fully the benefits of this move from 'nature' to 'environment', we must consider some recent features of the evolution of the world economic system. First, the growing role of intangible goods within the market economy and other economic spheres has led to, on the one hand, the evaluation of environment in terms of cost and, on the other hand, the concern for human resources as central for entrepreneurial success. Second, the influence achieved by the idea of sustainability has led to a search for endogenous resources in any given territory. In this sense, the postulate of a necessary connection between sustainable policies and the environment is a foregone conclusion. Third, there is now a far greater emphasis on endogenous resources, compared to the stress on (foreign) investment that characterised economic theory in the sixties and seventies. If that theory emphasised investment and training, the new paradigm highlights the multiplier effect of endogenous action on the territory. This is quasi updating of the famous phrase: 'do not give them a fish, give them a fishing-rod and teach them how to fish *in their own* river'. And fourth, the concept of territorial development (be that local, regional or national) as a deliberate instrument of political and social action is legitimised as hegemonic. It is important, in this context, to underline that the combination of endogenous resources and territory does not necessarily lead to an increase in territorialism. Moreover, the notion of territory does not refer to cultural or administrative criteria so much as to economically compatible spaces.

The combination of these various aspects has progressively extended its influence over the new types of capital: human resources, the environment, and culture. In fact, the phrase 'think globally, act locally' summarises the new philosophy and gives culture the status of goods, not only as a formula to reduce pressure on natural resources, but also as a means of stemming the depopulation of less-developed areas. However, the reductionist notion of 'environment' as synonymous with 'nature' persists in policy-making. Legitimised only by general discourse, policies for sustainable development do not take much account of human agency – that is, culture – because they are more concerned with the sustainability of the natural resources.

Dealing with Culture as Heritage

Given that this concern about natural resources somewhat restricts short-term material benefits of economic activity, the persistent notion of unrestrained development now focuses on 'culture' as a brand new resource to be exploited. If 'nature' was reduced to whales and rainforests, what we are seeing now is 'culture' being converted into 'cultural heritage'. Anthropologists must pursue this crucial matter further. Thus, in my view, anthropological research and debate ought to centre on the cultural definition of the geographical notion of territory, on the expressive nature of notions of place and space, and on how cultural heritage can reinforce identity while also being considered an economic resource. We should focus our research and discussion on 'ethnologically friendly' development as an outcome of socially meaningful practices.

The following discussion investigates how political practice copes with the relationship between culture and economy in Andalusia, the southernmost Autonomous Community of peninsular Spain. It is intended to demonstrate how culture in the region has been economically converted into cultural heritage (Spanish: *patrimonio*) in order to pursue sustainable territorial development, and how all this has developed into a culture-economy perspective. The significance achieved by the tourism industry within the economic reality of the Autonomous Community determines the entire process. The following sections describe how regional policy-making deals with the sustainability demands of a global cultural market without mortgaging the cultural identity of the region. The theoretical perspective used here is that of the conversion of *place* through the mediation of tourism *space*.

This conversion, and the implicit negotiation of meanings, is traced by a textual analysis of three policy documents. The contents and sequence of these documents (1993, 1997 and 1999) reveal Andalusian policy-making uncertainties during the 1990s at a time of coming to grips with the consumption of the region's culture through tourism. The study compares the convergence shown by regional policies on culture and on tourism, illustrating the influence post-industrial reasoning has, by means of quality control, over notions of sustainable tourism based on cultural heritage.

The tourism industry is considered in Andalusia today as the best approach to dealing with cultural intangibles within the framework of sustainable development discourse. Using an economically correct discourse, it could be said that successive Andalusian governments have opted for a quality tourism industry in order to keep growth rates steady and to reduce unemployment figures. From their point of view, it has been fortunate for traditional culture, for its preservation and enjoyment, that tourism exists not only as an expression of the dominant capitalist system, but also as a tangible material reality that directly benefits territories. Fortunately, tourism is based on the alterotropism of places and spaces, and fortunately for traditional culture, tourism collaborates in its very conversion into cultural heritage. Fortunately, then, traditional culture will be properly preserved if converted into an endogenous resource, that is, cultural heritage. Tradition and culture are useful only as commercial metaphors of our past. But is this conversion of cultural manifestations into 'cultural heritage' effected in accordance with the natives' expressive world, or rather more with reference to the values codified and revealed by tourists in motivational surveys? Are the profits suggested by hotel-nights, visits to monuments, and queries at information desks the actual referents?

Territorial Development, Endogenous Resources and Cultural Heritage

In 1990, the Directorate-General for Tourism of the *Junta de Andalucía* (Autonomous Government) distributed a folded leaflet containing graphs and tables about tourist arrivals, tourism-related employment, the number of restaurants and travel agencies, regional economic incentives for investment in tourist facilities such as hotels, camping, congress centres, golf clubs and recreational harbours. The front of the leaflet shows a glittery egg and the phrase '*El turismo pone mucho ... en cifras*' (tourism puts in a lot ... in figures). On the back, the Hen of the Golden Eggs winks while embracing the slogan '*Todos podemos poner mucho*' (we can all put in a lot). Since the early 1990s, the tourism policy of the Autonomous Government has sought to expand the offerings to tourists beyond traditional coastal and summer tourism, including an ambitious programme to face the challenges of the new millennium within a global free-market economy.

Ten years later, Andalusia bases its regional economy on the tourism industry. In 2000, the annual growth rate in the tertiary sector was about 8%, income from tourism reached 13% of the regional GDP, and the number of visitors reached 20 million, of which almost 75% sought the traditional three S's of sea, sand and sun. These commercial figures, however, do not reflect the anthropological production of meaning and culture in Andalusia. According to the State Ministry for Education and Culture, there were 1,945 cultural properties in Andalusia in 2000. These included historical town centres, gardens, monuments, historical sites, archaeological zones, museums and archives. Thanks to this heritage, the region has been able to attract a constantly increasing number of cultural visitors to these locations, reaching 4.5 million in 2000. The statistical profile of these visitors indicates that 51% of the tourists come from Spain; of these, 63% come from other regions. In terms of occupational background, the dominant group are professionals, with 37.6% of the 30-44 age group and 24.3% of the 45-64 age group falling into this category. However, the important datum surely must be that the cultural tourist spent at least three times more (€76.09) than the summer tourist (€25.36).

To mark the International Day of Tourism (27 September 1995), the Public Enterprise of Tourism published a pamphlet entitled 'Decalogue of Tourism in Andalusia' (all translations author's own), which tried to contextualise the shift towards a new type of 'quality' tourism whilst keeping the empathy with former conceptions. This new 'quality' tourism, in accordance with incipient global trends of quality standards as well as with the sustainable development paradigm, was mainly defined in terms of consumption of culture:

1. *Tourism is prosperity* Tourism involves the movement of millions of people and thousands of billions of dollars, and the economies of entire regions, areas and even countries rely on tourism.

2. *Tourism is an economic reality in Andalusia* Andalusia is one of the most touristically developed zones in the world. Income from tourism reaches six hundred billion pesetas, making it a pillar of the regional economy.

3. *Tourism generates employment* An increase of 6% is expected through creation of new enterprises. Some 17.8% of the total working population are directly or indirectly employed in the tourism sector.

4. *Tourism perfectly fits our geographical and cultural conditions* Our geography, weather, personality, cultural heritage and natural settings have a potentiality for growth that we must develop.

5. Tourism is culture. Tourism is sharing   During the 1950s and 1960s, some people maintained that tourism was related with underdeveloped countries and servile societies. Reality today is different. The five leading tourism countries now are the United States, Germany, France, Italy and Spain. At the end of the twentieth century, tourism has become a key form for the exchange of cultures, knowledge and experience. Tourism is sharing. It is to know other people, and to let other people to know us.

6. Tourism improves the level of services   Tourism demands, and always has done, an efficient and competitive level of service, facilities and infrastructure that benefits all the citizens of Andalusia.

7. Tourism moves underdeveloped areas forward   New trends in tourism, and particularly the growth of rural tourism, while only beginning, assist the economic advancement of deprived areas.

8. Tourism helps to care for environment   Global tendencies towards nature and ecology have reached tourism as well. Thus tourism is considered as an compelling force for the care and preservation of the environment and natural spaces.

9. Tourism indicates the new reality of Andalusia   Andalusia is becoming a modern region, dynamic and vigorous in economy and culture. Tourists are well placed to perceive the changes and, moreover, they are in the best position to diffuse it, in a positive way, in their own countries.

10. Tourism drives the conservation of the historical and art 'patrimonio'   Tourism has reminded us of the rich *patrimonio* that we have inherited, and obliges us, make us aware of the need, and drives us to conserve and protect it.

There are some features of this Decalogue that signal when the *Junta de Andalucía* took the path towards rationalising culture. For instance, the use of terms such as 'growth' and 'underdeveloped' can be traced back to the period when token gestures towards 'sustainable development' or the politically correct term 'less-developed countries' were not yet common. Growth is still characterised, in items 1 to 3, as an increase in the basic economic variables of employment and enterprise creation. Andalusia is presented in item 4 as a tourism territory where the industry can satisfy its needs by using the peculiarities of the region. Item 5 introduces tourism as the perfect channel to ease interculturality. It is worth stressing that this item also expresses how peripherality is perceived through class-related subordination in the tourism industry. An important point links this discourse up with item 6 – the sense of a general well being for 'all the citizens of Andalusia' manifested through the efficiency and quality of tourist services. Items 7 and 8 introduce the main ideas of tourism as economic motor within the basic sustainable development discourse. The last two items address the clash between culture and economy. Item 9 clearly embodies the idea of motion and constant adaptation. Conversely, item 10 takes a gamble on the conservation of cultural characteristics of the region as materialised in historical and art *patrimonio*.

The gap between economic dynamism and the concern for *patrimonio* expands as the continuous adaptation required by the exigencies of quality tourism turns out to be increasingly competitive. Nevertheless, this does appear to be the solution to the seasonality and harmful effects of tourism industry.

Tourism Planning in Andalusia in the 1990s

The *Junta de Andalucía* intends to find, if not an powerful and definite solution, at least an acceptable political strategy that, on the one hand maintains controlled social and economic growth (as a less-favoured region within the EU), and, on the other, does not mortgage the cultural identity of the region. How then do policy practices deal with the need for sustainability in a global market where the periphery seems to own the culture and the centre the economy? This negotiation is analysed through the following three strategic documents:

- The *Plan de Desarrollo Integral del Turismo en Andalucía DIA* (Plan for the Integral Development of

Tourism) dealt with key issues of modernisation and competitiveness of the tourist sector.

- The *Plan General de Bienes Culturales - PGBC* (General Plan for Cultural Assessts) tackled the challenge of both promoting and preserving the historical heritage of the country.

- The *Foro Andalucía Nuevo Siglo* (Forum Andalusia New Century) aimed to generate a new project for the future of the country, stressing multiculturalism as the basis for building an open society.

The Plan for the Integral Development of Tourism (DIA)

The 1993 DIA Plan is a direct consequence of the agreement reached between the Autonomous Government of Andalusia and the Confederation of Entrepreneurs of Andalusia in June 1991. It was conceived as a starting point to create new models for the tourist development of Andalusia, and aims to 'search for a new model of tourist quality that will not only maintain our present position in the international market but also open up and create new expectations' (Junta 1993:1).

The strategic instrument to meet this objective is the idea of professional qualification, and around this idea the DIA Plan is specially designed to promote the quality of services as an image of Andalusia. It centres on the quality of service through the permanent training of human resources within an enterprise; an increase in the competitiveness of tourism enterprises according to new motivations and to the market demands; the matching of the price of the service offered and the satisfaction with the quality perceived. Finally, the Plan centres on the design of an effective product given the objectives of the tourist enterprise, or what should be the same: the satisfaction of the attracted tourists and, as a macro-economic sum, its share in regional development.

If the Plan had gone no further, it would have just been another rationalising construction of the image of the product *Andalucía*, according to the tourist cognitive map. Far beyond this reductive objective, however, the Plan raises some rather interesting questions concerning the commodification of the region, and especially the notion of 'qualification'.

This process of 'qualification' must be considered as the difference between the tourist's expectations and the tourist's reality as perceived during the consumption of the tourist service in our region. That is, the notion of 'qualification' does not imply a quantifiable monetary system, but the definition of quality in terms of a service higher than the one expected by the consumer (Junta 1993: 4). Hence the challenge is not to attract a larger number of tourists, but to 'qualify' the Andalusian tourist product and, simultaneously, to sell to the consumers that product together with the raised expectation of quality.

However, from an ethnologically-friendly development point of view it can be noted that the Plan does not really study the characteristics of the product to be sold. The analysis of the Plan leaves the impression that the product is the quality of the services, quite independently of the location, the social context, the cultural heritage environment, and the diversity of landscapes. This Plan is, it seems, designed for the tourism industry, and according to the tourists' models, tastes and motivations.

The General Plan for Cultural Assets (PGBC)

The later PGBC (Junta 1997: 7) states that it is an instrument for *rationalising* and improving the activities of the cultural administration of the Autonomous Community of Andalusia with regard to historic heritage. The whole idea of planning is based on the evidence of

> ... the needs to shape an open, flexible, and respectful approach to our past. An approach able to generate the social, economic and cultural profitability of the heritage, both for Andalusian as well as for *other possible users* (Junta 1997: 8; emphasis added).

As tourism is, from then onwards, gradually introduced as one of the dynamic agents of social and economic reality in Andalusia, and as one of the best preservers of heritage, so rationalisation is presented as the foundation of a sustainable culture economy (ibid.):

To rationalise is the main aim of any plan. This concept must be understood as an attempt to establish a sequence that allows the maximum benefits from certain efforts and, besides, that such a sequence be inspired by the principles of equilibrium, justice and realism. To apply reason is not easy when managing cultural items, most of which possess a deep symbolic meaning. The term rationalise applied to the historic heritage forces respect for its inherent values along with the capability to generate development, in such a way that preservation, growth and transmission to future generations is guaranteed.

It is clear to see that the rationalisation process presented in here goes far beyond the one shown in the previous case. The consistent concern about the commodification of cultural heritage led policy practice to balance the different types of profit. Neither the authors of the Plan nor the policies could, however, advance this ethnologically-friendly development of cultural heritage any further.

Andalusia New Century

The Forum Andalusia New Century brought together about two hundred experts during the period July 1998 to February 1999. It was mass-mediated as a personal initiative of the president for whom

> ... it seems convenient to open a serene and meditated period of reflection over the future of Andalusia, its hopes and expectations. To share all our ideas, to exchange our opinions, worries and constructive critique (Presidential discourse on www.junta-andalucia.es/nuevosiglo/principal.html).

The Forum was built around seven themes: 'Andalusia in the World', 'Andalusia: a Competitive Economy Generating Employment', 'Andalusia: a Multicultural Reality', 'Andalusia: an Inclusive Society', 'Andalusia: a Young and Prepared Community', 'Andalusia: a Technologically Advanced Society', and 'Cohesive Andalusia'. Each of these workshops attempted various objectives and brought together professionals and specialists from the most diverse academic disciplines and entrepreneurial sectors, including intellectuals.

For the purpose of this chapter, I am concerned only with the workshop entitled 'Andalusia: a Multicultural Reality'. It focused on Andalusia as

> ... a politically autonomous society, rapidly changing its social structure, and culturally settled, with the important difference that previous explanations and theories on Andalusia mainly *came from outside*, and now we are ready, given the development of social sciences, to provide them from the inside (Junta 1999: 143; emphasis added).

In this context, the objectives of the workshop were, first, to deepen the cultural definition of Andalusia, reinforcing its identity, starting with its unity and the richness of its diversity, promoting it and opening it up to Europe and to the wider world.

Second, to encourage dialogue, tolerance and neighbourly relations among the diverse groups and cultures settled in the region. In order to achieve this, education in tolerance and solidarity is a must. Following this point being made, the economic implications of this reality became a central issue. Thus, all collaborators emphasised the need for promotion and diffusion of cultural heritage as well as proper protection, to ensure the sustainable management of cultural resources through tourism and planning strategies.

Consequently, the third objective was to promote a better understanding and diffusion, as well as the preservation and management of cultural heritage, by the population itself and the institutions. The main conclusion was that this cultural heritage could be properly maintained through sustainable tourism policies.

The intellectual debate in the workshop centred on the cultural definition of Andalusia and the reinforcement of its regional identity. The participants from different sectors of art and culture sought to encourage dialogue, tolerance and coexistence among all different cultural (territorial and non-territorial) groups settled in the region, including Africans, Castilians, European pensioners, Andalusians, and Gypsies. Culture, as a social asset, was conceived as an instrument to pursue future social equilibrium. Therefore the Andalusian way to understand Andalusia needed to be preserved and improved in order to ensure cultural continuity, with cultural heritage playing an important role in this instrumental logic.

The search for self-identification through preservation and conservation of cultural heritage is, however, not independent of the setting where tourists seek to satisfy their expectations. Actually, the reductionist notion of culture as *patrimonio* as stated during the 1990s is, ten years later, moving more towards a view of culture in Tylor's sense. The post-industrial economic dynamism, together with competitive adaptation, quality tourism and the commodification of cultural heritage predispose policy-makers to claim that

> ... historical heritage is those material and non-material items in which, like a mirror, the population seeks self-recognition, where it searches for explanation of the territory where it is rooted, and in which those people that preceded it will also follow it. A mirror people *offer their guests* to make explicable their jobs, their ways of behaviour and their intimacy (H. Rivière, quoted in Junta 1999: 154; emphasis added).

As we see, the perceived commodification of culture may threaten the basis of post-industrial rationalisation and the sustainability discourse. Facing this unresolved tension, the workshop stressed a main peculiarity of Andalusian culture: the cultural mixing (*mestizaje*) as a crossroad between Europe, Africa and America. While other cultures and people encourage the notion of identity as different from that of others, Andalusia shapes its identity through *mestizaje*, trying to find a middle point between chauvinism and cultural relativism in order to build an open society.

The Forum concluded by merging the different positions in this idea of *mestizaje*. Against the sense of durability and intransience involved in the notion of cultural heritage, the Forum sketched the idea of the dynamism of cultural contexts through *mestizaje* as one way to accomplish socially and economically sustainable development. As the document states, Andalusian heritage would be the materialisation of a historical continuum where societies have fused, so visitors could easily unearth those meaningful cultural traits without interfering too much in the real production of culture. It is a different way to approach the conversion of places through tourism space.

Tourism and Cultural Agency

According to the *Anuario Estadístico de Andalucía*, a tourist is any person who, having their permanent residence elsewhere, remained overnight in a place visited for purposes other than for monetary reward. This statistical concept of what a tourist is for the Andalusian Government differentiates between who is and who is not a tourist. It highlights the rational and instrumental reality of a person who travels, does not get paid for it and stays overnight in the destination; that is, the tourist is depicted as a consumer of goods and services and, consequently, the local residents as producers of those goods and services.

It might be assumed that the administrative and geographical territory that constitutes the Autonomous Community of Andalusia acquires a double nature when considered through that statistical construction. As we have seen above, on the one hand, Andalusia is presented as a territory where exploitation, transformation, appropriation and managerial tourism-related practices are carried out; in other words a *tourist territory*. On the other hand, Andalusia is also presented as a *tourist setting* through which visitors experience vivacity, satisfy their expectations, and which motivates them to travel.

However, Andalusia is also more than a tourist territory or setting. For local people, Andalusia is their expressive world, an objective reality where Andalusians dwell and work, and where, since long ago and without conscious effort, they have been historicising themselves as a cultural group. Andalusia is for them their *place*, although, as this essay argues, we might also consider the existence of a *negotiated ground*. Such a negotiated ground can be located in those areas where interrelation between visitors and residents is more evident, and where conflicts of appropriation are intensively manifest, as many ethnographic accounts demonstrate (Mandly 1996; Boissevain 1996; Provansal 1993; Nogués 1999, 2001).

At this point, I want to approach the shift from a reductionist perspective on cultural heritage towards one of culture-economy from a new angle. It seems to me that to understand this search for the most profitable meaning of culture, we should consider the generation of a sphere through which meaning is mediated both for the residents' and for the visitors' expressive worlds. And it is precisely in this dialectic between these two expressive worlds that a tourism space is generated. Such tourism space concentrates all the cultural expressions and represents the projection of ideals and myths of the global society (Chadefaud 1987). It is a frame of reference where all the images that offer contents and meaning converge, where all the referents and mediators in the interpretation of reality meet.

The generative process of a tourism space in Andalusia ran in parallel with the 'neocolonisation of quality space' (Gaviria 1974) and the advent of coastal mass-tourism during the 1950s. The corollary occurs when the 'place' is perceived, experienced, interpreted and understood through the perceptual and expressive world of the visitors; when, progressively, tradition disappears as cultural amalgamation, and is re-presented for residents in the same way as it is for visitors; when, in the end, the 'place' becomes 'tourism space' and the profit connotations of the tourism industry appear as the hegemonic discourse in the most diverse cultural, social, and economic daily activities and locations.

Here the analysis achieved a different, comprehensive dimension. In the first place, it is worth noting the presence of some dormant ideas that resemble, somehow, the former dependency theory dualism between centre and periphery. There is a clear identification between underdevelopment and servility as the bottom line of most policy practices in Andalusia since late 1970s. The progressive neocolonisation of quality spaces, including that of culture, has mediated the meaning of Andalusia as the place for Andalusians. Not surprisingly, the Forum faced the problem of the widespread stereotypes of Spain. Those cultural traits seen as 'typically Spanish' are, indeed, mostly Andalusian. This appropriation of Andalusian culture especially during the period of Franco's rule was especially emphasised by tourist imagery (Nogués 1996).

There is an element of performance in this negotiation. Indeed, while the Forum explicitly rejected the glamorous and exotic image of Andalusia, and the PGBC underlined the need for an inclusive perspective on culture heritage according to self-identity, the DIA Plan stressed the visitors' expectations as the referent to follow when planning both the tourist territory and setting.

To conceive cultural heritage as 'a basic instrument for social redistribution of wealth and territorial equilibrium' (Junta 1997: 21) and stress the profitable meaning of culture seems to turn the dependency issue on its head, proposing as a result a culture-economy based on the rationalisation of cultural heritage by means of quality tourism. This assumes that the periphery owns the culture, while the centre owns the know-how.

Tourism space speeds up the translating process and mediates in the introduction of the technical approach to the sustainable management of cultural heritage. From this point of view, tourism could be seen as one of the favourite forms of expression of the dominant capitalist system, ensuring the continuity of the system itself through the exploitation of endogenous resources, stemming the depopulation of rural areas, offering an alternative to industrial crisis and reducing unemployment rates.

Far from being a matter of the commodification of culture, or of staged authenticity, what results from this is the idea of establishing an administration of culture, understood as an attitude towards culture, which does not pay attention to the production of meaning. It is an administrative view that, on the one side, underlines the economic value of tourist time not only as an occasion for the consumption of culture, but also as the restorer of labour power, and on the other hand expands this instrumentality into the sphere where a society represents itself, produces meaning, and creates moral bonds of community – into culture, that is.

This playful context becomes more concerned with the technique of cultural heritage than with the social production of culture. The culture of technical knowledge, as the prominent army of experts in *patrimonio* illustrates, is the result of the negotiation of meaning between global trends and local practices.

Dedication

To the precious memory of Jorge, my dearest brother.

References

Boissevain, J. (ed.) (1996), *Coping with Tourists. European Reactions to Mass Tourism*, Berghahn.

Chadefaud, M. (1987), *Aux origines du tourisme dans les Pays de l'Adour (Du mythe à l'espace: un essai de géographie historique)*. Départament de géographie et d'aménagement de l'Université de Pau et des Pays de l'Adour, et Centre de recherche sur l'impact socio-spatial de l'aménagement, Pau.

Gaviria, M. (1974), *España a Go-Go: Turismo charter y neocolonialismo del espacio*. Ediciones Turner.

González Turmo, I. (ed.) (1993), *Parques Naturales Andaluces. Conservación y Cultura*, Consejería de Cultura y Medio Ambiente, Junta de Andalucía.

Junta de Andalucía (1993), *Plan de Desarrollo Integral del Turismo en Andalucía: objetivos y estrategias, programas y actuaciones*. Consejería de Economía y Hacienda, Junta de Andalucía.

Junta de Andalucía (1997), *Plan General de Bienes Culturales de Andalucía 1996-2000. Documento de Avance, Enero 1997*. Consejería de Cultura, Junta de Andalucía.

Junta de Andalucía (1999), *Foro Andalucía en el Nuevo Siglo. Consejería de Presidencia*, Junta de Andalucía.

Mandly, A. (1996), *'Echar un revezo'. Cultura: Razón común en Andalucía*. Diputación Provincial de Málaga.

Nogués, A.M. (1996), 'El concepto de espacio turístico y la andulización folklórica de España', in *Dos Algarves* 1, 24-29.

Nogués, A.M. (1999), 'Del cante al discurso: el juego de la re-presentación compartida en la Semana Santa', in Oliver Narbona, 141-153.

Nogués, A.M. (2001), 'Turismo. Patrimonio y desarrollo' in Rodríguez Becerra, 53-82.

Oliver Narbona, N. (ed.) (1999), *Jornadas de Antropología de las Fiestas: Identidad, Mercado y Poder*, Universidad Miguel Hernández-Expo Fiesta.

Our Common Future. World Commission on Environment and Development, United Nations, 1987.

Provansal, D. (1993), 'El Parque Natural de Cabo de Gata-Nijar: de la percepción de un paisaje a la transformación social', in González Turmo, 47-51.

Rodríguez Becerra, S. (ed.) (2001), *Antropología de Andalucía* II, Publicaciones Comunitarias.

Smith, V. (ed.) (1989), *Host and Guests: the Anthropology of Tourism*, 2nd ed., Pennsylvania.

Udo de Haes, H. (1991), *Environmental Science: Definition and Demarcation. Center of Environmental Science*, Leiden.

11 Creating a Cornish Brand: Discourses of 'Traditionality' in Cornish Economic Regeneration Strategies

Amy Hale

Creating a 'Cornish Brand' is just one of the exercises occurring in Cornwall at present, as part of the reshaping of the lagging Cornish economy. As Jim Dunne of the Dublin based Identity Business has argued in relation to Ireland, countries, as well as companies, need to be very clear about the messages they give about who they are, where they are going, and the type of visitor and investor they want to attract. In the case of Ireland, Dunne identified a number of somewhat 'mixed messages' that in the past have contributed to a perhaps confused 'visual Ireland' (Dunne 1997). He noted in particular contradictions about 'traditional' and 'modern' Ireland that featured prominently in images of the country in both tourist and in economic strategy documents. Dunne spotted a potential problem: Who wants to pursue high tech investments in a country apparently filled with rustic peasants? Luckily, Ireland has overcome any contradictions in these perceptions to become a fast paced, modern, successful economy. Cornwall, however, is at the very beginning of facing these challenges, and it, too, is sending contradictory messages.

Among the contradictions identified by the development agency Cornwall Enterprise are: successful yet impoverished, accessible yet peripheral, industrial, yet attractive to tourists. The Cornwall brand is far from clear. After a century and a half of decline in what is considered to be not only one of the birthplaces of the Industrial Revolution, but also one of Europe's first post-industrial economies, Cornwall is working toward reconceptualising its economic and cultural position, both in the United Kingdom (UK) and in Europe. But the decisions of planners and policy makers at these early stages will greatly influence the direction of the territory. In this essay, I will discuss how the discourses of 'traditionality' have emerged within economic policy making in Cornwall, and the potential impact of this strategy on Cornish development.

Tradition

'Tradition' has often been considered to be one of the defining, fundamental concepts of the field. Stith Thompson once said, 'tradition is the touchstone for everything that is to be included in the term folklore'. It is 'tradition' which in many ways is perceived as a key definer of the 'folk group', whether that group is ethnic, religious, occupational or so on. Yet what constitutes 'tradition' remains hard to define.

We do know that tradition makes for very impressive rhetoric, and regardless of the critiques and questions posed by folklorists, it has a real meaning and value for people. As the essays in Hobsbawm and Ranger (1983) have shown, tradition is often used as a legitimising force; by groups attempting to maintain power, and also by disempowered groups working to assert, reassert or even to construct their history and identity. Of course it is within these paradigms that some of the most interesting expressive behaviour occurs.

However, folkloristic considerations of 'marketing tradition' tend to focus on the ways in which expressive behaviour, often national, regional or ethnic is performed and consumed. It generally does not refer to making a case for developing e-commerce. It is how 'tradition' becomes implicated with the processes of defining 'peoplehood' and the language of distinctiveness, which is the basis for my argument. The ways in which expressive behaviours are used to this end – dance, music, costume and so on, have always been a popular topic for folklorists but entire industries can also become part of this process. We can probably all think of regions that are strongly identified with particular industries: in Britain, these include, for example, south Wales and the coal mines, Leeds and textiles, Sheffield and steel. In Cornwall, however, the 'traditional' industries have not only become linked with territory and identity, they are also linked with ethnicity. As Richard Handler has shown, discourses of 'tradition' often underpin the construction of cultural difference (Handler 1988). So, in Cornwall where demonstrating difference is now a key to regeneration, the language of folkloristics has become a guiding principle of economic strategy outside the sphere of the creative industries, which is where we might initially expect it.

Cornwall and Cornish Ethnicity

Cornwall is the very tip of the southwestern peninsula of Great Britain. It is bounded on the fourth side by the river Tamar, which makes the territory almost an island. As a result of a number of economic, linguistic, religious and political features, Cornwall has continually asserted a sense of difference from England. Many people in Cornwall do not consider themselves to be English, nor do they consider Cornwall to be a part of England. Since at least the eighteenth century, the Cornish have increasingly defined themselves (and have also been externally defined) as Celts, predominantly on the basis of the existence of the Cornish language, which is related to Welsh and Breton. From the mid-nineteenth century within the parameters of the growing pan-Celtic movement, a Cornish ethnonationalist movement slowly emerged, with the primary aims of promoting Cornish cultural difference and varying degrees of political sovereignty. The Cornish are industrial Celts. Mining, fishing and agriculture are considered to be the three traditional Cornish industries. Mining has been linked with Cornwall for over 2000 years. Fishing has continued to be a significant occupation, although somewhat troubled in recent years, and not as prominent as it was 150 years ago. The Cornish coat of arms features a miner and a fisherman, which gives some small indication of the prominence of these occupations in shaping conceptions of Cornwall.

Although assertions of Cornish ethnicity are not entirely linked to the economic position of Cornwall, there are certainly some useful correlations to consider. Payton and Deacon have both argued that a sense of Celtic ethnicity in Cornwall arose directly from the collapse of the mining and fishing industries in the last quarter of the nineteenth century, which created a need to redefine the Cornish identity at a time of crisis (Deacon 1993; Payton and Deacon 1993; Payton 1997). Although it could be argued that this is a rather simplistic and determinist model, there are some comparisons to be made with the assertions of ethnicity in Cornwall during the economic crises at the end of the twentieth century and those at the end of the end of the nineteenth.

Yet, one difference is that since the early 1990s the idea of a Cornish 'Celtic' ethnicity has probably been much more popularly accepted than at any time in the past. A large part of this may be a result of the discourses of ethnicity and difference becoming more mainstream (cf. Boissevain 1994). Some of this has probably also been linked to a wider international 'Celtic revival' which has seen a boom in Celtic inspired publishing, creative industries and festivals, as well, of course, in Welsh, Scottish and Northern Irish devolutionary measures. The Irish 'Celtic Tiger' economy has demonstrated that certainly within a European framework, cultural difference, rather than assimilation, has real economic benefits.

Throughout almost the entirety of the twentieth century, Cornwall has been in a state of economic crisis. By the 1990s, as prosperity was growing in other parts of the UK, Cornwall was consistently falling behind. Cornwall became one of the most deprived places not only in the UK, but also in Europe (Cornwall County Council 1999). Frustration was increasing. 'Incomers' and second-home owners from wealthy urban areas were pushing locals out of the housing market, which actually contributed to a greater sense of Cornish cultural distinctiveness as well as increasing the economic division between locals and those from outside Cornwall (Deacon, George and Perry 1988).

In 1999 Cornwall was awarded Objective 1 status for the purposes of the European (EU) Structural Funds – a generous funding program for the most deprived regions of Europe. Using Cornish cultural difference as a basis for economic development became a key feature of strategy documents prepared in conjunction with the Objective 1 program. It is here that we start to find an interesting intersection between the discourses of ethnicity, industry and 'tradition'.

In the 1990s a lot of the academic focus of Cornish Studies was centred on the issue of 'the Cornish identity' – what it was and what it is (Payton 1992; Deacon 1997; Westland 1997; Kent 2000). Certainly the rather modern construction of 'Celticity' was one element, but perhaps the most prominent features were the persistent links between Cornishness and industry. Mining, fishing and agriculture were identified by Bernard Deacon and others as the basis for a distinctive Cornish culture influenced also by Cornish Methodism (Deacon 1997). Importantly, it was industry, and mining in particular, which was credited with serving as the basis for Cornish identity overseas, as Cornish miners emigrated to Australia, North and South America and South Africa where they formed Cornish communities. The descendants of these Cornish migrants today still very heavily identify with mining history as being at the heart of their identity.

Yet this poses a very real problem. While agriculture and fishing are still viable industries (although neither as buoyant perhaps as a hundred years ago), hard rock mining is gone, only China Clay mining remains. Certainly the stackhouses and engines are still a characteristic feature of the Cornish landscape, but the mines themselves are not functioning, and this has created somewhat of an identity crisis for the Cornish. When South Crofty mine closed in 1998, it was presented in the media as an act of genocide. The press reported the closure with words like 'the heart has been ripped out of Cornwall'. As the battle to save South Crofty mine was being waged, a significant piece of graffiti was scrawled on the wall in front of the mine, taken from Roger Bryant's anthem 'Cornish Lads'. It reads 'Cornish boys are fishermen and Cornish boys are miners too, but now the fish and tin are gone, what are Cornish boys to do?' The link between identity and economy has been so strong, that although new industries are needed for regeneration, there seems to be a fear that introducing non-traditional industries may further jeopardise the distinctiveness of Cornish identity that has been so closely linked with industry.

To summarise, Cornish cultural distinctiveness has become a central theme in economic regeneration strategies. However, primary conceptualisations of that 'distinctiveness' and Cornish ethnicity itself are based in 'traditional' industries that are either no longer operational, or no longer central to Cornish life. Government bodies, mainly led by Cornwall County Council, which are charged with the onerous tasks of redefining the Cornish economy, are being especially careful to integrate this notion of 'distinctiveness' in every area of their strategies. Planners conceive of it as a 'value added' component to not only creative industries, heritage and tourism, but also, importantly, 'to primary production, energy and environmental management.' Often this distinctiveness is characterised with recourse to the language of 'historicity', 'continuity', and 'tradition' (Cornwall County Council 2000). The Cornwall Culture and Heritage Strategy, prepared in 2000 by Cornwall County Council is explicit on this point:

> The Strategy proposes a commitment to heritage and culture as a cornerstone of social and economic regeneration in Cornwall. It is based on those elements of Cornish cultural identity which connect past achievement to present practice (ibid: 3).

The result is sometimes an 'invention of tradition', where a historical justification for a new or developing industry is pushed and emphasised.

Surely there are a number of reasons for adopting this strategy. The first is economic – difference, especially within a European regional context, means funding. However, there may be domestic reasons as well. Planners may be hoping to convince the Cornish people themselves that development bodies are seeking 'appropriate' industries – a common stereotype of the Cornish is that they are conservative and very resistant to change and progress. This belief is certainly implied in the language of strategy documents. However, policy makers are also asserting that the Cornish identity, and perhaps ethnicity, will remain intact, if not strengthened.

Economic Strategies

For this chapter I have examined a number of planning documents and economic reports to see how 'traditionality' was being employed. The *In Pursuit of Excellence* guides, the *Objective One Single Programming Document* produced by Cornwall County Council in 2000, and the *Cornwall Enterprise Strategy and Action Plan* for 2000 were the most revealing, and they are also the reports that are currently shaping economic policy in Cornwall. There were a number of areas in which traditionality was used to justify development, among them Earth Sciences, Entrepreneurship, and Technology and Intellectual Capital. Here I will examine three examples: first, the general principle of small scale development, second, design, and third, information and communications technology.

An early example of this process surrounds the particularly Cornish settlement pattern of dispersed towns that comprises outlying villages, hamlets and farms, which was a result of complex economic, social and political factors. Cornwall does not currently have a major primary economic centre, but for decades planners argued that a 'city' would be a major step toward a modern economy. However, in 1993 economist and Cornish activist Ronald Perry argued for a holistic Cornish economy based on small-scale development, and an intersection of culture, society and environment.

Perry noted that small-scale developments and focused entrepreneurship have historically been very successful in Cornwall, which they have for a variety of reasons (Perry 1993). Subsequent planners have attributed this to what is commonly believed to be a uniquely Celtic (therefore ethnically based) social pattern of small-scale and dispersed settlement (Cornwall Enterprise 2000: 7). This notion of developing in accordance with 'natural Celtic settlement patterns' (although there is nothing necessarily 'Celtic' about them) has shaped conventional wisdom in Cornwall for years; it has also been the foundation for explaining the above average number of small and medium sized enterprises in Cornwall. The most recent appearance of this logic was in the Strategy and Action document written by Cornwall Enterprise (2000: 29), where it is argued that

> Cornwall is a Celtic region with cultural links with Wales, Ireland, Scotland, and Brittany ... Community identity is linked to an in built sense of place. The Cornish are resilient and independent, but they have strong family traditions. This influences many aspects of social and economic life in Cornwall, in particular the settlement pattern and economic structure.

This statement serves as much of the justification for policy in this 136-page document. Although this is not strictly invoking tradition, it is certainly an example of explaining and promoting development by recourse to historicity, ethnicity and essentialism.

Prior to the establishment of Cornwall Enterprise, during the mid 1990s the group In Pursuit of Excellence, a body comprised of businesses, planners, executives and marketing people, led the way in promoting Cornwall as a land of success and opportunity. They produced annual glossy guides designed to showcase Cornwall's more successful enterprises and to overcome the perceptions of potential investors that Cornwall was backward, inaccessible and basically an industrial backwater. In a 1996 edition of this guide Professor Alan Livingston, the Principal of Falmouth College of Arts sets the scene for a growing design industry with reference to the Newlyn and St Ives schools of painting. He refers to the 'rich tradition of artistic practice' into which can be placed architects, interior and graphic designers, and industrial designers (Livingston 1996: 12). It is an interesting comparison. The Newlyn and St Ives Schools were almost exclusively non-Cornish, and certainly not practically oriented. The major artistic tradition associated with Cornwall is landscape painting, much of it modernist. Yet the points of comparison are not as important here as justifying the growth of the industry.

The development of information and communications technology (ICT) is also rationalised through an appeal to tradition. The Strategy and Action Document Cornwall Enterprise 2000: 48) notes that

> Cornwall has traditionally been at the centre of developments in communications technology, largely because of its location. Cornwall was the location for the first overseas mail service, for the first transatlantic radio transmission, for the landing and distribution of high capacity cables, and for the reception of satellite communications.

Yet, the document then goes on to highlight the poor ICT infrastructure and the comparatively low number of ICT users in Cornwall. Therefore, although Cornwall may have been the site of several communications landmark events in history, it was hardly the centre. The overall effect of these moments has been rather fleeting, hardly comprehensive, and neither emerging from, nor transforming Cornish communities. What is compelling here is the way the section of the document was phrased: instead of emphasising Cornwall's ideal position for transatlantic communications, there is instead a resort to Cornish history and tradition.

This tactic has not gone unchallenged. In the Cornish daily newspaper, the *Western Morning News* of April 17, 2001, Cornish activist and author John Angarrack criticised the Objective 1 team for 'playing the distinctiveness card' to secure European funding, and then not using any of the funding to support Cornish culture. A spokesman for Objective 1 responded to Angarrack by arguing that in fact £142,000 has just been awarded for the development of a Marconi centre on the Lizard peninsula to commemorate the first transatlantic radio signal. Yet, Angarrack retorted that the Marconi centre is not Cornish and does not promote Cornish distinctiveness. Despite Angarrack's views, I have spoken with other Cornish activists who do believe that communications technology should be Cornwall's 'new' traditional industry precisely because of Marconi.

Consequences

What are the consequences of this paradigm? Most importantly, there emerges an essentialist conception of what kinds of activity can (or cannot) take place in Cornwall, legitimised by this notion of 'traditional' industries, and this can generate some very dangerous policies and perceptions. To give an example, I once had a conversation with an Englishwoman who was incredulously on the executive board of the Cornwall Racial Equality Commission. She explained to me that Cornish people were genetically suited to manual labour and that the transition to a knowledge and technology based economy posed a serious threat to the Cornish as a people.

Furthermore, for better or worse, tradition is often seen as the opposite of progress and modernity. To paraphrase Dan Ben Amos, 'Tradition and civilization (or modernity) are an oppositional pair'. Traditionality may be valued as quaint or even confident, but it can also imply a lack of progress, and an unwillingness to break from the past. Even when the concept of 'traditional' is valued, this opposition needs to be carefully countered by strategists; otherwise it will serve as a limitation.

Yet it is not all negative. It is important, that planners are even considering 'traditionality' and Cornish 'difference' holistically within their strategies. They are perhaps attempting a 'Cornish solutions to Cornish problems' approach rather than adopting centrist, assimilationist policies. Furthermore, although not all of the industries referred to in strategy documents are 'traditional' in perhaps the ways that mining was in the sense of being the centre of community activity, it is possible to promote some sort of historical continuity with some of these industries – especially with information technology. If this makes people in Cornwall think more deeply and broadly about their achievements and their culture, this is a positive step.

Cornwall is currently in the first stages of developing a 'Cornwall Brand' as part of this wider economic strategy. Authorities, industry and marketing professionals are conducting research and conjuring concise images to communicate to both those inside and outside Cornwall a clear set of values. It is only hoped that the use of discourses of 'tradition' promotes the notion of a developing Cornwall that is inspired by the past, but not one that is fettered to it.

References

Boissevain, J. (1994), 'Towards an Anthropology of European Communities', in Goddard et al., 41-56.

Cornwall County Council (1999) *Socio-Economic Profile of Cornwall*, Truro.

Cornwall County Council (2000) *Heritage and Culture Strategy*, Truro.

Cornwall Enterprise (2000) *Strategy and Action Plan*, Truro.

Deacon, B. (1993), 'And Shall Trelawny Die? The Cornish Identity', in Payton, 200-23.

Deacon, B. (1997), '"The Hollow Jarring of the Distant Steam Engines": Images of Cornwall between West Barbary and the Delectable Duchy', in Westland, 7-24.

Deacon, B., George, A. and Perry, R. (1988), *Cornwall at the Crossroads*. COSERG.

Dunne, J. (1997), 'Creating a Visual Language for Ireland', in *Design Management Journal* 8(1), 45-9.

Goddard, V., Llobera, J. and Shore, C. (eds) *The Anthropology of Europe: Identities and Boundaries in Conflict*, Berg.

Handler, R. (1988), *Nationalism and the Politics of Culture in Quebec*, Wisconsin.

Hobsbawm E., and Ranger, T. (eds) (1983), *The Invention of Tradition*, Cambridge.

Kent, A. (2000), *The Literature of Cornwall: Continuity, Identity, Difference*, Redcliffe.

Livingston, A (1996), 'The Creative Mind: Design Education in Cornwall', in *In Pursuit of Excellence: The Green Book*, Hawkins.

Payton, P. (1992), *The Making of Modern Cornwall: Historical Experience and the Persistence of Difference*, Dyllansow Truran.

Payton, P. (ed) (1993), *Cornwall Since the War*, Dyllansow Truran.

Payton, P. (1997), 'Paralysis and Revival: The Reconstruction of Celtic-Catholic Cornwall 1890-1945', in Westland, 25-39.

Payton, P. and Deacon, B. (1993), 'The Ideology of Language Revival', in Payton, 271-90.

Perry, R. (1993), 'Economic Change and "Opposition" Economics', in Payton, 48-83.

Westland, E. (ed.) (1997), *Cornwall: The Cultural Construction of Place*, Patten.

12 'The Tiger No Longer Speaks Celtic': Economic Conditioning and the Irish Language

Máiréad Nic Craith

The Republic of Ireland is affectionately known as the 'Celtic Tiger'; a phrase that refers to its current prosperity. Since Celts never had tigers and those animals are not indigenous to the country, the slogan is rather dubious. Even more uncertain is the notion that contemporary Ireland is Celtic. In this essay I explore the link between economic conditioning and the Irish language, arguing that policies towards this Celtic language have consistently reinforced its association with poverty. Although Irish is not inherently a language of the poor, British and Irish governments have consistently portrayed it as such, and Irish people have been conditioned to associate the language with deprivation. This condition is, however, not irreversible!

The Irish government's position with regard to the state's first official language has always been an ambivalent one. When the Republic of Ireland joined the European Economic Community in 1973, administrators in Brussels found it difficult to classify the Irish language. Since Irish bureaucrats had no particular desire to categorise Irish as an official working languages of the Union, a special class of official, non-working languages had to be devised to cater for this 'exceptional' case.

In reality, Irish has much more in common with other regional or lesser-used languages, such as Welsh, Catalan or Basque. Yet the Irish Government refuses to sign the Charter for Regional and Minority Languages, on the grounds that Irish is the first and official language of the Republic. Irish politicians do not wish to see Irish formally classified as a regional or minority language – and there are many good reasons for this.

The concept of a 'minority' language appears to devalue the language. Anthropologists, linguists and politicians have struggled for decades to find suitable terminology for the non-official, non-working languages of the European Union, and have constructed categories such as 'lesser-used', 'minorised', 'less-widely taught', or 'less widely used'. All of these imply some qualification of the language and appear to detract from its status.

In any case, this terminology is meaningless. We are all familiar with the case of Catalan, which has considerably more speakers than Danish. Yet Catalan is classed as a lesser-used language whereas Danish is an official, working language of the Union. In the context of Quebec, French is a lesser-used language but in the world order, French is hardly a lesser-used language.

The primary difference between majority and minority languages pertains to power, rights and privileges. Perhaps the only factor uniting speakers of minority languages is their lack of majority status in government. It is also the case that these minority languages have been associated with poverty and backwardness. In this chapter, I wish to explore the process by which Irish became associated with penury whereas English came to be regarded as the language of commerce.

Education and Anglicisation

Much of Ireland's history reflects a colonial pattern. Nandy (1983) has argued that historically there were two distinctive genres of colonisation at play worldwide, and these were usually separated chronologically. The first focused on the physical acquisition of new territories, whereas the second was 'more insidious in its commitment to the conquest and occupation of minds, selves, cultures'. Usually, greed and a simple desire to expand one's holdings generated the first. In contrast, the pioneers of the second genre of colonisation were 'rationalists, modernists and liberals who argued that imperialism was really the messianic harbinger of civilisation to the uncivilised world' (Gandhi 1998: 15). Both genres were present in Ireland's history, but in this essay I wish to focus primarily on the second.

In nineteenth-century Ireland, the British colonial power embarked on a system of education designed to enhance the British imagined community in Ireland. A 'national' system of education was established in 1831. Skills of literacy and numeracy were offered entirely in and through English even where children were largely speakers of Irish. The emphasis on English was designed to establish homogeneity and commonality within the British Empire, and to reduce any 'regional' differences. Many inspectors' reports throughout the country lamented the problems encountered by the sole use of English as a medium of instruction (Nic Craith 1994).

A similar situation prevailed right throughout Britain. Here the 1870 Education Act encouraged a homogenous print community and sounded the death knell for Celtic languages in the regions. Welsh and Scottish Gaelic were banned in the schools of Wales and Scotland. In Cornwall, the operation of the Education Act 'made everything Cornish seem "rough ready and rude"' (Burton 1997: 155). The spread of transport and communication networks especially towards the end of the nineteenth century generated considerable homogeneity throughout Britain, and the concept of an Anglophone print community was particularly pertinent. Newspapers in English were widely available in the towns. The dissemination of the Bible in English and the tradition of English Christian writing had generated a high degree of cultural integration.

The Anglicisation policy was not confined to Ireland and Britain, but extended throughout the entire Empire. In Newfoundland, for example, teachers with no knowledge of Gaelic were appointed by the Scottish Education Department, despite the fact that most of the pupils were Gaelic-speakers. It was assumed that children would adapt easily and acquire the English language:

According to the Inspector's Reports it was the deliberate policy of the Scottish Education Department to appoint someone from outside the area who spoke only English, someone who made no attempt to learn Gaelic, someone who expected the pupils to conform immediately to the ways of the outsider   (Bennett 1989: 64).

A similar policy prevailed throughout many empires in the nineteenth century. Dutch was the medium of instruction in schools in West Friesland at the beginning of the nineteenth century, and spoken Frisian was banned from the classroom. In a school almanac of 1816, teachers were urgently advised not to permit children to speak Frisian. Economic reasons were put forward for the advancement of Dutch rather than Frisian, because 'to get by in their profession as a merchant, an artisan, a bargeman or something like it they had to learn Dutch' (Feitsma 1981: 166).

In all these instances the role of formal education was regarded as crucial in the construction of a print community in the language of the coloniser. However, the impact of schools in the Anglicisation process in Ireland is a matter for debate. Coolahan (1981: 7), for instance, argues that national schools merely formalised a tradition of learning in English, since this was already established in the more informal hedge schools of Ireland. As English was required for successful economic transactions, and was widely perceived as the language of commerce, the native language had already been disregarded by educators in Ireland in the older and more informal educational institutions of the seventeenth, eighteenth and early nineteenth centuries.

There is no doubt that the Anglicisation process was primarily a consequence of the urge to improve one's living conditions (Nic Craith 1994). For economic reasons, the desire to learn English was very strong. The Head Inspector, Patrick Joseph Keenan, in 1856 commented on the social impact of the association of English with commerce. When Irish-speaking islanders met with strangers to the islands, they noted that 'prosperity has its peculiar tongue as well as its fine coat'. They associated prosperity with the English language and saw 'that whilst the traffickers who occasionally approach them to deal in fish, or in kelp, or in food, display the yellow gold, they count it out in English'. Also significant was the fact that the legal process was conducted entirely through English. 'English is spoken by the landlord, by the stray official who visits them, by the sailors of the ships that lie occasionally in their roadsteads'. For all these reasons, Irish-speakers 'long for the acquisition of the "new tongue", with all its prizes and social privileges' (Keenan 1856: 143f.).

This implies that the primary motivation for the acquisition of English in nineteenth-century Ireland was economic rather than educational. While the national schools provided the mechanism by which English replaced Irish, they were hardly responsible for the change that occurred. National education offered people the opportunity to acquire the language of the coloniser, but it did not oblige them to learn English (Akenson 1969: 382f.). Formal education constituted merely a part of the Anglicisation process.

Hindley (1990: 14) suggested that the role of schools in the decline of Irish and the expansion of English are greatly exaggerated. His principal point was that universal and compulsory education was not enforced until the final decade of the nineteenth century. From 1831 onwards, the process of education was largely under the management of the Catholic Church with the voluntary support of parents. A process that was voluntary for more than half a century could hardly be held responsible for the decline of the native language. In my assessment, however, Hindley underestimated the desire for education on the part of the native Irish. Although schooling may not have been compulsory, it is certainly the case that Irish people have always been interested in education and would have been quite enthusiastic about any opportunity to acquire literacy skills in whatever language.

Moreover, it is important not to underestimate the significance of the colonisation process in generating the desire to assimilate. The Anglicisation process in nineteenth-century Ireland is a prime example of hegemony as defined by Gramsci (1971). His concern was with the assent given by the great masses to the general direction imposed on their social life by the dominant group. Historically, this consent is generated by the economic prestige enjoyed by the dominant culture (Burton 1997: 153).

As English was the language of the coloniser, education and, particularly, literacy marked social differentiation and offered a discourse of commerce and professionalism. It was a moral force offering children the opportunity to transcend the poor conditions of their birth. Children were taught literacy and numeracy, and were imbued with new values. Ideally, the idea of education in English was to enable Irish children to meet with British people as equals. Its purpose was to facilitate their citizenship and their commercial participation in the British Empire.

Parents were determined that their children would acquire the English language and the associated literacy skills. Oppression enhances the desire of a socially inferior group to conform to the dominant community. This is particularly the case when the inferior group believes that it can overcome the barriers of discrimination that are imposed upon it by the dominant group (Segre 1980: 9). The oppressed try to escape their condition by demonstrating unconditional adaptation to the cultural model of the dominant group, and through the rejection of their native cultural style:

> In every colonial situation, therefore, there is a stage at which the elites of the conquered society consider that self-alienation is an indispensable step towards achieving self-determination, and that the imitation of the conqueror will eventually reveal the secret of his strength and ultimately lead to freedom (ibid.).

The 'natives' perceive their own cultural style as inferior, associate their culture with poverty and backwardness, and abandon their traditional cultural forms and language. They endeavour to appropriate the whole way of life of their oppressors:

> Having judged, condemned, abandoned his cultural forms, his language, his food habits, his sexual behaviour, his way of sitting down, of resting, of laughing, his general behaviour, the oppressed flings himself upon the imposed culture with the desperation of a drowning man (ibid.: 43).

In nineteenth-century Ireland, literacy in English was deemed a valuable tool. Writing was feared among illiterates generally, as literacy had been used to steal property from them in the form of land maps and the civil surveys of earlier centuries. This is the subject of Brian Friel's renowned play *Translations*. Schools would help children to gain knowledge about the forms of control over them, and people needed to

have access to these power structures. Education was trans-
formative. It should have enabled children to transcend the
poor social status of their parents, to supersede local
commercial standards and provide them with cultural capital.
Instead, it perpetuated the very inequalities it promised to
overcome.

Education fulfilled the same role in each empire in that it
rationalised difference. It reflected the pattern by which the
colonising group was extolled and the socially inferior group
became stigmatised and associated with poverty. Education
rationalised the relationship between the dominant and the
dominated, and it did so always to the advantage of the
dominant. For many children in Ireland, it conceptually
linked the Irish language with ignorance and poverty (Crowley
2000; De Fréine 1978; Ó Huallacháin 1994; Purdon 1999).

In Wales, the Welsh language was similarly considered a
hindrance to commercial progress (e.g. Durkacz 1983). It was
a barrier to prosperity. A report on the Welsh people in 1847
noted that 'the Welsh language is a vast drawback to Wales,
and a manifold barrier to the moral progress and commercial
prosperity of the people'. The writer commented that the
language

> ... dissevers the people from intercourse which would greatly
> advance their civilization, and bars the access of improving
> knowledge to their minds. As a proof of this, there is no Welsh
> literature worthy of the name (J. C. Symon's report 1847, cited in
> Grillo 1989: 87).

English was the language of commerce and civilisation,
and in particular 'correct' English was the manifestation of
status. The focus on language in education was really on
linguistic skills and the ability that these skills would give
you in later life. English was useful. Irish had no practical or
commercial value. As their parents spoke poor English – if
any at all – pupils learnt to associate this with poverty and a
lack of intelligence, and internalised a sense of shame about
their indigenous culture. Children absorbed the idea that
Irish exercised a damaging influence on their acquisition of
English.

Even more significantly they learnt that local knowledge
does not travel:

Local languages had low status, whether they were used in education (for initial literacy, as in the British and Belgian empires, and in South Africa and pre-independence Namibia) or not (as in the French empire in Africa), such literacy in no way challenging the dominance of the colonial language in secondary and higher education, administration, etc. (Phillipson-Rannut and Skutnabb-Kangas 1995: 339).

Folklore, folk medicine or other indigenous knowledge was never transported via the written page. Moreover, the value of that folklore was open to question. Education was perceived as an opportunity for civilisation – an opportunity to gain access to scientific and rational knowledge, which would replace superstitious and barbaric concepts. At the same time, their limited literacy in English did not really afford Irish children the option of integration. Schooling reinforced the dichotomy it had promised to overcome. It reaffirmed a cleavage between the colonisers and the natives, literate and illiterate, educated and uneducated, rich and poor. Schooling indulged the fantasy of national participation, but in reality, it reproduced a powerful sense of inadequacy and the need for redemption in generation after generation. It confirmed the notion of the state as something existing outside the local community, and taught pupils that effective communication with the state required effective segregation of English and Irish.

Emigration and English

Several other factors influenced the association of English with material progress. In the late eighteenth and early nineteenth centuries, two thirds of Ireland's emigrants were from Ulster. As they were primarily Presbyterian and Anglican, a majority were, presumably, English-speakers. Those migrating from the South were mostly Protestant and, probably, largely unfamiliar with Irish. By the mid-1820s, some of Ireland's relatively poorer classes had begun to emigrate. In some cases, the British government had prompted this relocation by providing free passage and land grants in foreign countries. In all probability, some of these migrants had knowledge of Irish, although the precise details cannot be ascertained.

For many decades, the poorest and largely monoglot Irish-speaking peasantry continued to resist the lure of emigration:

> On the western coasts and other remote, mountainous regions sheltered from Anglicizing influences ... Irish-speakers still clung to their clachan settlements, rundale and joint tenancies, partible inheritance, and other customs which materially reinforced archaic 'dependent' or 'interdependent' outlooks, including strong communal and familial inhibitions against individual initiative and improvement (Miller 1988: 236).

The Great Famine of 1845-1851 precipitated a change as the numbers emigrating from Ireland increased dramatically, and continued to remain high for several decades. Table 12.1 indicates the numbers leaving Ireland from the time of the Famine until partition. A large proportion of those emigrating in the post-Famine period were small cottiers and labourers who were driven from their land by opportunity-seeking proprietors. Irish emigrants during the Famine years were poorer, younger, less skilled, and more likely to have Irish than previous migrant groups.

Table 12.1 Numbers of emigrants from Ireland, 1851-1920

Decade	Number of Emigrants
1851-1860	1,163,418
1861-1870	849,836
1871-1880	623,933
1881-1890	770,706
1891-1900	433,526
1901-1910	346,024
1911-1920	150,756

Source: Adapted from Miller (1988: 570f.)

The mid-nineteenth century exodus had a decidedly Gaelic character. During the late 1840s, port officials occasionally reported that entire shiploads to America were unable to speak

English. In many cases, migrants were unable to complain about the poor conditions on board because of an inability to speak English. Despite the need to emigrate for the purpose of economic survival, traditionally monolingual Irish-speaking communities in the west of Ireland resisted movement to a new country. Table 12.2 provides an estimate of the numbers of Irish-speaking emigrants from selected counties immediately after the Famine years.

Table 12.2   Estimates of Irish-speaking emigrants from counties with the highest proportion of Irish-speakers in the years 1851-1855

County	Emigration 1851-1855	% of Irish speakers 1851	Irish-speaking emigrants 1851-1855 (est.)
Cork	90,552	47.2	42,740
Tipperary	59,597	18.9	11,264
Limerick	44,423	31.4	13,949
Kerry	39,520	61.5	24,305
Clare	37,368	59.8	22,346
Galway	37,609	69.1	25,988
Donegal	26,437	28.7	7,587
Kilkenny	25,000	15.0	3,750
Waterford	25,071	55.4	13,889
Antrim	24,039	1.2	289
Total	409,616		166,107
% of total emigration	54.8		22.3

Source: Kallan (1994: 30)

In the post-Famine decades, large numbers of bilinguals left Ireland in a quest for economic progress. The resistance to emigration in the western, more monolingual Gaelic regions did not abate fully until the early 1880s. The effect of emigration was not merely a dilution of the numbers of Irish-speakers in Ireland. It also proved a remarkable motivational factor for the acquisition of English and the abandonment of Irish. School-teachers and parents collaborated in their efforts to ensure that children learned the language of opportunity (Corrigan 1992). The decline of Irish weakened the desire to remain at home, and a continuous stream of emigration from the country consolidated the Anglicisation of several generations. Chain migration provided the financial assistance necessary for many of those going abroad. Table 12.3 gives the numbers of Irish-speakers leaving the selected counties in 1891.

Table 12.3   Estimates of Irish-speaking emigrants from counties with the highest proportion of Irish-speakers in the years 1891-1900

County	Emigration 1891-1900	% of Irish speakers 1891	Irish-speaking emigrants 1891-1900 (est.)
Cork	77,456	27.3	21,040
Mayo	40,835	50.4	20,514
Kerry	38,718	41.4	15,980
Galway	36,852	62.2	22,902
Clare	18,156	37.7	6,798
Roscommon	16,298	10.4	1,699
Limerick	14,537	10.7	1,544
Sligo	14,197	21.8	3,066
Donegal	13,067	33.4	4,364
Waterford	10,059	38.1	3,832
Total	433,526	24.4	105,866

Source: Miller (1988: 571, 580; totals refer to Ireland as a whole)

Economics and the Gaelic Revival

Despite the increasing association of Irish with poverty, there were some advocates of an Irish revival towards the end of the nineteenth century. One of the best-known promoters was Douglas Hyde, who called for the de-Anglicisation of Ireland in 1892 (Hyde 1986). Hyde protested that the Irish had diverged from their 'true' path by ceasing to be Irish without successfully becoming English. They had acquired the language of the coloniser at the expense of their native tongue, had translated their own names and indulged in English literature.

Hyde's promotion of cultural separation made a strong impact. He pointed to the curious anomaly that existed as the Irish regularly protested their antipathy towards England yet rushed to imitate its culture (ibid.: 153):

> I should also like to draw attention to the illogical position of men who drop their own language to speak English, of men who translate their euphonious Irish names into English monosyllables, of men who read English books, and know nothing about Gaelic literature, nevertheless protesting as a matter of sentiment that they hate the country which at every hand's turn they rush to imitate.

Cultural rather than political independence, according to Hyde, would mark the authenticity of the Irish imagined community, but it seemed to him that the Irish people were more interested in material progress than in cultural capital. Thus he himself reinforced the image of English as the language of commerce and Irish as the language of poverty.

Hyde appealed to 'every Irish-feeling Irishman' to 'set himself to encourage the efforts which are being made to keep alive our once great national tongue' (ibid.: 160). It was important to

> ... arouse some spark of patriotic inspiration among the peasantry who still use the language, and put an end to the shameful state of feeling – a thousand-tongued reproach to our leaders and statesmen – which makes young men and women blush and hang their heads when overheard speaking their own language.

If Ireland ever gained political independence, the new state should endeavour

> ... to bring about a tone of thought which would make it disgraceful for an educated Irishman ... to be ignorant of his own language – would make it at least as disgraceful as for an educated Jew to be quite ignorant of Hebrew (ibid.: 161).

Culture and Economy
Contemporary Perspectives

Edited by Ullrich Kockel

| December 2002 | 219 x 153mm | 256 Pages |
| Hardback | 0 7546 1923 0 | £45.00 |

For further information, please contact
Debbie Fattore *at the address below*

Ashgate

Gower House • Croft Road • Aldershot • Hampshire GU11 3HR • UK
Tel: +44 (0) 1252 331551 • Fax: +44 (0) 1252 368595
e-mail: info@ashgatepub.co.uk • www.ashgate.com

Hyde was one of the founder members of the Gaelic League, which promoted the concept of the Irish nation as a distinct language community. One of its primary aims was the enhancement of a sense of difference from the British, reinforcing the concept of two separate traditions. This involved the development of a sense of respect for the indigenous language and culture and the undermining of the automatic deference to British culture (Ó Giolláin 2000: 120).

Although Hyde primarily focused on the revival of the Gaelic culture and language, he also referred to economic activities, which were relevant to the revival of the language. Hyde encouraged people to wear Irish-spun clothes rather than English alternatives, asking (Hyde 1986: 168):

> Why does every man in Connemara wear home-made and home-spun tweed, while in the midland counties we have become too proud for it, although we are not too proud to buy at every fair and market the most incongruous cast-off clothes imported from English cities, and to wear them?

This gives the impression that Irish people were rushing to demonstrate their prosperity through the acquisition of English clothes as well as the language.

The revival of Irish towards the end of the nineteenth century should be set in the context of the literary revival, which sought to establish the native voice in Irish literature. Many writers at the turn of the century emphasised the significance of the peasant as a necessary ingredient to Irish authenticity. No doubt this was influenced by the Romantic Movement, which equated modernity with material progress and assumed both would impact negatively on traditional languages and cultures.

In the case of Ireland, certain upper-class Irish people, mostly Protestants, portrayed their empathy with the Irish peasants and their disdain for material possessions, but unlike the peasant, they already enjoyed the possessions they derided:

> The peasant may not have had worldly goods but he certainly wants then, though generations of poverty may have taught him to tell others in self-compensation that the opposite is the case (Foster 1987: 301).

Wealthy Protestants who collected peasant lore were frequently black sheep among their own families and were hardly representative of the gentry.

For many Gaelic leaders, such as Patrick Pearse, Irish was to be the language of the new Ireland. Newly emerging Irish language literature endeavoured to represent the peasant in all his noble poverty. In his forward to *Íosagán agus Sgéalta Eile*, Pearse outlined his vision of a new Ireland, which was romantically close to nature, but hardly commercially viable:

> I see before my eyes a countryside, hilly, crossed with glens, full of rivers, brimming with lakes, great horns threatening their tops on the verge of the sky in the north-west; a narrow, moaning bay stretching in from the sea on each side of a 'ross', the 'ross' rising up from the round of the bay, but with no height compared with the nigh-hand hills or the horns far off; a little cluster of houses in each little glen and mountain gap, and a solitary cabin here and there on the shoulder of the hills. I think I hear the ground-bass of the water-falls and rivers, the sweet cry of the golden plover and curlew, and the low voice of the people in talk by the fireside (cited in Foster 1987: 305).

The Irish-speaking Peasant

With the establishment of independence in the early twentieth-century, the Irish Government designated certain peripheral areas on the west coast as Irish-speaking known collectively as the *Gaeltacht* (Fig. 12.1). In retrospect, the designation of specific *Gaeltacht* areas has been perceived as an attempt at 'freezing the language borders at a particular point in the geographical recession of the language' (Akutagawa 1987: 131). While the original intention was to award a special status to *Gaeltacht* regions, these internal borders also fulfilled the state's cultural objective. *Gaeltacht* regions would enable the rest of the state to become Gaelic-speaking, and activities in these areas were motivated by national rather than regional interests. Government policy in these *Gaeltacht* regions, implemented from Dublin, aimed primarily at the maintenance rather than the development of local indigenous industries. There was some concern that economic progress could contaminate the purity of Irish.

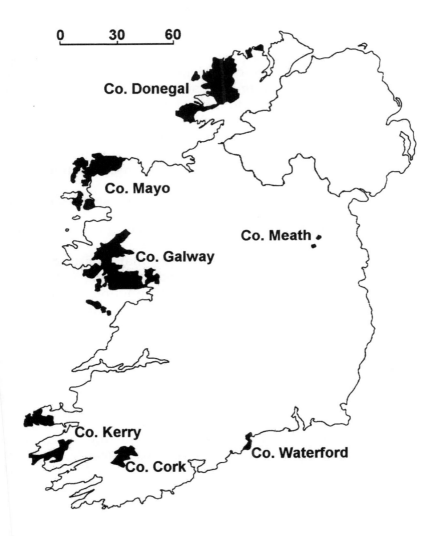

Figure 12.1 The Irish *Gaeltacht* regions

This image of the peasantry was carefully nurtured in Irish language literature. Foreign and native visitors to the Great Blasket Island in the early twentieth century spurred literati such as Tomás Ó Criomhthain (O'Crohan in English), Muiris Ó Súilleabhain (O'Sullivan in English) and Peig Sayers to narrate their lifestyles in print. The initial catalyst for these books was the peasant autobiography of Maxim Gorky, which portrayed Russian poverty in a style that was recognisable to the Blasket Islanders.

The impact of Gorky's peasant voice on writings from the Great Blasket Island was considerable, and Ó Criomhthain's autobiography *The Islandman* first appeared in Irish and was subsequently translated into many languages. Once again the image of poverty became strongly associated with linguistic perfection in Irish. The blurb on the Oxford paperback edition explains that while Tomás was tutor to scholars from many different countries, he lived the life an ordinary Islandman:

> He shared to the full the dangerous life of a primitive community, often stormbound, going hungry when the fish or crops failed, living well when the storm drove a wrecked cargo up the strand.

Twenty Years A-Growing, the next major autobiography from the Great Blasket, was promoted as a more jovial book. However, the brief postscript to the introduction explains that paltry economic circumstances forced many islanders to leave their native homes: 'As for the Blasket Island, all the old people who figure in the story are gone; the school was closed many years ago; and the village is in ruins'. George Thomson (1951: xi) tells us that the population of the Island was reduced to a mere five households with only one child among them:

> The mainland is being devastated in the same way. Nearly all the young people have emigrated. Everything seems to show that this corner of Ireland is destined to become as desolate as parts of the Scottish Highlands.

The third book in the series, *An Old Woman's Reflections* by Peig Sayers, was marketed as similarly frugal. The blurb explains that

> ... Peig lived through great hardships and 'clouds of sorrow', but was compensated with friendship which 'was like a little rose in the wilderness' and with the natural beauty of the Great Blasket.

In each instance, the potential reader was alerted to the poverty of the lifestyle before reading the book, and the images on the covers were suitably desolate. Inevitably, such marketing – rather than the books themselves – reinforced the concept of Irish as a 'natural' and 'beautiful' asset, but hardly advantageous if one desired material success in life.

The association of Irish with poverty was such that Flann O'Brien penned *The Poor Mouth*, satirising the 'excellent poverty' of the Irish autobiographical genre. While reactions to O'Brien's book noted the strong association of the Gaelic condition with poverty, some commentators argued that the book reflected on Irish life in general, rather than on Irish-speaking areas in particular. *The Poor Mouth* was conveying Irishness or the state of 'being Irish' as utterly dismal:

> Words such as 'hard times', 'poverty', 'drunken-ness', 'spirits' and 'potatoes' recur in the text with almost monotonous regularity. The atmosphere reeks of the rain and the downpour and with relentless insistence he [O' Brien; MNC] speaks of people who are 'facing eternity' and the like (Power 1973, cited in Cronin 1989: 130).

Negativity towards Irish

During the early years of the independence, Irish was taught to every schoolchild, but the language remained strongly associated with poverty at this time – a fact that hardly enhanced its appeal to schoolchildren. This is an image that is difficult, but not impossible, to reverse. In a large-scale attitude survey in 1973, the *Committee on Language Attitudes Research* (CLAR) observed the general perception that

> ... Irish speakers were smaller, uglier, weaker, of poorer health, more old-fashioned, less educated, poorer, less confident, less interesting, less likeable, of lower leadership ability, lazier and more submissive compared to an English speaker (cited in Ó Cróinín 1991: 64).

While the average individual seemed to place considerable value on Irish as a symbol of ethnic identity, its significance was qualified by a general pessimistic view of the language's future and a feeling that Irish was inappropriate for contemporary life. More recent surveys confirm the stability of this pattern. If anything, the role of the Irish language as a symbol of ethnic identity has strengthened, but there is general public pessimism about its future viability.

Conclusion

While there is nowadays a renewed interest in Irish in some urban regions, a substantial proportion of Irish people still associate the language with backwardness and material poverty. The economic potential of the language is as yet un-harnessed and under-appreciated. Many would react with disbelief to any suggestion that the widespread use of Irish could alleviate poverty and inequality in Irish society.

Instead, the attitude appears to be that the continuing love of Irish exacerbates economic problems, and that it is time for everybody to acquire a 'useful' language such as English, French or German. There is an implicit belief that Irish is a rural, parochial and anti-modern tongue, and encouraging a more widespread use of it would make Ireland even more insular, more parochial, and less economically successful.

Yet perhaps it is our use of English rather than Irish that makes Ireland's role in world economics just a local variety of a larger (British or American?) culture. At its most extreme, the 'Englishness' of Irish life compels a view of Ireland as an island 'off the mainland' of Great Britain. To assume that the use of Irish enhances parochialism is to fall into the error of equating any minority language or culture with all the characteristics of non-modern, non-progressive society. It is to look at the minority culture from the perspective of the coloniser and to ignore the success of local initiatives, such as, for example, *Tiobraid Árann ag Labhairt* (Ó Muircheartaigh 1996) or *Gaillimh le Gaeilge* (Nic Uidhir 1996).

As yet the link between language and economy is grossly under-researched. A language that is spoken by people of wealth does not die. A language that is spoken by those in authority or in government does not die. Language death seldom if ever occurs in communities of wealth and privilege. Rather, it occurs among the dispossessed and disempowered. The perception of wealth makes a language infinitely more attractive to a learner.

The implications of this are obvious. If a language is to flourish, significant attention must be paid to the economic well-being of its speakers. Irish-speakers do not wish merely to survive on government grants. If they are to be persuaded to continue speaking a language on more than a token basis, then the prospect of economic success must be available to them in that context.

There are some examples of wealthier communities speaking a so-called lesser-used language. Catalan is an obvious case study that could usefully be researched. More attention needs to be paid to the development of economic resources in our 'minority' language. It is the economic prosperity of speakers of a language rather than any inherent quality of a language itself that will ensure its survival.

Now that Ireland has become economically successful in English, it may be time to review economic policies for Irish-speaking regions and Irish-speakers, and to consider the potential of the language for the economy of the country. Ireland has many emigrants for whom the language has a natural appeal. The Celtic brand sells all kinds of goods, from CDs to tattoos. Now that the 'Tiger' has become economically prosperous, it is time to focus attention on its Celtic attributes, which could be harnessed to market uniquely Irish products on a worldwide scale.

References

Akenson, D. (1969), *The Irish Education Experiment: the National System of Education in the Nineteenth Century*, Routledge & Kegan Paul.

Akutagawa, M. (1987), 'A Linguistic Minority under the Protection of its own State: A Case Study in an Irish *Gaeltacht*', in MacEoin et al., 125-45.

Bennett, M. (1989), *The Last Stronghold: the Scottish Gaelic Traditions of Newfoundland*, Canongate.

Burton, R. (1997), 'A Passion to Exist: Cultural Hegemony and the Roots of Cornish Identity', in *Cornish Studies*, 2 (5), 151-63.

Chaney, D. (1994), *The Cultural Turn – Scene-setting Essays on Contemporary Cultural History*, Routledge.

Coolahan, J. (1981), *Irish Education: its History and Structure*, Institute of Public Administration.

Corrigan, K. (1992) 'I gCuntas Dé Múin Béarla do na Leanbáin': Eisimirce agus an Ghaeilge sa Naóú hAois Déag' ('For God's sake, Teach the

Children English': Emigration and the Irish Language in the Nineteenth
   Century), in O'Sullivan, 43-61.
Cronin, A. (1989), *No Laughing Matter. The Life and Times of Flann O'Brien*,
   Grafton.
Crowley, T. (2000), *The Politics of Language in Ireland 1366-1922*, Routledge.
De Fréine, S. (1978), *The Great Silence*, Mercier.
Durkacz, V. (1983), *The Decline of the Celtic Languages: A Study of the
   Linguistic and Cultural Conflict in Scotland, Wales and Ireland from the
   Reformation to the Twentieth Century*, Edinburgh.
Feitsma, A. (1981), 'Why and How do the Frisian Language and Identity
   Continue?' in Haugen et al., 116-38.
Foster, J. (1987), *Fictions of the Irish Literary Revival: A Changeling Art*,
   Syracuse U.P.
Friel, B. (1981), *Translations*, Faber.
Gandhi, L. (1998), *Postcolonial Theory: A Critical Introduction*, Columbia.
Gramsci, A. (1971), *Selections from the Prison Notebooks and the Study of
   Philosophy*, Lawrence and Wishart.
Grillo, R. (1989), *Dominant Languages: Language and Hierarchy in Britain
   and France*, Cambridge.
Haugen, E., McClure, J. and Thomson, D. (eds) (1981), *Minority Languages
   Today*, Edinburgh.
Hindley, R. (1990), *The Death of the Irish Language: A Qualified Obituary*,
   Routledge.
Hyde, D. (1986), *Language, Lore and Lyrics. Essays and Lectures*, B. Ó
   Conaire (ed.), Irish Academic.
Ihde, T. (ed.) (1994), *The Irish Language in the United States: a Historical,
   Sociolinguistic and Applied Linguistic Survey*, Bergin and Garvey.
Kallan, J. (1994), 'Irish as an American Ethnic Language', in Ihde, 27-40.
Keenan, P. (1856) 'General Report for 1856' in *Appendix to Twenty-Third
   Report of Commissioners of National Education*, HMSO, 143-4.
MacEoin, G., Ahlqvist, A. and Ó hAodha, D. (eds) (1987), *Third International
   Conference on Minority Languages. Celtic Papers*, Multilingual Matters.
Mac Póilín, A. (ed.) (1991), *Krino*, Galway.
Miller, K. (1988), *Emigrants and Exiles: Ireland and the Irish Exodus to North
   America*, Oxford.
Nandy, A. (1983), *The Intimate Enemy: Loss and Recovery of Self under
   Colonialism*, Oxford.
Nic Craith, M. (1994), *An Ghaeilge i gCorcaigh sa Naóú hAois Déag*, 2nd ed.,
   ESIS.
Nic Craith, M. (ed.) (1996), *Watching One's Tongue: Issues in Language
   Planning*, Liverpool.
Nic Uidhir, M. (1996), 'Gaillimh le Gaeilge: an Effective Bi-lingual
   Movement', in Nic Craith, 103-10.
O'Brien, F. (1973), *The Poor Mouth*, Hart-Davis MacGibbon.
O'Crohan, T. (1978), *The Islandman*, Oxford.
Ó Cróinín, M. (1991), 'Stranglehold: Irish in the Land of the Living', in Mac
   Póilín, 64-7.
Ó Giolláin, D. (2000), *Locating Irish Folklore, Tradition, Modernity, Identity*,
   Cork.

Ó Huallacháin, C. (1994), *The Irish and Irish – A Sociolinguistic Analysis of the Relationship between a People and their Language*, Irish Franciscan Provincial Office.

Ó Muircheartaigh, L. (1996), 'The Tipperary Irish Language Project: a Typology of Minority Language Education', in Nic Craith, 131-44.

O'Sullivan, M. (1983), *Twenty Years A-Growing*, Oxford.

O'Sullivan, P. (ed.) (1992), *The Irish in the New Communities*, Leicester.

Phillipson, R., and Skutnabb-Kangas, T. (1995) 'Language Rights in Postcolonial Africa', in Skutnabb-Kangas et al., 335-45.

Purdon, E. (1999), *The Story of the Irish Language*, Mercier.

Sayers, P. (1962), *An Old Woman's Reflections*, Oxford.

Segre, D. (1980), *Crisis of Identity: Israel and Zionism*, Oxford.

Skutnabb-Kangas, T., Phillipson, R. and Rannut, M. (eds) (1995), *Linguistic Human Rights: Overcoming Linguistic Discrimination*, Mouton de Gruyter.

Thomson, G. (1951), 'Postscript', in O'Sullivan, M. (1983), xi.

13 Language and Equity: A Development Perspective

Jane Saville

In any multilingual country, a government's choice of language to be used in official situations or as a medium of instruction in educational institutions will advantage certain groups and disadvantage others – not only in their social and cultural lives, but in terms of their ability to participate in political and economic life. People have always learned languages for economic reasons. In much of Africa, public markets are multilingual environments where people need to acquire a lingua franca in order to be able to trade food and goods. They will adopt a common language – a specialised market pidgin or one of the languages from the surrounding area.

Regardless of the variety used, language acquisition results from the immediate need to communicate and the actual use of that language in the interaction of buying and selling. Similarly, both national and world economic systems require a lingua franca, which will most likely be the official or national language and English respectively. Unlike the lingua franca of a market, however, both the non-native official or national language and English is typically acquired in school. Therefore, those who cannot afford schooling, have no access to effective tuition, or have no time to attend school may be prevented from obtaining jobs or participating in decision-making systems that require those languages.

This chapter analyses the link between language and equity and, using examples from different countries, shows that language is considered as both an economic resource and, conversely, as a hindrance to economic development. It concludes with a critical look at the activities of the World

Bank and the British Council in promoting English as a global language.

Language and the State

In a post-industrial economy the linguistic skills of workers at all levels take on a new importance (Cameron 2000; Cope and Kalantzis 2000; Gee et al. 1996). The need to be competent in 'communication skills', the new literacies prompted by new technologies and at least one foreign language all represent what Bourdieu (1991) called 'linguistic capital'. It has been suggested that languages are now being viewed more commonly as economic commodities rather than as symbols of identity (Heller 1999). This affects which languages people choose (if they are able) to learn and their motivations for learning. It also affects the choices that institutions make in the allocation of resources for language learning (Block and Cameron 2000: 5) and raises questions regarding the equality and equity of such choices and their consequences.

Tollefson (1991) argues that while modern social and economic systems require a certain language competence, governments simultaneously create conditions ensuring that large numbers are unable to acquire it. Education is the concern of the state, and its policies play a decisive role in determining who has access to the institutions of the modern market and therefore to political power. According to Paulo Freire (1985), power as a form of domination is not simply something imposed by the state via institutions like the government, police, courts and army, but is also expressed by the way in which power, technology and ideology come together to produce forms of knowledge, social relations and other concrete cultural forms that function to actively silence people. The oppressed then internalise and participate in their own oppression. Schooling, at whatever level, plays a most vital role as an efficient mechanism for social control, and there is strong evidence that inequalities among ethnic groups are reproduced through 'systematic elements of schools' (Bullivant 1987; Giroux 1983; Shannon 1989, cited in Tollefson 1991: 5-7). Many educators' idea of education is 'to adapt the learner to her environment' rather than teaching them to be critical of it (Freire 1985: 116). Instead, according to Freire (1985: 68), the educators' role should be to raise consciousness of this conditioning, to allow people to at least understand, and at most shape their own equality. Tollefson concludes that inadequate language competence is not due to poor materials, low motivation, inadequate methodologies and so on, but is directly related to government language policy.

Education is also closely associated with economic class. In Africa, lifetime salaries of people who completed higher education were seven to ten times the earnings of those who had only completed elementary education (Tollefson 1991: 8). It is suggested that schools serve as a 'gatekeeper' for the labour force, determining which individuals and groups will have which jobs. Large numbers of unskilled and semi-skilled workers are required in contrast with a small number of technicians and managers. Language is one criterion for determining which people will complete which level of education, and thus rations access to jobs with higher salaries, sustains economic and social divisions, and maintains state control of the labour force. This can be clearly seen in the case of the Philippines.

The Philippines

The Philippines, a former colony of both Spain and the United States, has at least eight major native languages and a number of smaller language groups, totalling over seventy indigenous languages (Clampitt-Dunlap, 1995). There are two official languages; English and Filipino, a linguistically engineered language which is based on Tagalog, the vernacular spoken on the main island, Luzon, and in Manila, but also containing elements of the other main languages. Filipino is the national language. Between 1974 and 1987, English and Pilipino were the languages of instruction in schools. English was used for teaching maths, science and technology and Pilipino for all other courses. In 1987, Filipino replaced Pilipino both as the national language and medium of education. It must be noted that although Pilipino and Filipino are often used interchangeably, Pilipino is largely considered to be a literary form of Tagalog while Filipino is the correct name for the composite, engineered language. English still dominates in higher education, however, and less than two-thirds of the population of the Philippines speak Filipino as their first language, despite it being used in the school system (Clampitt-Dunlap, 1995).

The Philippines face considerable social and economic problems, notably poverty and the unequal distribution of wealth. Secondly, most Philippinos do not own land, landless peasants being 'hired' by the owners of huge plantations. A third issue is increased rural-urban migration, resulting in problems of homelessness and unemployment. Fourthly, a few rich families with private armies dominate the political process with private armies; and finally, the population is growing rapidly, rising from 43 million in 1975 to a predicted 96.7 million by 2015. The urban population increased by 21 million between 1975-97 (United Nations 1999).

The choice of an official language was considered of crucial significance for access to economic resources, policy-making institutions, and political power. It was seen not purely as a struggle between the instrumental value of English and the symbolic, integrative value of Pilipino, but as one aspect of a struggle between competing economic interests, with Pilipino and English serving fundamentally different groups. Before Martial Law was imposed in 1972, there had been a move by political agitators and student bodies towards the use of Pilipino as opposed to English. From 1972, however, the elementary and high school curricula were transformed into 'work-oriented' programmes, to prepare young people to work in commercial and industrial enterprises.

When the World Bank funded new materials designed to help the education system to respond to the needs of the new economic policy largely financed by foreign capital, there was an increased emphasis on English. However, most students were educated for low-paying jobs requiring little English, even if located with multinationals. Since native languages were not used in schools, students remained illiterate or semi-literate in those as well. The educational system thus ensured that the rural poor provided cheap unskilled or semi-skilled labour. In general, the better jobs went to students from private colleges and elite schools, which taught English more successfully. This system of education supporting economic policy continued long after Martial Law was lifted. The success and support of the New People's Army (NPA) – a revolutionary group demanding political change, estimated in 1991 to have more than 20,000 fighters and countless sympathisers – was a direct result of the exclusion of the majority of Philippinos from the policy-making process and lack of access to economic resources. The NPA's language policy of ending the dominance of English as a national language aimed to redress this. It did, however, not deal with the issues of vernaculars other than Tagalog (Tollefson 1991).

In 1987, the Department of Education, Culture and Sports of the Aquino government adopted two 'department orders' regulating language in education and clarifying the issue of the national language, since neither the 1935 nor the 1973 Philippine Charters had been clear on this. This policy stated that Filipino and English should be used at the primary and secondary levels, with English only to be used for science, maths and technology and Filipino for other subjects. Its use in teacher-education and the improvement of materials and syllabuses is recommended. It is also thought that university lecturers proficient in Filipino should use that language in their subject areas in the hope of a trickle-down effect. Finally, the goals of the Bilingual Education Policy (BEP) include promotion of Filipino as the sole language of literacy, in scholarly discourse, and as a linguistic symbol of national unity and identity. English was reserved as an international language for the Philippines and as a 'non-exclusive' language of science and technology (www.ncca.gov.ph).

Bilingualism has been a policy in the Philippines for decades. Nevertheless, although successive governments have implemented a curriculum that should promote bilingualism, they have failed to take into account the development of the vernaculars of the people whose first language is neither English nor Tagalog. The need to use 'regional' languages as an auxiliary medium of instruction and an initial language for literacy is acknowledged, but this is swamped by the heavy focus on the increased use of Filipino and carries no specific guidelines. Higher education courses in the Humanities and Social Sciences are to be taught in Filipino. More ominously, Executive Order No. 335 instructs government departments, offices and agencies to use only Filipino exclusively in official transactions and communications. The reason given is that its use will result in 'greater understanding and appreciation of government programs, projects and activities throughout the country, thereby serving as an instrument of unity and peace for national progress' (www.ncca.gov.ph). However, it was reported in 1990 that English was still the primary language of education in the schools and universities of the Philippines (Clampitt-Dunlap, 1995) and that the government had continued to use English as its principle means of written and oral communication. It seems that, in reality, little has changed since the arrival of the American colonisers, when participation in government was dependent on the ability to use English. This is borne out by Arcelo (1990) who concludes that the type of bilingualism that occurs depends on the socio-economic situation of the speakers – whereas manual workers switch between their vernacular and Filipino, Philippino professionals rely mostly on English. However, the language debate in the Philippines now is focused on the imposition of Filipino as the national language to the exclusion of other indigenous languages from schools. This is a complex, unresolved issue. Recent studies in non-Tagalog speaking areas have shown that the everyday usage of other languages is widespread (Phillipson 2000: 166). Although Senior High school students, questioned in a survey, accepted triglossia in their communities – Filipino, English and their native tongue –, use of their mother tongue in school was sometimes perceived as rude or disrespectful of their teachers. At Elementary level, the children of the rural poor have to learn two completely new languages, English and Filipino, and yet only achieve a 'halting' level of fluency in both while failing to acquire adequate literacy in their mother tongue (Gonzales 1996: 43, cited in Phillipson, 2000: 167).

Phillipson (1992:47) has explored language polices at some length and argues that governments are often guilty of linguicism, which he defined as

> ... the ideologies and structures which are used to legitimate, effectuate and reproduce an unequal division of power and resources (both material and non-material) between groups which are defined on the basis of their language (i.e. of their mother tongue).

According to Phillipson, linguicism takes various forms. It may be overt – e.g., prohibition of a language in schools – or covert – while not forbidden, it is not used in teacher training, aid activities, or as a language of instruction. Those who support a Filipino/English bilingual education policy believe that, by eliminating all but one indigenous language for all educational and official functions and, in effect, relegating speakers to illiteracy in their first language, they are preventing English from dominating. In reality, the opposite is occurring, as educated young people (the elite of other Philippine language groups) are turning towards English in preference to Filipino, which they perceive as less useful for advancement in an increasingly globalised society (Smolicz and Nical 1997, cited in Phillipson 2001: 168). They attend extra-curricular English language classes, or private schools where English is the medium of instruction, seeing English as an economic resource and, conversely, the promotion of their national language as holding back economic development.

Those unable to receive their education in their native tongue are still disenfranchised. Since most people are unable to acquire English fluently, and over a third of the population does not speak Tagalog as a first language, they are stuck with poorly paid, marginal employment with little hope of advancement. Although, as Tollefson (1991) predicted, there have been signs of awakening language consciousness in the form of advocacy of Cebuano in Cebuano speaking provinces, to replace Tagalog as the official language, it is paradoxical that in order to influence the government to change policy in favour of the majority, pressure groups have to be competent users of English or Filipino. Language policies requiring widespread second language acquisition may help maintain a system in which language is a key indicator of socio-economic class and power. English was sold as the 'great equaliser' and Filipino is sold as the 'unifier', but in reality the ability to use either fluently depends on your status in society or your first language.

India

In India, there are around eight hundred different languages and over sixteen hundred dialects spoken. Hindi is a lingua franca as there are over three hundred million speakers, of which at least two hundred million use it as a first language, and it is a regional language in the northern and central states. The government is constitutionally committed to spending resources for its spread and development. However, English is still regarded as a necessary second or 'associate' official language, despite its colonial associations, especially for the southern and eastern states, where Hindu nationalism may be offensive to those who have a different language and religion (Ager 2001: 27). Moreover, English also remains the language of the elite. Interestingly, Indian English, as a recognisable variety, is widely accepted, and, according to Ager (2001: 26), 'a source of pride ... an elitist possession and a passport to riches in career terms'.

The government's language policy theoretically supports all linguistic groups, but this is not converted into everyday reality for many citizens. There is, for example, controversy over the status of regional languages such as Urdu. In the biggest state, Andhra Pradesh, the official language is Hindi; however, Urdu-speaking Muslims make up at least 15% of the population, and constitute 50% or more of the population in some large western cities such as Meeruta. Literacy rates in Andhra Pradesh rose from 21.2% to only 45.11% between 1961 and 1993/4, whereas in Kerala, where there is relatively little language conflict, the rise was from 46.8% to 90.59% (www.indiadecides.com, 1999). While there may be several reasons for this discrepancy, it is likely that the imposition of an official language may be one of the reasons why literacy rates remain low in states where the native language of a large group is not official. Illiteracy is a clear obstacle to equality and development.

For Urdu speakers to obtain language rights in education and central government development committees in Andhra Pradesh, Urdu has to be listed in the Eighth Schedule to the Constitution as an official regional language. Ager (2001: 28) notes that pressure for change is generally resisted because of the expense involved. In areas like Tamil Nadu, which has a very strong regional, nationalist, Tamil-speaking party, the Congress party, whose members are largely Hindi speaking, has not regained power since 1967. Kohli (1990) has studied this erosion of authority and claims that what was once a legitimate and modernising, stable State has become reactive, omnipresent but feeble, highly centralised and interventionist but apparently powerless. It does not initiate action to foster the 'life-chances' of its diverse social groups and seems neither capable of dealing with the concern of diverse groups nor of directing planned development.

This situation is, according to Kohli, partly due to the growing conflict between contending social groups (1990: 17). In the run-up to the election of 1998, prominent members of the coalition party attacked the dominance of English in government business and as a language of instruction in private schools. The Defence Minister at the time, Mulayam Singh Yadav, said 'We've had enough of leaders who ask for votes in their mother tongues but spend their parliamentary tenures speaking in English', and Sonia Gandhi, who made a political speech in English, was criticised for not speaking an Indian language. In addition, while the Ministry for Education funds schemes to promote both modern Indian languages and English (www.nic.ecucation.in, 2002), the Department of Official Language in the Ministry of Home Affairs has a Quarterly Progress Report Proforma regarding the progressive use of Hindi in government ministries and departments (www.dol.nic.in/qpreng, 2002). This may be seen as a possible indication of a move towards Hindi as the sole official language and more of the emerging backlash towards the dominance of English. Ager (2001: 30) suggests that the linguistic component of Indian identity is both stable and yet potentially explosive.

According to Nederveen Pieterse (2001: 60f.), culture has been introduced to the development discourse in response to increasing globalisation, since Western ethnocentrism is no longer regarded as acceptable. In addition, reference to culture is often used as a device in nation-building. However, when applied to culture in this context, dependency theory – characterised by protectionism, dissociation and endogenous development – can actually create cultural dependency. In multicultural societies such as India, the equation of national identity with a cultural identity using language as a centre-piece is wrong. Nederveen Pieterse claims this 'subsumption' of cultural identity under national identity is deliberate, as the politics of nation-building requires indigenous and other minorities to be discriminated against and peripheralised. Language policy, as a mechanism for exclusion, is frequently fundamentally exploitative. This is evident in educational systems that impose disadvantages on minority students, and in restrictions on bilingualism among both subordinate and dominant populations. Research into education highlights the necessity for policymakers to take into account the attitudes of people towards the language chosen. How learners and their families perceive the status of a language has been correlated with rejection or acceptance of a Language of Instruction (Roy-Campbell 1992; Okwany 1993, cited in World Bank 1997: 36).

Bilingual education may provide a way of reconciling loss of cultural identity and pressures to assimilate (British Council 1999). Furthermore, a multilingual approach to language planning may help to decrease tensions where one language has been forced upon part of a population. An example of this is in Southern Sudan, where the imposition of Arabic and several conflicting language policies has led to a slowing down of growth and development, and eventually to civil war (Nyombe 1997, cited in British Council 1999). In Ecuador, some sections of the indigenous, Quichua-speaking population rejected early attempts at bilingual education, as they saw it as another form of oppression. The case of the Atlantic coast of Nicaragua provides a clear example of how the cultural and linguistic needs of all groups have to be ascertained before policy is formed.

Nicaragua

Unlike the rest of Nicaragua, where Spanish is spoken universally, the Atlantic Coast hosts a multilingual society, with Miskitu, Creole, Spanish, Carib, Sumu and Rama all spoken as first languages by different sections of the population. Freeland (1988: 80) asserts that language was often used as an instrument of repression in this part of the country and became an important mark of ethnic identity and resistance to domination. Under the dictatorship of the Somoza regime, for example, teachers were required by law to teach through the medium of Spanish, even though their classes could not understand them, and there were huge dropout rates among Miskito-, Sumo- and Creole- speaking children.

The ban was lifted immediately when Somoza fled in 1979, though at the time of the revolution, illiteracy in any language stood at 80%. Very few Miskitos and Sumos had ever seen anything written in their languages, and literacy in English, the first language of the Creoles, Ramas and Black Caribs, depended on privileged access to private schools. Education presented a difficult problem to the revolution.

Through the organisations MISURASATA (Miskitos, Sumos, Ramas and Sandinistas United), SUKAWALA (Nicaraguan Association of Sumo Communities) and SICC (Southern Indigenous and Creole Community), the ethnic minorities claimed the right to bilingual education in their own languages and Spanish, and in 1980, the government added mother-tongue literacy programmes in the three written languages of the region – Miskito, English and Sumo – to that for Spanish. Despite initial progress, however, the civil war worsened and prevented further progress until the ceasefire agreements in 1986 made travel easier again and a special bilingual/bicultural branch of the Ministry of Education co-ordinated development of bilingual programmes in schools.

The initial reaction of parents was that mother-tongue teaching would hold their children back, but the programmes were designed to develop children's pride in their language and culture, the communities were closely involved in the development of materials in their language, and the Spanish materials were designed to encourage children to evaluate the dominant culture critically in relation to their own. The Autonomy Process for the region was asking the people to shape their own political and social development in their own languages. The call for adult literacy rose in response to the opportunity to participate actively in decisions, which would be their own futures.

All the languages now have equal status in the country's Constitution, people have pride in them again, and ethnic tensions have been decreased. There is a peaceful struggle for their rights, with the realisation that the government is now receptive because it belongs to them too (Freeland 1988: 81f.).

Africa and the World Bank

The spread of European languages can be seen as supporting unequal relationships between developed and developing societies in that access to information does not depend solely upon language fluency, but also on institutional structures and relationships, such as small or non-existent computer networks, complex and slow bureaucratic systems, and political influence. Nations need to develop the necessary institutions, like research universities, development offices and so on to gain access to European language resources. This often requires the assistance of the major world powers, which engenders a potentially unequal relationship, in which developing countries are forced to open up their institutions to direct influence and control.

Furthermore, European languages are associated with the institutionalisation of inequality within developing countries, as most colonial and post-colonial societies have a dual system of institutions – a 'developed', 'Westernised', industrial sector, and an 'underdeveloped', pre-industrial, traditional one. Migration occurs from the largely rural 'underdeveloped' to the largely urban 'developed' sector, due to differences in wealth and income, but this does not reduce the effects of the dualism, as there are still acute divisions within the urban centres. The economic and geographical division is often accompanied by a linguistic one. Those in the 'Western' sector are much more likely to learn European languages, which may be a criterion for membership in this sector (Tollefson 1995).

The children of the political elites of many developing countries, such as the Nehrus, the Bhuttos and the Nyreres, have received a western education. Those in the 'traditional' sector may not have an opportunity to learn. This situation helps to institutionalise the gap between sectors and creates a barrier to progress. Outside education, national languages ration access to political institutions of power. The adoption of a national language depoliticises one variety while making it a symbol of national unity. Resistance to a national language, therefore, is seen as opposition to national unity.

Furthermore, the importance of language policy is fundamentally rooted in the rise of the modern State. It is one mechanism available to the state for maintaining its power and that of the groups that control state policy. Language policy is likely to be seen as a threat by those groups who are excluded, yet the hegemonic approach interprets language policy as the benevolent arm of the state in serving national interests. Thus it cannot analyse the role of language planning in creating and sustaining economic inequality through language education. Neo-classical economic theory, with its emphasis on market-led growth and the need to liberalise state structures, misses completely the role that language policy plays in exploitation (Giddens 1982, cited in Tollefson 1991: 201).

Colonisation still continues to influence language policy, which is increasingly being internationalised. Rassool (cited in Phillipson 2000: 56) points out that the influential policy makers are now transnational organisations such as the International Monetary Fund (IMF), the World Bank (WB), the European Union (EU) and the British Council (BC), and that these are increasingly replacing the nation-state in terms of their power in the realm of language rights and policy. In developing countries, aid and Structural Adjustment Packages (SAPS) are often 'tied' to conditions that impinge on linguistic choices and rights or force a country to curtail spending in areas like education. Social inequalities are therefore exacerbated.

In the current battle over the language of instruction and academia in Africa, the World Bank states, in the face of criticism, that it is unable to force an educational language policy on any African country and in the last ten years has moved towards acknowledging the value of mother tongue instruction in schools. However, this 'lack of intervention' policy is seen as inconsistent, rather than an appropriate attitude. In the current 'contest' between English and indigenous languages as the medium of instruction in Africa, the World Bank persists with its policy of encouraging the cutting of government subsidies for education. Subsidies are vital to instruction in mother tongues, for example, to ensure investment in the production of materials to promote the vernaculars. Encouragement to use vernaculars at primary levels, if it is possible after SAPs have been implemented, may actually help the acquisition of a former imperialist language, at higher levels. Thus, Mazrui (1997: 40) argues that

> ... under World Bank-IMF structural adjustment programmes, the only path open to African nations is the adoption of the imperial languages from the very outset of a child's education.

Never does the Bank raise the question of using the vernacular beyond elementary levels, and it does not seem to consider the 'linguistic Africanisation' of upper levels of education. Its publication on strategies for stabilising and revitalising universities (Saint 1993) makes no mention of the place of language at tertiary level.

Furthermore, the Bank has argued that the majority of students, who mostly come from affluent backgrounds, can afford to pay for their own education. Subsidies to public universities are considered to be rather inefficient, and even 'regressive' social spending (World Bank 1994). This does not tally with their figures, however, that an average of 60% of students come from the peasantry, workers and small traders who could definitely not afford to pay for their children's education. There are two consequences of this. Firstly, dropout rates among students from poorer backgrounds are increasing. At Kenya's Moi and Egerton Universities, for example, which educate 6,000 students, over 2,000 were removed from the registration rolls in early May 1996 over non-payment of tuition fees (*Daily Nation*, 4 May 1996; see Tollefson 2002: 279). It can be assumed that these were from lower-income families. The second, long-term consequence is the transformation of African universities into 'middle-class' institutions. Middle-class families that are the most likely to use the colonial languages, not only in education, but in all areas of life, and the consolidation of the English language to the detriment of African languages is therefore seen as directly exclusionary regarding access to education. Mazrui (1997) sees the bank's withdrawal from higher education as a possible hope for the future, depending on the willingness of the African elites to promote their native languages through extensive usage in academia. Currently, the net effect of both the Bank's SAPs on African education and the unwillingness of the African elites to use their mother tongues is the creation of further inequality in society.

Finally, if we view the place of language in imperialist control from the economic perspective, it has a labour and a market side. On the labour side, the World Bank's policy on educational instruction in Africa can be seen as part of a wider agenda to supply labour for foreign capital. The Bank, after all, has recommended restructuring African universities into regional polytechnics to meet the demand needed by African economies (WB 1994, cited in Mazrui 1997: 44). European languages will be the medium of instruction, of course.

However, the needs of African economies have been shaped by former colonial powers, and the labour hierarchy could be a direct result of the languages used when these were created. Thus, the Bank is promoting the continuation of this hierarchy and an economy dominated by foreign owned interests. It is the poorer children who are destined to supply the lower ranks of the hierarchy, since they will have the least chance to obtain higher education in a foreign language. The market motive of the World Bank involves the role of English as a medium of global capitalism. The consolidation of that capitalism is now dependent on the language. As leading institutional representatives of international capitalism, the World Bank and IMF have a vested interest in this interplay between linguistics and economics.

The British Council

The English Language Teaching (ELT) business has become one of the major growth industries around the world in the past thirty years. The British Council, with its network of 243 offices and teaching centres in 110 countries, aims to promote cultural, educational and technical cooperation and to 'enhance the reputation of the United Kingdom in the world as a valued partner' (Mission statement, Annual Report, 1998-99). In 1995/96, over 400,000 candidates sat the worldwide English language examinations administered by the Council, over half of which were in English as a Foreign Language (EFL), and there were, at any time, 120,000 students learning English and other skills through the medium of English in Council teaching centres. The Council's website (www.britcoun.org) tells us that the spread of English has increased due to the 'perceived benefits seen to accrue to its native speakers', and two economists are reported as saying that the use of English in a global market gives native-speaker countries an economic comparative advantage. This is supported by Kachru (cited in Phillipson 1988: 1), who tells us that English is considered a 'symbol of modernisation, a key to expanded functional roles, and an extra arm for success and mobility in culturally complex and pluralistic societies'.

In a discussion on the professionalism of English Language Teaching worldwide, Phillipson says that the dominance of English is part of a general failure to deliver educational aid. A survey of theories of educational aid and dependency and the empirical evidence by a World Bank consultant ends with the statement that

> ... there is a good deal of evidence that much Western educational curricula, technology and institutions have failed in the Third World because of their inappropriateness (Hurst 1984: 33, cited in Phillipson 1992: 260).

It is argued that the English language appears to be an integral part of the global structures of dependency. Naymith (cited in Tollefson 1995: 43) suggests that English language teaching

> ... has become part of the process whereby one part of the world has become politically, economically and culturally dominated by another and that the core of this process is the fact that English has become the language of international capitalism.

Phillipson maintains that the international linguistic hegemony of English, largely in the name of 'development', has over the last twenty-five years adapted to a constantly changing situation, ranging from the 'colonialist' to the 'neo-colonialist', and he points out that native speakers of British and American English, and 'experts' using English as a second language, 'have served to secure the establishment or perpetuation of linguistic bridgeheads throughout the global periphery' (Phillipson 1988: 341). From his analysis of many organisations – economic, political, military, communicational and cultural – Phillipson believes that it has been deliberate government policy in English speaking countries to promote the worldwide use of English for economic and political purposes: 'The British empire has given way to the empire of English' (ibid.: 342). The increasing link between education – specifically language education or Languages of Instruction – and politics provoked Pennycook to call for all teachers of Applied Linguists and English around the world to

> ... become political actors engaged in a critical pedagogical project to use English to oppose the dominant discourses of the West and to help the articulation of counter-discourses in English (Tollefson 1995: 55).

As an English language teacher and teacher-trainer myself, and having worked abroad for the British Council, the largest employer of English language teachers in the world, I have seen both the possibilities and the limitations of this call to arms. While teachers can certainly equip their students to be fluent communicators of their opinions, and even to be critical of the world they live in, there is always an element of control in that syllabuses and materials are usually fixed and already provided, knowledge is tested, and teaching is assessed and monitored throughout. Teacher training is almost totally aimed at disseminating best practice from the West, regardless of whether it is appropriate for different cultures and settings. There may be a nod in the direction of how to adapt the methodologies for their classrooms but it is, in my opinion, very cursory. Furthermore, the University of Cambridge English Language Exams System is universally marketed, but is totally Euro- or, rather, British-centred, with no reference to other varieties of English.

Furthermore, teachers are encouraged to be 'globile' – the council often provides only short contracts, teachers have little opportunity to establish themselves in that country, and are expected to spread 'good practice' around the different teaching centres of the world. Graddol (1997) reports on a British Council survey of its teachers. Most English language teachers believe that English is essential for progress, but do not think that it leads to negative social consequences. On closer examination, the specific statements the respondents were asked to agree or disagree with referred to the necessity of English to gain access to high-tech communication and information over the next twenty-five years. The second question was worded thus: 'Competence in English encourages elitism and increases socio-economic inequalities' (see Graddol 1997: 38). Notably, only 59% disagreed, which is encouraging, but secondly, and more importantly, bearing in mind the points above regarding 'globility' of British Council teachers, the result of the survey should not be taken too seriously. In my experience, a large proportion of these teachers is neither well informed about the socio-economic situation in the country hosting their employment, nor are they interested.

Graddol's book, 'The Future of English' (1997) was commissioned by *English 2000*, an initiative, led by the British Council, that 'seeks to forecast future uses of English worldwide and help develop new means of teaching and learning English' (www.britcoun.org/english/pdf/future). The project team worked to 'position' British English language teaching goods and services 'to the mutual benefit of Britain and the countries with which it works' (ibid.). This appears reasonable, until it becomes clear that the commission was born out of a fear that the future of English as the global language is not as certain as most may think. At the end of the foreword, written by HRH Prince Charles, the book is commended to 'all who are concerned to see a strong and vigorous future for our language'. Although Graddol attempts to take an objective standpoint, including anti-English viewpoints and a section on global inequalities in his presentation – in which the link between social inequality and the teaching of English is admitted grudgingly, and with the use of many modal verbs of possibility and much tentative language – he is clearly conscious of who commissioned his writing. He warns native speaker readers that the book may contain facts and ideas that may be 'uncomfortable'. For example, as the number of native speakers of English will soon be exceeded by non-native speakers, 'the centre of authority regarding the language will shift from native speakers as they become the minority stakeholders in the global resource' Graddol 1997: 3); English will diminish in world importance, possibly replaced by an oligarchy including Chinese and Spanish. Language is continually referred to as a resource (ibid.: 2f.):

> To put it in economic terms, the size of the global market for the English language may increase in absolute terms, but its market share will probably fall.

It is noted that the decisions of organisations, governments and consumers in the future will have to be made with reference to a shift in social values and public opinion, which is increasingly making social equity as important as income in personal life choices. Those responsible for promoting a global English will, it is suggested, be 'burdened' with new social responsibilities and 'may have to engage in a more complex public agenda, including ethical issues relating to linguistic human rights' (Graddol 1997: 3). This appears to imply that this is a new consideration, even for organisations like the British Council.

The United Nations' Human Development Report for 2001 (United Nations 2001) concentrates on the link between development and technology. A recent technology that uses predominantly English, the Internet, is the fastest-growing tool of communication ever, with an estimated 700 million users in 2001. The vast majority of websites, almost 80%, are in English. However, the technology is limited to a few countries. In mid-1998, industrial countries, with only 15% of the world's population had 88% of Internet users. In Cambodia, in 1996, there was less than one telephone per 100 people – in Monaco there were 99. Most telephone lines in less developed countries are in the capital, and thereby inaccessible for the majority of citizens; connections are poor in the rainy season, and user costs are very high (United Nations... 1999: 58). The monthly Internet access charge as a percentage of average monthly income in Nepal is 278%, compared to 1.2% in the US (United Nations 1999: 58; 2001: 81).

The typical Internet user worldwide is male, under thirty-five years old, with a college education and high income, urban-based and English-speaking – a member of a very elite minority (United Nations 1999: 63):

> Current access to the Internet runs along the fault lines of national societies, dividing educated from illiterate, men from women, rich from poor, young from old urban from rural (United Nations 1999: 62).

The advantages of speed and accessibility of information from electronic communication are clear – if the choice exists. Until a population is literate, it cannot use the Internet. In addition, if they are not competent users of English, they cannot access the information. The inability to use the Internet is, therefore, at the moment, not without its costs. Those who fail to acquire English may have their life chances reduced. Things are changing, however, with the numbers of other languages increasing, especially Chinese.

However, Gray (2002) sees a positive side to the use of English on the Internet and points out that there is the possibility that it will become the language of global resistance to exploitation and injustice. He gives the example of Zapatista statements that are regularly posted in English and Spanish, and the recent campaigns against Nike and Gap in the USA that were organised online and were aimed at improving conditions for workers in developing countries. The most striking line I read on this topic, however, was in the British Council commissioned 'The Future of English', where the author stated that a possible consequence of the fact that many African universities have poor connections to e-mail was that 'many students will have to study overseas' (Graddol, 1997: 39). This, I suggest, is not an obvious consequence to many people, and reads more like a poorly-disguised commitment to the continuation of selling an overseas education in an English-speaking country, in this case, the United Kingdom, to the elites who can afford it and will then further the use of English in their native countries.

Conclusion

Skutnabb-Kangas (1990) makes the point that while people used to be divided into groups with unequal access to power and resources on the basis of biological 'race' and culture, the criterion now is language. Due to migration and globalisation, the number of linguistically homogenous states is rapidly decreasing, and one political approach to managing the diversity of most countries is the extension of democratic pluralism. This necessitates the eradication of discrimination and the reduction of the social and political distance between ethnolinguistic groups created by excessive inequalities in the distribution of economic resources (Tollefson 2002). Language policies in education are therefore critical to ensure that all groups in society acquire the language competences they need for economic advancement, and the languages they need to retain to maintain their fundamental sense of identity or to provide a basis for the learning of other languages. Tollefson warns us that failure to establish effective policies will result in increasingly unequal distribution of economic resources and escalate the likelihood of ethnic and linguistic conflict. He predicts that language rights will become increasingly important to counteract the new forces of hegemony.

The monolingualism of the majority of citizens in Britain and the USA may become a liability in the future, offsetting any economic advantage they now have as native speakers of the current global language. Experiments as to whether the spread of English as a lingua franca might be causing comprehension problems between speakers of the different varieties of English, with their different cultures, found no evidence for this, but discovered that native speakers from the UK and the USA were not the most intelligible, nor were they best able to understand the other varieties of their language (Graddol 1997: 56). The development of varieties of English is likely to continue, as second-language countries will almost certainly develop their own curricula, materials and training that they will sell to neighbouring countries. A more sensitive approach to the teaching of English is needed, and even David Graddol (1997: 63) admits that English is not a 'universal panacea for social, economic and political ills', and that teaching methods, materials, and educational policies need to be adapted for local contexts. Ager (2001: 105-119) encourages us not to view the spread of English as a conspiracy, but to recognise the need to standardise a form of communication where the use of language is accompanied by a rejection of the cultural norms of the native-speaker nations. However, he also tells us that the correction of inequality is an unlikely motive for policy-making.

It is to gain equality in the distribution of resources that the Indian language groups that are not officially recognised at national or regional level are seeking that recognition (Ager, 2001: 116-7). We have seen how a government's choice of language may produce inequality in the employment market in the Philippines. Income disparities may, over time, increase a society's tolerance for inequality, undermine public policies likely to advance human development and erode social capital, including citizen responsibility (United Nations 2000: 17). It is to gain economic advantage that the elite of non-Tagalog speakers in the Philippines wish to learn English, and why the other non-Tagalog speakers wish to reject Filipino and use their mother tongues in official spheres. The latter group do not have access to private schools to learn English, and need to redress the imbalance of power against Tagalog speakers.

Language can be both a resource for, and an obstacle to economic development. Development is not imported, but is generated from within by the people themselves. Education should empower people to create their own development. The mother tongue 'sets the stage for the empowerment of ... children' (Vasques 1993, cited in Roy-Campbell and Qorro 1997: 75-76). An 'understanding' of processes that produce economic disadvantage is achieved through education. This needs to include an understanding of underlying political and economic processes, and not merely of the culture that is produced by a particular political economy. To facilitate this process, students need to understand their materials and teachers, and to be enabled to develop cognitive processes and express their opinions. This can only be done through the mother tongue and, as the example of Nicaragua shows, can be highly effective. Thus language policy can be used to transform as well as reflect power relations. Tollefson tells us that language policy is inseparable from the power relations that divide societies (1991: 202), and Freire that 'education worldwide is political by nature' (1985: 188). Chris Brazier's report on education in the North and South, concludes that, in the twenty-first century, we should be able to focus on improving the quality of teaching and learning, and on 'educating children to be critical thinkers rather than clones, active democrats rather than drones' (Brazier 1999: 29). The social context in which language policy takes place is essential for an understanding of its social meaning.

Different developing countries may need different mixes of European languages and vernaculars. The most appropriate language policy for an individual country may not necessarily be monolingual or bilingual, but it needs to be decisive, clearly considered by the government, widely accepted by the population, and adequately resourced. Different languages may suit different subjects and different levels in the cycle from primary to tertiary levels. However, all social groups must be able to make an informed choice about their futures, aware of how the local, regional, national and international situation affects them, and what options are available to them. Language is an economic resource, but currently, some languages are more valuable than others. It is to be hoped that the Universal Declaration of Linguistic Rights, which is now circulating for approval, will contribute to the eradication of inequity and inequality on the grounds of language.

References

Ager, D. (2001), *Motivation in Language Planning and Language Policy*, Multilingual Matters.

Albrow, M. (1990), *Max Weber's Construction of Social Theory*, Macmillan.

Block, D. and Cameron, C. (eds) (2002), *Globalization and Language Teaching*, Routledge.

Bourdieu, P. (1991), *Language and Symbolic Power*, Polity/Blackwell.

Brazier, C. (1999), 'Making it Happen', in *New Internationalist* 315, August, 29.

Bunyi, G. (1999), 'Rethinking the Place of African Indigenous Languages in African Education', in *International Journal of Educational Development* 19 (4-5), 337-50.

Cheshire, J. (ed) (1991), *English Around the World. Sociolinguistic Perspectives*, Cambridge.

Clampitt-Dunlap, S. (1995), *Nationalism, Native Language Maintenance and the Spread of English: A Comparative Study of the Cases of Guam, The*

Philippines and Puerto Rico, Dissertation, University of Puerto Rico, www.ponce.inter.edu/ul/tesis/sharon/diss.

Cornia, G., Jolly, R., and Stewart, F. (eds) (1987), *Adjustment with a Human Face*, 2 vols., Clarendon.

Crystal, D. (1997), *English as a Global Language*, Cambridge.

Freeland, J. (1988), *A Special Place in History. The Atlantic Coast in the Nicaraguan Revolution*, Nicaragua Solidarity Campaign (London).

Freire, P. (1985), *The Politics of Education. Culture, Power and Liberation*, Macmillan.

Graddol, D. (1997), *The Future of English? A Guide to Forecasting the Popularity of the English Language in the 21st Century*, British Council.

Gray, J. (2002), 'The Global Coursebook in English Language Teaching', in Block and Cameron (eds), 151-68.

Greaney, V. and Kellaghan, T. (1996), *Monitoring the Learning Outcomes of Education Systems*, World Bank.

Grin, F. and Vaillancourt, F. (1999) *The Economics of Multilingualism: Overview of the Literature and Analytical Framework*, accessed at www1.worldbank.org/wbiep/decentralization/grin.htm (10/7/99).

Hettne, B. (1995), *Development Theory and The Three Worlds*, Longman.

Kachru, B. (1986), *The Alchemy of English: the spread, functions and models of non-native Englishes*, Pergamon.

Kohli, A. (1990), *Democracy and Discontent. India's Growing Crisis of Governability*, Cambridge.

Mazrui, A. (1997), 'The World Bank, the language question and the future of African education', in *Race and Class* 38 (3), 35-48.

Meara, P. and Ryan, A. (eds) (1991), *Language and Nation*, British Association for Applied Linguistics in association with Centre for Information on Language Teaching, Regent's College, London.

Mercer, N. and Swann, J. (1996), *Learning English: development and diversity*, Routledge.

Nederveen Pieterse, J. (2001), *Development Theory: Deconstructions/ Reconstructions*, Sage.

Patrinos, H. and Ariasingam, D. (1997), *Decentralization of Education. Demand-Side Financing*, World Bank.

Pennycook, A. (1994), *The Cultural Politics of English as an International Language*, Longman.

Phillipson, R. (1988), 'Linguicism: structures and ideologies in linguistic imperialism', in Skutnabb-Kangas and Cummins, 339-58.

Phillipson, R. (1992), *Linguistic Imperialism*, Oxford.

Phillipson, R. (ed.) (2000), *Rights to Language, Equity and Power in Education*, Lawrence Erlbaum.

Roy-Campbell, Z. and Qorro, A. (1997) *Language Crisis in Tanzania. The Myth of English versus Education*, Mkuki na Nyota (Dar es Salaam).

Ruggie, J. (ed.) (1983), *The Antinomies of Interdependence*, Columbia.

Schuurman, F. (ed.) (1993), *Beyond the Impasse. New Directions in Development Theory*, Zed.

Sengupta, A. (2000), 'Realising the Right to Development', in *Development and Change* 31 (3), 553-579.

Skutnabb-Kangas, T. and Cummins, J. (eds) (1988), *Minority Education: From Shame to Struggle*, Multilingual Matters.

Tollefson, J. (1991), *Planning Language, planning inequality. Language policy in the community*, Longman.

Tollefson, J. (ed.) (1995), *Power and Inequality in Language Education*, Cambridge.

Tollefson, J. (ed.) (2002), *Language Policies in Education. Critical Issues*, Lawrence Erlbaum.

United Nations Development Programme (1999), *Human Development Report*, Oxford.

United Nations Development Programme (2000), *Human Development Report*, Oxford.

United Nations Development Programme (2001), *Human Development Report*, Oxford.

Working Group on Educational Research and Policy Analysis, Association for the Development of Education in Africa (1997), *Languages of Instruction. Policy Implications for Education in Africa*, International Development Research Centre, Ottawa.

World Bank (1980), *Education Sector Policy Paper*, 3rd ed., World Bank.

World Bank (1988), *Financing Adjustment with Growth in Sub-Saharan Africa 1986-1990*, World Bank.

World Bank (1995a), *Priorities and Strategies for Education. A World Bank Review*, World Bank.

World Bank (1995b), *World Development Report 1995. Workers in an Integrating World*, Oxford.

World Bank (1997), *Primary Education in India*, World Bank.

Web Sites

British Council
   www.britcoun.org/english/englit3.htm (18/2/99).
   www.britishcouncil.org/work/news.htm (13/5/99).
   www.britcoun.org (22/1/02)
Indian Government
   www.education.nic.in (16/1/02).
   www.dol.nic.in/qpreng (16/1/02).
India Today
   www.indiadecides.com/reference1/literacy.shtml (17/8/99).
Philippines Government
   www.pids.gov.ph (20/1/02).
   www.ncca.gov.ph (20/1/02).
World Bank
   Education Sector Strategy Document, at www.worldbank.org (7/10/99).

14 The EU as Manufacturer of Tradition and Cultural Heritage

Reinhard Johler

Compared to the nearby 'European Pavilion', the 'Global House' at the last World Exhibition in Hannover was a great success. The Austrian region of Vorarlberg contributed to the exhibitions in that 'Global House' one of the visionary models concerning 'the future of work'. Its project 'Nature and Life in the Bregenzerwald' presented a curious mix of, on the one hand, modern, open-minded design with, on the other hand, regional and traditional culture, underlined by several stage performances in folk costume, which created an obvious contrast for the audience. And yet, this contrast indicated exactly what the project was about: It was an example of a regional 'bottom up' development, ecologically and consumer (in a European, networked sense) oriented, which actually had contributed to structural improvements in agriculture, commerce and tourism in the Bregenzerwald area, and it was sustained in this valley by a multifaceted and intense search for 'cultural roots'. In this area, 'cultural heritage' has come to be associated with nature-based agriculture; low transport, small-scale handicraft production; a cultural landscape defined as 'natural'; and, a newly re-discovered local folk culture, branded with the seal of authenticity. In other words: a reinforcement of regional identity has been the driving force and the aim of this regional development as presented in the 'Global House'.

In this exhibition, particularly 'typical' products, such as cheese and wood, were meant not only to represent regional identity, but also to enable the region to gain access to niches of the European market. These products demonstrated, therefore, the 'local roots', the Own, and the identity of the valley – in short: they represented the now-so-important 'cultural heritage', with the aid of which local producers hope to succeed in the global market.

'Heritage is Everywhere'

This Austrian example is anything but an exception. Muriel Faure, for example, recently showed how a local kind of cheese was transformed into an 'objet culturel' and became a symbol of the French 'Alpes du Nord' (Faure 1999). Similar activities can be observed in Sweden (Svensson 1998), Spain, Italy, Greece (Caftanzoglou-Konvani 1997), or even, with a Celtic twist, in rural development in the north of Scotland (Gray 2000; 2002). It is no coincidence that Jane Nadel-Klein gave her ethnographic study on the cultural consequences of economic crisis in the north Atlantic fishing industry the meaningful title 'Fishing for Heritage'. With this title she emphasised the intense 'creation of Scottish heritage' that one can currently observe (Nadel-Klein 2002).

It is, therefore, with good reason that one could speak of a 'Heritage Crusade', as David Lowenthal describes it. And, no doubt, his observations are accurate when he says that, all of a sudden,

> ... [h]eritage is everywhere – in everything from galaxies to genes. It is the chief focus of patriotism and a prime lure of tourism. One can barely move without bumping into a heritage site. Every legacy is cherished. From ethnic roots to history theme parks, Hollywood to the Holocaust, the whole world is busy lauding – or lamenting - some past, be it fact or fiction (Lowenthal 1998: xiii).

This is not the place to discuss Lowenthals analysis in detail. And although it is true that 'tradition' and 'cultural heritage' have become the main pathways world wide for the production of identity in the late twentieth century (cf. Bendix 2000; Boniface-Fowler 1993; Chevallier 2000), this general development is still worth investigating in detail to determine more precisely its agencies or causes. In this chapter, I want to deal with the European Union as a powerful 'manufacturer' of 'tradition' and 'cultural heritage', influencing everyday-life in Europe. At the same time, it seems equally important in this context to address the role of European ethnologists – both in the past, when they were functioning as the constructors of tradition and cultural heritage, and as participants in the present process of Europeanisation (Borneman and Fowler 1997) – a process that changes deeply what cultural heritage is.

Tradition and Change

It was not so much the terminology, but rather the content that was clear to our ethnological forefathers – 'tradition' and 'cultural heritage' to them were not only concepts and central themes of study, but also something very real and tangible, something that existed in the 'real world' (Bausinger 1969).

Within this frame of mind, tradition and cultural heritage always referred to the Own as something original, something typical, something distinguishable, handed down unchanged from the past. Tradition, as well as cultural heritage, was seen as static, given, fundamentally shaping 'folk cultures' (customs, folk costume, farmhouses, folk music or folk art) usually conceptualised within ethnic or national discourses. This search led the researchers into a pre-industrial past, for in the present time tradition and cultural heritage seemed to be fundamentally compromised and therefore endangered by the process of modernisation, existing therefore only as relics, reminders of an earlier time in that survive in certain areas of refuge that become cultural reservations.

It was this theoretical basis that determined the role and tasks of ethnologists. Their inherently ethnic view of their own culture led them to become constructors of a long gone 'authentic' heritage. They saw themselves as researchers and saviours of this cultural heritage as well as taking on the role of influential protectors. In these efforts, early ethnologists were extremely successful, offering a role model for a broader public. Seen in this context, the efforts of organisations like UNESCO, the Council of Europe, and indeed the European Center for Traditional Culture, founded in Budapest in 1996, (Verebély 1997), may sound familiar. The fact that 'Europe' is part of the name of the centre in Budapest is no coincidence. It has to do with EU subsidies, and this is a point we will return to later. For the moment it is more important to note that the 'Europe' of the late nineteenth century was, to the early ethnologists, modern, urban and a place of international high culture, which stood in stark contrast to local tradition and national cultural heritage. The 'Euroculture', propagated presently by the EU, shows an interesting continuity with this earlier vision, which is important to emphasise here. It too is seen as a primarily economically motivated, uniform and hegemonial culture, which is a threat to the local, regional and national variety in Europe.

We do not agree with this interpretation – neither for present-day Europe, nor for the European past. But its popularity comes directly from an ethnological train of thought, which, as mentioned earlier, saw tradition and cultural heritage in a purist perspective as static. In other words, tradition and cultural heritage were constructed as 'authentic', original forms of 'folk culture'. The process of modernisation was seen as a threat, and the adaptation of 'folk' cultural elements in this process was denigrated as 'folklorism' (cf. Moser 1962; Bausinger 1969). But that mindset blocked the perspective on cultural change and the commodification of cultural heritage, and thus has made it difficult understand how the present situation has developed.

Let us therefore now broaden our perspective by returning to the Austrian example presented at the EXPO in Hanover. The protagonists presented the project 'Nature and Life in the Bregenzerwald' as a counter-movement, as an antithesis to uniform Europeanisation. The truth, of course, was far more complex. The fact that the term 'Europeanisation' was used so widely in the local context was not simply a coincidence: these projects were directly supported by European subsidies, and in the valley there is a quite strong and visible local EU infrastructure. The rhetoric, the contents, the intention and the goal of 'Nature and Life in the Bregenzerwald' lead us directly to its real basis – the EU LEADER programmes for the development of economically disadvantaged rural areas. Networking and 'Europe-wide performance' are expected just as much as the mobilisation of 'cultural heritage'. In the Bregenzerwald, this is realised by an initiative referred to as the 'rural market place', an Internet project encompassing western Greece, the Rhône-Alps area, and Andalusia. Culturally manufactured regional differences are seen as an opportunity for tourism and economic development. Defining, or better: re-working cultural heritage is therefore a central policy goal. Ann-Kristin Ekmann is surely right when she observes that 'the role of traditional culture' became in Sweden – and one could add in the whole of Western Europe – 'a guiding metaphor in a process of regional transition' that is led by these European programmes (Ekman 1999).

Mobilising European Heritage

In many parts of Europe one can nowadays observe a massive mobilisation of cultural heritage. The 'local' has become musealised (Albertin 1999), regional foodstuffs are extremely popular (Tschofen 2000), and trade fairs, farmers markets, regional festivals and customs are revitalised in many places all over Europe (Boissevain 1992). This no doubt has to do with a defending of, but much more with the re-defining of identity. Europe, or rather the EU, takes on a key role in the mobilisation of cultural heritage that should not be under-estimated, and has become one of the foremost agencies in the definition of cultural heritage in Europe. One could say, as Susan J. Smith remarked, that the presence of Europe has turned the sameness and difference of social life into a prime political interest (Smith 1999). But this diagnosis should be seen from different angles. The EU seems successful where the support of local and regional diversity is concerned. But it has generally failed, as the lack of interest in the 'European Pavilion' at the EXPO in Hanover proved, in the creation of 'sameness', the establishment of a common, identity-shaping 'European culture'.

This apparent contradiction should, however, not stop us from seeing the many – in EU-speak – 'EU-Success-Stories'. These not only include the already mentioned project in the Bregenzerwald. The EU primarily subsidises projects aiming to support processes of economic homogenisation. Culturally, however, its subsidy programmes have contributed massively to the production of difference in Europe. Observing this on a local as well as on a European level greatly improves one's ethnologic understanding of the present, but also shows that tradition and cultural heritage have become important factors of powerful EU policy making in the process of 'Building Europe' (Shore 2000).

These EU subsidy programmes cannot be explained in detail here, but it should be noted that they all accord a high significance to cultural heritage at a European and national as well as at a regional level. The endowment programme for arts, 'Culture 2000', contains the stipulation that projects should aim to 'make the cultural heritage of Europe more accessible to all'. In EU structural and regional policies, the LEADER programmes, a suite of development programmes for disadvantaged areas, include subsidies that are conditional on the exploitation of 'cultural heritage' as a possible resource for planning and a potential for development. Even 'Agenda 2000', the EU's programme for developing rural space, targets the maintenance of 'cultural heritage' through a combination of subsidies for promoting different cultures and traditions.

One should not forget that there are tens of thousands of well-financed projects across Europe pursuing directly or at least rhetorically one or more of these EU-programmes. These subsidy programmes have given many small groups and individual actors the political power to establish a new relationship with their nation state, a development that can hardly be overestimated. And they have led to a massive mobilisation of cultural heritage, and increased the emphasis on cultural heterogeneity (cf. Ray 1997; Johler 2001). This intense culturalisation of Europe may, at first glance, appear to contradict economic homogenisation. So what are the intentions connected to it, according to article 130 of the 'Treaty of Maastricht' (Der Vertrag 1998: 205-206) and the subsequent 'Declaration of Cork', in which the protection and promotion of traditions and cultural heritage are mentioned?

The EU subsidises cultural heritage in order to achieve political, cultural and economic goals. Politically, pronounced regionality weakens the nation states and turns the EU into a protector of heterogeneous culture (Bausinger 1994; Kockel 1999). This intention is closely tied to the cultural goals and the development of a 'new European Identity'. Since the early 1980s the EU has been trying hard – as determined in the

'Treaty of Maastricht' – to directly address the 'European citizen', and actually to create 'the European' characterised by a shared European culture, history and identity. Both intentions have had an earlier career of their own as political slogans, namely of a 'Citizens Europe' (Shore 1993; Shore and Black 1994), and of 'Unity in Diversity' (McDonald 1996). Both are intended to signify, and ultimately engender, a common 'Euroculture', thought to be created through mutual respect as well as the financial support to the many national, regional and local cultures – in other words: through diversity proclaimed as typical of Europe.

The EU institutions see this diversity – and that is the economic goal of the EU-propagation of 'cultural heritage' – as an economic opportunity. Local traditions and heritage are seen as specific foundations for the economic development of tourism or agricultural production. This 'heritage policy', as it is practised by the European Union, must be seen as an instrument for European identity politics. It turns the recent construction of regional or local cultural heritages into a central political issue, and, as a consequence, heterogenises Europe. Supported by the EU, innumerable people are now seeking cultural or historical uniqueness, simultaneously and in direct competition with each other. This has lead to a definite bureaucratisation of culture, identity and cultural heritage. Moreover, the local has been made suitable for the global arena. It has become in many cases a specific, well known and, most significantly, consumable part of the new 'world culture'.

Consequences

One may find this process encouraging or regrettable, but as European ethnologists, we should not ignore it. For our perspective on 'tradition' and 'cultural heritage', this has two consequences. The first concerns the EU and its promotion of 'Euroculture'. 'Like the people of Europe', Thomas Wilson once said, 'anthropologists can either make their war or their peace with it, but cannot ignore it' (Wilson 1993). I think our ethnological perspective must include not only a vista onto the local of everyday life, but also the scrutiny of the big and powerful institutions. EU-Europe must be included in a discipline that carries the word 'Europe' in its very name (Johler 2002).

As a second consequence, 'tradition' and 'cultural heritage' can no longer be taken out of their local context in order to be understood (Giddens 1996). In late modernity they have become the issue of many disputes in the controversial 'identity politics', and they are scarce goods in the field of global economy. It is this that will demand new thoughts and ideas from us European ethnologists as well as a new and more dynamic concept of cultural heritage.

References

Albertin, L. (1999), 'Regionale kulturelle Identität. Selbstgenügsames Refugium oder europäisches Handlungselement', in Viehoff and Segers (eds), 321-332.

Anttonen, P. (ed.) (2000), *Folklore, Heritage Politics and Ethnic Diversity. A Festschrift for Barbro Klein*, The Multicultural Centre (Tumba).

Bausinger, H. (1966), 'Zur Kritik der Folklorismus-Kritik', in *Populus Revisus. Beiträge zur Erforschung der Gegenwart*, Tübingen, 61-76.

Bausinger, H. (1969a), 'Folklorismus in Europa. Eine Umfrage', in *Zeitschrift für Volkskunde* 65, 1-55.

Bausinger, H. (1969b), 'Kritik der Tradition. Anmerkungen zur Situation der Volkskunde', in *Zeitschrift für Volkskunde* 65, 232-250.

Bausinger, H. (1994), 'Region – Kultur – EG', in *Österreichische Zeitschrift für Volkskunde* 48/97, 113-40.

Beck, U., Giddens, A. and Lash, S. (eds) (1996), *Reflexive Modernisierung. Eine Kontroverse*, Suhrkamp.

Bendix, R. (2000), 'Heredity, Hybridity and Heritage from One Fin de Siècle to the Next', in Anttonen, 37-54.

Boissevain, J. (ed.) (1992), *Revitalizing European Rituals*, Routledge.

Boniface, P. and Fowler, P. (1993), *Heritage and Tourism in the 'Global Village'*, Routledge.

Borneman, J. and Fowler, N. (1997), 'Europeanization', in *Annual Review of Anthropology* 2, 487-514.

Brednich, R., Schneider, A. and Werner, U. (eds): *Natur – Kultur. Volkskundliche Perspektiven auf Mensch und Umwelt. 32. Kongreß der Deutschen Gesellschaft für Volkskunde in Halle v. 27.9.-1.10.1999*, Waxmann.

Caftanzoglou, R., and Kovani, H. (1997), 'Cultural Identities and Integration in Rural Greece', in *Sociologia Ruralis* 37, 240-54.

Chevallier, D. (ed.) (2000), *Vives campagnes. Le patrimoine rural, projet de société*, Éditions Autrement.

Der Vertrag (1998), *Europäische Union – Europäische Gemeinschaft. Die Vertragstexte von Maastricht mit den deutschen Begleitgesetzen*, Ed.by T. Läufer, Presse und Informationsamt der Bundesregierung (Bonn).

Ekman, A. (1999), 'The Revival of Cultural Celebrations in Regional Sweden. Aspects of Tradition and Transition', in *Sociologia Ruralis* 39, 280-93.

Faure, M. (1999), 'Un produit 'affiné' en objet culturel. Le fromage beaufort dans les Alpes du Nord', in *Terrain* 33, 81-92.

Giddens, A. (1996), 'Tradition in der post-traditionalen Gesellschaft', in Beck et al., 113-94.

Goddard, V., Llobera, J. and Shore, C. (eds) (1996), *The Anthropology of Europe. Identities and Boundaries in Conflict*, Berg.

Gray, J. (2000), 'Rural Space in Scotland. From Rural Fundamentalism to Rural Development', in *Anthropological Journal on European Cultures* 9, 53-79.

Gray, J. (2002), *At Home in the Hills. Sense of place in the Scottish Borders*, Berg.

Johler, R. (2001), '"Wir müssen Landschaft produzieren": Die Europäische Union und ihre "politics of landscape and nature"', in Brednich et al., 77-90.

Johler, R. (2002), 'Wieviel Europa braucht die Europäische Ethnologie. Anmerkungen zur deutschsprachigen Volkskunde in einer transitorischen Gegenwart', in Köstlin et al. (in press).

Kockel, U. (1999), *Borderline Cases. The Ethnic Frontiers of European Integration*, Liverpool.

Köstlin, K., Niedermüller, P. and Nikitsch, H., (2002), *Die Wende als Wende? Orientierungen Europäischer Ethnologien nach 1989*, Institut für Europäische Ethnologie Wien (in press).

Lowenthal, D. (1998), *The Heritage Crusade and the Spoils of History*, Cambridge.

McDonald, M. (1996), '"Unity in Diversity". Some tensions in the construction of Europe', in *Social Anthropology* 3, 47-60.

Macdonald, S. (1993), 'Identity Complexes in Western Europe: Social Anthropological Perspectives', in Macdonald, 1-26.

Macdonald, S. (ed.) (1993), *Inside European Identities. Ethnography in Western Europe*, Berg.

Martin, S. (1993), 'The Europeanization of Local authorities – challenges for rural areas', in *Journal of Rural Studies* 9, 153-65.

Massey, D., Allen, J. and Sarre, P. (eds) (1999), *Human Geography Today*, Polity.

Moser, H. (1962), 'Vom Folklorismus in unserer Zeit', in *Zeitschrift für Volkskunde* 58, 177-209.

Nadel-Klein, J. (2002), *Fishing for Heritage. Modernity and Loss along the Scottish Coast*, Berg.

Parman, S. (ed.) (1998), *Europe in the Anthropological Imagination*, Prentice Hall.

Ray, C. (1997), 'Towards a Theory of the Dialectic of Local Rural Development within the European Union', in *Sociologia Ruralis* 37, 345-62.

Shore, C. (1993), 'Inventing the people's Europe: critical approaches to European Communities and the construction of Europe', in *Man* 28, 779-800.

Shore, C. (2000), *Building Europe: The Cultural Politics of European Integration*, Routledge.

Shore, C. and Black, A. (1994), 'Citizens' Europe and the Construction of European Identity', in Goddard et al., 275-98.

Smith, S. (1999), 'The Cultural Politics of Difference', in Massey et al., 129-50.

Svensson, B. (1998), 'The Nature of Cultural Heritage Sites', in *Ethnologia Europaea* 28, 5-16.

Tschofen, B. (2000), 'Herkunft als Ereignis: local food and global knowledge. Notizen zu den Möglichkeiten einer Nahrungsforschung im Zeitalter des Internet', in *Österreichische Zeitschrift für Volkskunde* 54/103, 309-24.

Verebély, K. (1997), 'Europäisches Folklore-Zentrum in Budapest', in *Hessische Blätter für Volkskunde* 32, 157-61.

Viehoff, R. and Segers, R. (eds) (1999), *Kultur – Identität – Europa. Über die Schwierigkeiten und Möglichkeiten einer Konstruktion*, Suhrkamp.

Wilson, T. (1993), 'An Anthropology of the European Community', in Wilson and Smith (eds), 1-23.

Wilson, T. (1998), 'An Anthropology of the European Union, from Above and Below', in Parman (ed.), 148-56.

Wilson, T. and Smith, E. (eds) (1993), *Cultural Change and the New Europe. Perspectives on the European Community*, Westview.

15 Culture and Economy: Towards an Agenda for Further Research

Máiréad Nic Craith and Ullrich Kockel

Culture has been described as the pattern of meanings embedded in symbolic forms, including actions, utterances and meaningful objects of various kinds, by virtue of which individuals communicate with one another and share their experiences, conceptions, and beliefs (Thompson 1990: 132). Many contemporary economists would see the market as the most efficient transmitter of communicating and sharing meanings, values and objects of all kinds between individual actors. The essays in this volume cover a wide range of geographical, political and institutional contexts in which the relationship between culture and economy is played out.

Rather than offering an evaluative summary of the essays in these concluding pages, we would like to outline an agenda for further research, based on debates at the two conferences from which most of the book's contributions are drawn, and also on the wider academic and political debate concerning culture and economy. We have chosen the format of a discussion paper to do this because it allows greater flexibility and openness than more conventional formats of presenting concluding remarks.

It is not our intention to offer a comprehensive catalogue of issues or even broad themes to be investigated. Instead, we highlight what we see as particularly significant areas for further study. Some of these appear to have been rather neglected in the debate so far. Others may seem 'well grazed', perhaps even 'overgrazed', from a particular methodological or theoretical angle, but merit a fresh approach all the same.

Economic Development, Power, and Cultural Change

Most contributions to this book emphasise the significance of power relationships for the interplay of culture and economy. Power takes many forms. It is not limited to institutionalised political or economic forms like the state or the corporation.

Gender Divisions of Labour

This is most evident in the gendering of economic activities, which in Western social science has come to be regarded as a clear expression of power relationships where men occupy the more prestigious, better paid and more influential positions, whereas women end up with menial and subsistence tasks. It can hardly be disputed that this is indeed an empirical fact in most societies. However, this does not warrant the belief that any gender division of labour is oppressive by definition. We need to examine critically the different cultural and economic contexts in which such divisions occur, and take into account possible alternative explanations. Lithuanian women living in Latvia, producing souvenirs in a cottage industry manner, may keep aspects of their culture alive in everyday practice while at the same time mediating between different cultures. It would be important to understand more fully the kind of power that this may engender. This will become increasingly important in situations where we are dealing with groups that are culturally less close to Western societal ideals than the groups discussed in the present book.

Invention of Traditions

The development of any culture involves the invention of new things and the forgetting of old ones (Bauman 1999: 73). In this context, cultural traditions – culture 'handed down' – are always 'culture in progress', rather than immutably fixed patterns and practices (cf. Kockel 2002). Investment in the stock market may be perceived as the very antithesis of 'traditional' economic activity, even though as the structure of the global economy changes, it is rapidly becoming just such an activity. Moreover, navigating one's way through masses of information and learning to 'read the market' relies as much on processes of 'handing down' as a peasant's ability to the signs of nature for the purposes of subsistence farm These processes, and the skills and power games involve ... them, need to be studied more thoroughly. A new 'virtualism' (Carrier and Miller 1998) is progressively compelling everyday lives to conform to the requirements of economic thought in much the same way as the Medieval Church once developed its own complex eschatology as a normative framework that would guide everyday praxis.

Creative use of received notions of 'tradition' and 'heritage', encouraging economic growth through cultural means, can generate significant benefits, and regions like Andalusia or Cornwall have long tried, with varying success, to reap these. In most cases, an essentially instrumental understanding of 'culture' and 'tradition' underpins such policies, giving rise to an alleged commodification of culture. However, culture as praxis cannot be quite so readily commodified. When we look at informal economy, as several of the essays in this volume do, we may find ourselves drawn to the hypothesis that what anthropologists call the 'substantivist' approach may perhaps be as appropriate for the study of highly developed economies as it is acknowledged to be for the study of more 'primitive' ones. Whether this will, in time, produce a viable alternative theory of the economy depends *inter alia* on how convincingly empirical case studies can be analysed in terms of such a theory. More importantly, it depends on how economic, social and political change will shape the hegemonic structures that determine which theories are acceptable at any point in time.

Transculturation and Indigenisation

Some authors examined transculturation processes whereby cultural forms, quite literally, move through time and space, interacting with other cultural forms and settings, influencing each other, producing new forms, and changing the cultural settings involved. Transculturation creates hybrids, a fusing of cultural forms, which is not simply the 'impregnating of one culture with the contents of another', but 'involves an ambivalence about both of the original cultures', creating a sense of freedom, nomadism, even opportunism (Naficy 1993: 127). This may include processes of indigenisation, that is, the 'localisation' of imported cultural elements (cf. Lull 2000: 244). In the history of anthropology and European ethnology, studies of cultural diffusion have played a significant role, but these were guided by a different set of paradigms. It might be worthwhile to look at cultural fusion using a paradigmatic fusion of old and new models, rather than relying only on one or the other. Little work has been done in this direction.

There has been in recent years a widespread celebration of hybridity as what one might almost call a cultural utopia. Two crucial aspects of this utopia should, however, be borne in mind by the celebrants. We need to be aware that a vision of cultural hybridity suits the 'virtual reality of economic thought' very well, and that we therefore should ask who stands to profit most from cultural fusion of any sort in a particular case. A second point is that, however similar in outward appearance, when it comes to reproduction a mule is not the same as a hinny – some hybrids are able to reproduce while others are not. This aspect should concern anyone interested in the utilisation of culture for promoting endogenous development – a low-input concept of economy premised on an endogenously renewable resource base rather than dependency on endless exogenous subsidies.

Intercultural Communication

For many regions, and the more peripheral ones in particular, cultural tourism has come to be regarded as the solution to problems of economic development. The reasoning is simple. As Western societies grow more affluent, better educated, and aware of the dangers of overexposure to sunlight, tourists are seeking out alternative opportunities for recreation, including the contact – mediated or otherwise – with different cultures. Peripheries are rich in culture (whereas centres tend towards civilisation), which they should marshal as a resource for development. 'Culture' in this sense is generally perceived as an endogenously renewable resource by virtue of the fact that 'the locals' have a vital interest in doing everything they can to keep it alive. This interpretation suits the neo-liberalist contempt for any kind of subsidy, but it fails to understand that exploiting a region and then leaving it to its own devices to repair the damage is not what the principle of subsidiarity is about. For endogenous development to work, in tourism or any other sector, we need thorough assessments of what each region's resource potential actually is. Earning power is a key factor, but there are many others. Like earning power, these may well differ between regions, and between various cultural resources within them. We also need to address the question of value, if we do not want to end up in a situation where the only cultural traits considered valuable will be those that are attracting a price tag. The problem of 'fake-lore' has long been recognised (e.g. Boissevain 1989), and the authenticity issue remains unresolved. But the question of value points beyond that debate. Will it be possible to find a way of acknowledging the value of cultural traits that avoids pricing them without falling into the trap of essentialism?

Reterritorialisation and Diasporas

Tourism is a special case of culture contact through, in this instance short-term, migration. Longer-term migrants usually attempt to establish a new cultural 'home' wherever they go (Tomlinson 1999: 148). Such cultural ambitions and activities contribute to processes often described as reterritorialisation. Fusing imported traditions with cultural resources in the new territory, immigrant groups all over the world create local versions of distant cultures. Cultural goods such as foods, clothing, and domestic items of all kinds flow rapidly around the world now, thanks mainly to transportation advances and market incentives for global import/export businesses. This is changing the everyday experience of individuals and groups living in some form of modern diaspora.

However, there are notable differences between migrants moving within those few, highly developed world regions who between them account for three quarters of world trade, and migrants who enter these regions from elsewhere. The postmodern dictum that 'we all live in the diaspora' signifies an individualistic utopia only for privileged Westerners who may indulge in the economic virtue of perfect mobility. It is normative rather than empirical. Moreover, on a closer inspection it reveals new identities formed not so much by a fusion that results from genuine culture contact, but by an acquisition – both literally and metaphorically – of cultural icons that almost clinically avoids engagement with anything other than the Self. There is a large, underexplored area for research here, which centres on ideas of intercultural communication. As taught at many universities, this refers at present mainly to communication between different business cultures, to the virtual exclusion of other spheres of culture contact. The different interpretations of the food aid situation in Moscow illustrate that there is far more to intercultural communication than how to get the most profitable deal from foreign business partners by playing their cultural games. In this regard, the Commission on Intercultural Communication of the International Society for Ethnology and Folklore (SIEF) is now breaking new ground, opening up this field for more broadly based interdisciplinary inquiry.

Networks

In Moscow people used informal exchange networks to locate goods and services. Money was of secondary importance to social access. The lack of food was a consequence of the lack of social connections. But the study also highlighted the new networks generated by the soup kitchens, new social spaces that cultivated a sense of belonging.

Effective networks enable a flow of products from the local to the national and to the international. Some of the essays in this volume have looked at the deterritorilisation of identity building. Deterritorialisation represents the initial step in the formation of new cultural territories. Lull (2000: 239) defines that process as a 'partial tearing apart of cultural structures, relationships, settings and representations'. Cultural signs become separated from particular locations in time and space, and are uprooted from the places we expect them to be (Giddens 1990; Rowe and Schelling 1991).

The Significance of Symbols in Economic Contexts

Symbols are given meaning by interpretation, which takes place in a cultural context and serves a cultural purpose. In many of the essays we have seen how symbolic power has been articulated in specific cultural situations. In Stockholm, the stock exchange has become a significant symbol as just over 60% of the population now participate in the stock market, either directly through stockholdings, or indirectly via mutual funds. The environment of theory and belief, feeling and rhetoric that dominates this symbol in the Swedish context finds parallels in the behaviour of investors in *Berkeley Hathaway*. Superficially, these investors may well appear anything but specimen of rational *homo oeconomicus*. However, their rationality may simply be different from that prescribed by neo-liberalist economics. Pragmatically, if such alternative rationalities 'deliver the goods', on what basis can we continue to classify them as inferior to market rationality?

As industrial work patterns developed over more than two centuries appear in terminal decline, the significance of work for individual identity and, more widely, as a cultural symbol has been highlighted, in this volume especially by the essays on Eisenerz and Leipzig. Apart from its illegitimate treatment of labour – like land and capital – as a commodity, economics fails to conceptualise labour in any form other than as wage employment, a form of utilisation of labour power which is inseparably linked with the capitalist mode of production. In regions where other modes are in operation, 'employment' as conventionally perceived is no longer a suitable concept. But what are viable alternatives, and how do we define 'viability' in this context?

Andalusia and Cornwall demonstrated the 're-packaging' of regions as cultural products for a global tourist as consumer, using symbolic references both for marketing the region, and for 'selling' the vision of a new region domestically, that is, to rally support for the policy and practice necessary to pursue success in the global market place. The case of Lithuanians in Latvia showed how traditional textile patterns and colours signified symbolic references carrying associations with the homeland, transmitted from one generation to the next.

Using tradition as a force for change is a strategy implicit in much of the contemporary debate on culture and economy at the policy level, not least within the EU institutions. A first glance may suggest that such a strategy serves to emancipate a periphery that has been 'internally colonised', revaluing its cultural heritage, which is thereby accorded status along with resources such as crude oil or precious metals. However, this new enthusiasm for things cultural, especially where they relate to the past, is far from unproblematic. To begin with, the entire terminology of 'tradition', 'heritage', 'culture' and so on serves to confuse rather than clarify the issues.

Culture as a Resource for the Twenty-first Century

While the final decades of the twentieth century witnessed a heritage boom, the EU 'discovered' culture as a vehicle for integration. Its discovery has engendered 'factional' historical trajectories by which individuals essentialise their past and locate their future. Heritage centres have mushroomed in many locations. In a world that is increasingly perceived as culturally fragmented, the recovery of a sense of the past constitutes an industry in itself. In the process, 'heritage' has become a commodity and a resource. Group identities and historical narratives are often constructed retrospectively, with groups vying with one another for a particular version of heritage as 'their' resource, and cultural disputes emerging from conflicting claims and reclamations.

The nature of heritage and the heritage experience needs to be carefully examined. At an empirical level, we need more case studies illustrating the invention or re-conceptualisation of heritage. In economics, the concept of 'futures' refers to a process whereby profits expected from the exploitation of resources not yet discovered are traded for profit. As heritage has become a commodity, is there such a 'futures market' for heritage not yet invented or 'reclaimed', and what role do the anthropological disciplines play in it? Beyond a critique of the retrospective construction of heritage, can anthropologists anticipate such future narratives?

Modes of Transaction

We envisage an interdisciplinary research programme that will explore the discourses of heritage and its futures, both empirically and theoretically – anthropologists, geographers, folklorists, political economists, social historians and others working together to review the role of heritage in generating a sense of continuity. Particularly needed at this juncture are theoretical explorations of the significance of the past for Europe in the twenty-first century, based on case studies of regions where heritage is, on the one hand, a key factor in locating identity and a sense of place, and, on the other hand, a significant means of generating jobs and revenue. The presence of varied modes of transaction in a particular region implies that these occur within a cultural nexus not defined by any specific mode of production. To date, no suitable models for analysing such situations, potentially involving several distinct modes of transaction, seem to exist, although most theorists are acutely aware of the need for them.

We are using 'mode of transaction' here as a shorthand for 'modes of production and exchange'. Unlike some economic anthropologists, and indeed most economists, we believe that the two must always be considered together, and that they are equally relevant. They need not be of the same quality – one might, for example, be feudal, the other capitalist. The production/exchange debate in economic anthropology (cf. Clammer 1987) has glossed over this problem and, likewise, economics has neglected it, with the result that conceptual tools for the analysis of hybrid systems have hardly been developed. The concept of a dual economy goes some way in this direction, but remains firmly rooted within modernisation theory, and hence based on a priori value judgements about the nature of the two sectors it postulates, contributing little to an understanding of hybrid modes of transaction.

Agency Motivation

Agency motivation is a key factor in development (Kockel 1992). Considering field-based evidence, it seems that it is not simply profit, nor even utility – in the economic sense – which is being maximised in many cases. Recourse to utility has been the response of mainstream economics to the earlier assaults on *homo oeconomicus*. But this was an unfortunate choice: If defined economically, utility means, in the last instance, profit. Otherwise, if defined trans-economically, utility can be used to explain just about anything, and thus explains nothing. It seems almost ironic that economic theory has no concept to explain economic rationality.

Unfortunately, the assumptions behind *homo oeconomicus* cannot be easily dispensed with, since, as Holy and Stuchlik (1983: 116) have noted, 'the analysis, to be able to proceed, needs to assume the purposiveness, intentionality or goal-orientation of human behaviour'. But the analyst must not fill these assumed qualities of behaviour with any content, as it were, a priori, since otherwise 'irrationality' might be nothing but non-compliance of the actors with the expectations of the researcher. Rationality is always bounded, and determined by the context of any action as known to the actor (cf. Holy and Stuchlik 1983). Economic analysis has no way of dealing with motives other than profit, financial or otherwise. We need an alternative framework for the analysis of agency motivation, to understand better how people 'causally' connect what they do, and the way they do it, with all the pasts they anticipate having had when their time comes to move on ....

References

Bauman, Z. (1999), *Culture as Praxis*, Sage.

Boissevan, J. (1989), 'Tourism as anti-structure', in Giordano et al., 145-59.

Carrier, J. and Miller, D. (eds) (1998), *Virtualism: A New Political Economy*, Berg.

Clammer, J. (ed.), *Beyond the New Economic Anthropology*, Macmillan.

Giddens, A. (1990), *The Consequences of Modernity*, Stanford.

Giordano, C., Schiffauer, W., Schilling, H. and Welz, G. (eds), *Kultur anthropologisch: eine Festschrift für Ina-Maria Greverus*, Institut für Kulturanthropologie und Europäische Ethnologie, Universität Frankfurt/Main.

Holy, L. and Stuchlik, M. (1983), *Actions, Norms and Representations: Foundations of an Anthropological Inquiry*, Cambridge.

Kockel, U. (1992), 'Provisory economy and regional development: Towards a conceptual integration of informal activities', in Tykkyläinen, 101-19.

Kockel, U. (2002), *Regional Culture and Economic Development: Explorations in European Ethnology*, Ashgate.

Lull, J. (2000), *Media, Communication, Culture: A Global Approach*, 2nd rev. ed., Polity.

Nacify, H. (1993), *The making of Exile Cultures*, Minnesota.

Rowe, W. and Schelling, V. (1991), *Memory and Modernity: Popular Culture in Latin America*, Verso.

Thompson, J. (1990), *Ideology and Modern Culture*, Polity.

Tykkyläinen, M. (ed.) (1992), *Development Issues and Strategies in the New Europe: Local, regional and interregional perspectives*, Avebury.

Index